"To live an extraordinary life is something everyone aspires to, yet so few attain. Why is it so elusive? *The Values Factor* unveils the simple yet so very powerful secret to a life of fulfillment and meaning. Immerse yourself in this book and be prepared to spend the rest of your life living extraordinarily!"

—Vanessa Talbot, Success Guide, Life Expander, author of *Extraordinary You: The Art of Living a Lusciously Spirited, Vibrant Life*

"From my experience of John Demartini's work, this book does a wonderful job of capturing the absolute key strategies John teaches to help you live a fulfilling and inspired life. The book is like a manual on how to get the absolute most from your life; it really demonstrates that you are here for a reason, that your life has a definite purpose. The message becomes clear that your progress in life is the result of your thinking and the hierarchy of your values, and that with the strategies in this book you will learn how to free yourself from your many self-imposed restrictions and those adopted from society. It's the most complete book I have ever read from the personal development field."

—Scott Cranfield, PGA Master Golf Professional

T0053916

THE
VALUES
FACTOR

The Secret to Creating
an Inspired and Fulfilling Life

DR. JOHN DEMARTINI

BERKLEY BOOKS, NEW YORK

THE BERKLEY PUBLISHING GROUP
Published by the Penguin Group
Penguin Group (USA) LLC.
375 Hudson Street, New York, New York 10014, USA

USA I Canada I UK I Ireland I Australia I New Zealand I India I South Africa I China

Penguin Books Ltd., Registered Offices: 80 Strand, London WC2R 0RL, England
For more information about the Penguin Group, visit penguin.com.

This book is an original publication of The Berkley Publishing Group.

Library of Congress Cataloging-in-Publication Data

Demartini, John F.
The values factor : the secret to creating an inspired and fulfilling life /
Dr. John Demartini. — Berkley trade paperback edition.
pages cm
ISBN 978-0-425-26474-4
1. Values.   2. Self-realization.   3. Meaninglessness (Philosophy).   I. Title.
BF778.D46   2013   2013016084
170'.44

PUBLISHING HISTORY
Berkley trade paperback edition / October 2013

PRINTED IN THE UNITED STATES OF AMERICA

15th printing

Cover design by Erika Fusari.
Text design by Tiffany Estreicher.

CONTENTS

THE
VALUES
FACTOR

What Is the Values Factor?

Your beliefs become your thoughts,
Your thoughts become your words,
Your words become your actions,
Your actions become your habits,
Your habits become your values,
Your values become your destiny.

—MAHATMA GANDHI

What is the most important step you can take to achieve the inspired and fulfilling life you've dreamed of?

You might think the answer was something like, "Start saving money," "Get a better job," or "Land that big promotion."

Or maybe your response would be more like, "Find my life partner," "Have a baby," or "Improve my marriage."

Perhaps your thoughts turn to such general answers as, "Go back to school," "Take more time to travel," or "Spend more time pursuing a spiritual practice."

Any of those actions might help you create a more well-rounded life—perhaps even a more meaningful one. But none of them alone will be the key to fulfilling your destiny—none of them alone may even come close.

Why? Because until you understand specifically what you truly value most, what truly inspires you, who you truly are, and what your true purpose is, a completely inspired, fulfilling life will elude you. You're likely to attempt to live the life that someone else wants you to live, trying to follow someone else's values or priorities—those of a parent, teacher, boss, or spouse. That is a recipe for frustration: the job that never quite satisfies you, the relationship that has somehow gone stale, and the vague sense that you're living a quiet life of desperation.

What if you *are* living according to your own highest values, but you're not completely aware of those values, nor appreciating what they actually are? If so, you're not able to experience the full rewards of your daily efforts. Our highest values are the key to helping us define and meet our goals. They alert us to opportunities we might otherwise have missed, and they allow us to tap into our own physical, mental, and spiritual powers. Being only partly aware of your highest values can cause you to overlook many of life's opportunities while blocking you from full access to your own abilities.

That is why I say that *determining your highest values is one of the most important actions you could ever take.* Determining your highest values is the key to living your inspired destiny. You'll be able to build a career where every day can feel like a vacation—because you love the work you do. You'll be able to find the life partner that you seek or transform your current relationship into the intimate, nourishing partnership that you would love. You'll be able to activate your own unique genius, grow your financial freedom, expand your influence, and unleash your vitality. Ultimately, you will be able to achieve your immortal vision, fulfilling your purpose for being here on earth. Understanding your highest values and then using those values to achieve your most meaningful goals is the key to transforming a quiet life of desperation into an amazing life of inspiration.

And what is the secret to understanding your highest values? That's where *The Values Factor* comes in.

LIVING BY YOUR VALUES

I'm going to make a confession.

Although I'd like to think of myself as a hardworking, dedicated person—and although my family and colleagues would probably describe me as such—I seldom *feel* as though I'm working hard. Those eighteen-hour days and that intense travel schedule to fulfill my international speaking engagements do not seem like hard work. Quite the contrary: they seem like the best vacation in the world—exactly what I'd love to be doing, even though I am at a point in life where I don't have to work.

Likewise, if you saw my dozen or so international bestselling books, or if you looked at the research I do to keep my work fresh and up-to-date, you might think that I'm a disciplined person. I'm not so sure that I am. But it doesn't matter, because when you're doing something you love, you don't think of it in terms of discipline. Fulfilling your purpose is so rewarding, you just can't wait to get out there and do it.

That's how I feel about my life: I can't wait to get up each day to research, write, travel, and teach. The teaching I do, the books I write, the research I conduct, and the travel I undertake are the most inspiring and satisfying activities I can envision. I can't wait to begin my next seminar. I look forward to meeting my next client. I am enthused about sitting down with new material to prepare my next book. And my intense travel schedule, which often has me visiting numerous cities and countries in a matter of days, is the icing on the cake.

Why has my life worked out to be so inspiring to me? Not because I'm unusually lucky, or ambitious, or effective at making money. My life has blossomed because I live according to my highest values—researching, writing, traveling, and teaching—and I set my goals and intentions accordingly.

I've reaped enormous rewards from understanding my highest values and using them to set my goals. Knowing that my highest values are researching, writing, traveling, and teaching has enabled me to choose a career and build a business based on realizing these values at their highest level. Because I'm pursuing and living according to my highest values wholeheartedly, I have complete access to my physical, mental, and spiritual resources: my leadership, my creativity, and my energy. Because everything in my life is aligned toward meeting my values, my whole life feels meaningful and rich.

Work is meaningful and fulfilling when it's something that you truly *love* to do. Life is intensely satisfying when it's full of people and activities that align with your highest values. And relationships based on mutual appreciation of both people's highest values are fulfilling at a level that is hard to imagine until you've experienced it for yourself.

Understanding the Values Factor has enabled me to live an extraordinary life. As soon as you understand the Values Factor, you can live a life that is equally extraordinary. You already have within you everything you need to create such a life. The key is knowing and understanding your highest values and then using them to determine your goals. In this book, I'll show you exactly how to do that.

HOW I DISCOVERED THE VALUES FACTOR

The first time I became aware of the power of the Values Factor, I was only seventeen years old. I was born with my hand and foot turned inward, so I had to wear hand and leg braces in early childhood. And I was also born left-handed, which in those days was considered "sinister." The efforts of my parents, teachers, and doctors to correct my "problems" created a number of additional learning challenges besides contributing to my sense that something was not exactly normal with me.

Accordingly, I was diagnosed with dyslexia and a speech impediment, conditions that made it difficult for me to read, write, and speak. In first grade, my teacher told my parents that I would never amount to much, and I had a challenging time in elementary school from then on.

Finally, at age fourteen, I dropped out of school and left home. I headed first for the Texas beaches, then for California, and finally on to Hawaii, where I became a full-time surfer, living hand to mouth. My plan was to learn to make surfboards and occasionally work other odd jobs to sustain my free-spirited surfing lifestyle, which I assumed would go on indefinitely.

A few years later, though, I almost died of strychnine and cyanide poisoning as a result of inadequate nutrition in combination with the consumption of excessive numbers of Hawaiian Baby Woodrose seeds, psilocybin mushrooms, and other toxic, psychedelic hallucinogens. My life was headed downward fast.

But the downward spiral was interrupted at age seventeen, when a local woman just happened to find me deathly sick, partly unconscious, and dehydrated in my tent in the Haleiwa Point jungle. This kind woman ran immediately to get me fresh fruit juices to rehydrate me. She helped me recover, cleaned up my tent, and then took me to a nearby health food store in Haleiwa called Vim and Vigor, where she helped replenish my body with quality, nutritious food.

I became a regular customer at Vim and Vigor, and a few days later, I noticed a flyer on its door inviting people to a special guest lecture at the Sunset Recreation Hall on the North Shore of Oahu to be presented by famous naturopath and longevity specialist Paul C. Bragg.

I had never before been to a lecture of this type, and I had never heard of Paul Bragg. But my intuition told me to attend. I later found out that millions of people around the United States knew Paul Bragg for his teachings on how to enhance vitality and well-being and possibly also to extend lives.

That evening changed my life. I sat with a few dozen other teenagers listening to this inspired, wise, elderly gentleman, the remarkable legendary figure who had once inspired health and fitness pioneer Jack LaLanne.

Paul inspired me, too. When I heard him explain how to use universal or natural laws along with our inner powers to become ageless and vital and to fulfill our unique, amazing purpose, it awakened something dormant deep within me. I realized that I had the power to mold my own life into any shape I chose.

This sense of empowerment was a revelation to me. As a high school dropout who had been told in first grade that I would probably never be able to read, write, communicate, or amount to anything, I had a secret, suppressed desire to be intelligent and well-read like my older sister, Lynn. I wanted to learn more about the world and to become important enough to make a difference in it. But I had accepted everything I had been told about my so-called limitations, and so I had held myself back.

Upon hearing Paul Bragg share his wisdom and inspiration that night, I felt for the first time in my life that just maybe I could break through my learning limitations and actually read and become intelligent. At that age, I understood that goal to mean becoming a teacher—someone who could understand and teach these natural laws.

My love for traveling also inspired a vision that night of traveling to every country on the face of the Earth and sharing what I learned with millions of people. Paul Bragg's inspiring words helped me to understand my previously hidden highest values: *researching* and *studying*, so that I could understand the universal laws of which he spoke; and then *writing*, *traveling*, and *teaching* so that I could share them with my fellow humans all over the globe. These are the highest values that were awakened in me that night and that have guided my life for more than forty years.

Understanding my highest values and purpose has enabled me to achieve remarkable things. First, I was able to overcome obstacles that had previously defeated me. When you actually begin to take the high-priority actions that are truly most meaningful to you, your self-worth and self-confidence increase, making you feel as though you can overcome any impediment that seems to block your chosen path. And that is what happened to me. Bringing my life into congruence with my true purpose inspired me to keep practicing my reading. I also drew strength from the affirmation that Paul Bragg encouraged me to say to myself each day: "I am a genius and I apply my wisdom."

And so I gradually broke through my dyslexic learning limitations. With steadfast dedication, I gradually mastered reading and writing. I went on to get a B.S. from the University of Houston and then to get special honors from Texas Chiropractic College when I got my doctorate there.

But I didn't wait to finish school to start teaching. As early as age eighteen, I began working with students who just seemed to be spontaneously attracted to whatever I was learning and inspired by. My first pupil was a large African-American woman who came to me to learn more about health. Then an Iranian man came to me, also seeking a healthier way of life, followed by a German man. Soon I was meeting with sixteen students every day in the college library. Then I was leading an open-air class of more than a hundred students in the central park at the University of Houston. By the time I was twenty-three, I was teaching students nearly every night in a wide variety of venues: in my apartment, in nearby health food stores, at local colleges, and at my professional school.

I continued teaching for several years, until I had finally graduated from Texas Chiropractic College and opened my practice. At that point, I began offering regular evening events for the public. Then I appeared on local radio and television shows. Eventually, I began speaking to even larger live audiences: first at state conventions, then at national meetings, and finally to huge global audiences from all walks of life.

Ultimately, then, I was able to fulfill my mission by serving millions of people all around the world while creating for myself a life that is so fulfilling, it feels almost like a vacation even when I am working eighteen hours a day, seven days a week. Being true to myself and to my highest values enabled me to access my deepest reserves of power, inspiration, genius, and creativity, as I will explain further in the chapters that lie ahead. To see the power of knowing your own highest values, however, you have only to compare the homeless seventeen-year-old working odd jobs and risking his health with the vital, creative educator delving deep into his research and sharing his knowledge with millions of people around the globe. I experienced the benefits of the Values Factor firsthand, which is why I believe in its extraordinary power.

These benefits are not available only to me. They are the rewards that await all people who are true to themselves and their highest values. They are based in a profound truth that I have been exploring ever since that fateful day more than forty years ago: everybody has a hierarchy of values. And when you live according to your highest values, that's when you liberate the most authentic you, the most empowered you, the most inspired you, and the most creative you. *Living according to your highest values is the secret to living an inspired and fulfilling life.*

USING THE VALUES FACTOR

Although Paul Bragg helped me unlock the secret of the Values Factor for myself, I did not immediately understand how to communicate this secret to others so that I could help them create their own extraordinary lives. This understanding emerged from years of teaching my signature seminar program, the Breakthrough Experience, where I have helped tens of thousands of people set goals and break through their limitations.

Some of my insights into the importance of the Values Factor came from my observations as I worked with thousands of students over several decades. As I helped people achieve their breakthroughs, I began to notice the underlying structure that enabled people to move forward more quickly with their lives and that empowered them as they made ongoing changes. This underlying structure, I came to realize, was twofold: the *values* that each person held, as well as the *voids*, *apparent lacks*, or *challenges* that he or she had experienced. (I'll explain this notion of values and voids more extensively later in this chapter and also in Chapter 3.)

My observations were supported by my ongoing research into the structure and function of the brain, as well as into psychology, philosophy, and physics. I also studied the lives of high achievers and leaders, seeking to understand what had driven them to their exemplary achievements while enabling their striking accomplishments. As we shall see throughout this book, people who live extraordinary lives of inspiration and fulfillment have aligned their goals with their highest values; that is, they have chosen goals that are congruent with their highest values, rather than seeking to live out the values of others; or, in some cases, they have found ways to align their values in service of their chosen goals. (I will explain how you can identify your own deepest values in Chapter 3, and I will show you to align your goals and your highest values in many chapters throughout this book.)

All of these insights into the Values Factor flowed naturally from the Breakthrough Experience seminar, where I helped people realize that they hold within themselves, at every moment, everything they need, want, or admire in others. This realization held undeniable power, and it led my students to achieve greater fulfillment in numerous areas of their lives, including business, love, finance, education, and relationships of all kinds.

But I also saw that many people could attain even greater personal and professional power if they only became aware of their own highest values. By definition, these people were in fact living out their own highest values, focusing on what was *really* most important to them, because that is what all humans do. However, they were not necessarily aware of these true highest values, or in some cases were uncomfortable about acknowledging them. As a result, they were at odds with themselves, unable to be fully honest or aware about who they *really* were and what they *really* wanted. Consequently, they were not fully able to mobilize all of their physical, mental, and spiritual resources to make their goals come true. Becoming aware of their highest values would enable that kind of mobilization, potentially bringing them greater fulfillment in all areas. Also, I found that students who *were* aware of their highest values had a clear advantage, because their self-awareness enabled them to more easily and quickly make the decisions that would most fulfill their purpose in life, while inspiring them with the energy and stamina to work tirelessly toward that purpose.

Over my decades as a human-behavior specialist, I honed these concepts as I worked with educators, schools, and some of the world's largest corporations and organizations, as well as with tens of thousands of students in my seminars. Based on my work in education, business, and human development, I was able to create a set of exercises to help my students realize their highest values and set their goals accordingly. I share those exercises with you in this book.

The power of the Values Factor is extraordinary. The people I've worked with have used this approach to build businesses, find their life partners, recover from chronic pain and illness, repair relationships with spouses, parents, and children, and reconnect to their deepest spiritual callings. These exercises embody the methods I have used to create and sustain my own extraordinary life. Both my own achievements and those of my students remind me, every day, of the immense power in realizing your highest values and setting your goals accordingly.

If there is one thing my time on earth has taught me, it is the remarkable ability of human beings to overcome obstacles, transform their most challenging situations, and find profound meaning in their lives. But the key to this transformation—each and every time—is the Values Factor. Knowing your highest values enables you to align your life's actions with the things that mean the most to you. Not being aware of those highest values makes it exponentially more difficult to create a meaningful, fulfilling life. It really is as simple as that.

WHAT VALUES ARE . . . AND
WHAT THEY ARE NOT

When I ask you to think about what your values are, what words come to mind?

If you're like most people, you might find yourself listing abstract qualities: honesty, integrity, trust. Or perhaps you would refer to a set of religious beliefs, a patriotic ideal, or a code of morality.

These are probably not really your own personal values. Rather, they are what I call *social idealisms*: socially acceptable ways of thinking and behaving. Social idealisms sound nice. But they don't necessarily reflect the true driving force that shapes your perceptions, decisions, actions, and feelings. You might genuinely believe that you are inspired by these ideals. But they are more likely to reflect your ideas of how you *should, ought to*, or *have to* behave—not what you truly value most.

You can recognize social idealisms because they are usually presented as general statements and abstract categories:

People should be honest.
Treat others the way you want them to treat you.
A good person goes to church, synagogue, mosque, or temple.
An "evolved" person is always generous or altruistic.

True values, by contrast, are as specific to you as your fingerprint, your retinal pattern, and your voiceprint. Perhaps what you truly value most is spending time with your family, listening to beautiful music, and the chance to play basketball several times a week. Or perhaps you value stylish clothes, nursing injured animals back to health, or expanding your enterprise's global reach. Your highest values may change throughout your life—most people's do—but they are still the very essence of *you*: what you're drawn to, what you inevitably seek out, what you live for. They are a kind of internal compass, pointing you toward the activities, people, and places that most fulfill you and away from the situations and people that are likely to feel unfulfilling. If you think of which activities and relationships truly nourish your innermost being, *those* are your highest values.

Just as no one else can choose your fingerprints or alter the pattern of your retina, no outside authority—no parent, teacher, political leader, or religious figure—can define your values. Only you can look into your own mind, heart, and soul and discover what is truly most important to *you*. Of course, you may find some similarities between your values and those of others. For example, both you and another person may love learning. But one of you may love to learn facts and figures, while the other revels in mastering profound philosophic concepts. Or perhaps one of you delights in mastering the ins and outs of investments in the stock market, while the other loves to invent complex financial instruments. In the domain of home and family, perhaps two parents equally value nurturing their children. But one expresses that nurturing through providing challenges and discipline, while another expresses that nurturing through long conversations about feelings and offering comfort in times of difficulty.

As you can see, even when two sets of values seem to be similar, one person's values will never be quite like anybody else's. If you and another person had exactly the same values, one of you would not be necessary! The world needs many different individuals, each with a unique set of values. Your unique purpose is to understand and fulfill your highest values. It is both a spiritual quest and the key to a fulfilling life.

This is why I suggest that you focus on your own personal journey of self-discovery and not allow social idealisms or possibly stagnant traditions or conventions to cloud the clarity of what really matters to you. Social idealisms that you learned from your parents or teachers may lead you to believe that you *should* save money . . . but if buying a movie ticket, a motorcycle, or a more expensive house is more in line with your *true* values, you will spend instead of save. Social idealisms picked up from your family or the culture around you might cause you to think that you *should* put in more time at work . . . but if going home to be with your children, meeting a beloved friend, or keeping a date with a potential life partner reflects what you *really* value, you will consistently find yourself leaving work early to fulfill that true desire.

People will naturally act in accordance with their own true highest values—spending money on what they truly value, spending time in ways that reflect what is most important to them. However, if they are not aware of their own values—and particularly if they believe they *should* follow the values of another—they will likely experience frustration and other self-depreciating emotions when they expect themselves to live outside their true highest values or even attempt to do so.

So if you want to know why you are not doing something you think you should, or why you can't stop doing something you think you shouldn't, the answer will almost always be the same: you are inevitably going to do what you truly value most. You may be frustrated with yourself because you *expect* yourself to live outside your own true highest values. But however you feel about your "shortcomings" or your "bad behavior," you will in fact continue to behave in whatever way aligns with your own true highest values.

By contrast, when you become aware of your own highest values and wholeheartedly pursue the goals that express them, your life will begin to embody the kind of fulfillment and inspiration experienced by history's extraordinary leaders and achievers. Awareness of their highest values is the secret of their achievement—and it can be the secret of yours.

This is why becoming aware of those true highest values is so important. This is why I have written this book: to share with you the power of the Values Factor.

How do you know when you are expressing your true highest values and when you are reflecting social idealisms? I'll offer some powerful exercises in the next chapter that will reveal your true highest values. Then, throughout this book, I'll show you how to use those most important values to help you reach goals that have been eluding you, from finding a life partner or establishing a business to saving money or losing weight.

Meanwhile, here's an important clue: anytime you find yourself saying, "I should . . . ," "I need to . . . ," or "I really must . . . ," you can be pretty certain that you are talking about social idealisms or the values of some external authority instead of expressing your own true highest values. When you hear yourself saying, "I desire to . . . ," "I choose to . . . ," or "I love to . . . ," then you know that you are talking about a goal that is truly valuable to you. Those are the goals you will inevitably achieve because they align with your highest values. But when you take on goals that are not aligned with your highest values, then you will, in all probability, struggle. External influences often seem to make it difficult to achieve your goals. Going within to choose your goals means that those goals are far more likely to be achieved.

VALUES COME FROM VOIDS

One of the things that's most powerful about our values is how they reflect what has been perceived as lacking in our lives—the seeming difficulties, challenges, obstacles, sorrows, or voids. Whatever we perceive is missing sets off a powerful hunger for precisely that thing. The perception of lack or void creates a corresponding value that drives us until we feel fulfilled.

For example, when I was a child, I felt restricted by the braces I was forced to wear. I perceived that restriction as a void—a lack of freedom. At age four, I begged my father to release me from that void. I promised to keep my hands and feet straight on my own if only I didn't have to wear the braces.

My father agreed. I was so thrilled to have filled that void—to have replaced restriction with freedom—that I have placed a very high value on physical movement and travel ever since. As a child, I simply ran everywhere, glorying in my ability to move without braces. Throughout my boyhood and youth, I placed a very high value on physical activity and went on to excel at sports. As an adult, I value travel, and I have vowed to visit every country on earth. To this day, I love being unrestricted, either by my physical location or by any type of limiting belief. Today, the universe is my playground, the world is my home, and every city is another platform where I can share my heart and soul.

Isn't it remarkable to think that my lifelong value on *freedom* came at least partly from the early-childhood experience of a void—a perception of a severe lack of freedom? Thus at a very early age, I began to experience the way *voids* create *values*.

I soon encountered another void that became another equally

important value. When I was five, I entered kindergarten, where the teacher frequently had us draw pictures. For some reason, my drawings were like the ones made by the girls: houses and trees and sky and sun, which we colored green, blue, and yellow. I seemed to have some gift with perspective and dimension, and I liked drawing those things. The other boys, on the other hand, preferred sketching armies and cars, which they colored black and red. So during drawing period, I repeatedly went to sit with the girls.

Well, that didn't suit my teacher. "You're *not* a girl!" she scolded me. "And you belong with the boys!" For days, she would drag me over to the boys' side of the classroom, put a black or a red crayon into my hand, and tell me to draw like they did.

Even at that early age, I just couldn't do what other people told me to do unless I believed in it myself. I couldn't draw like the other boys, and as soon as the teacher walked away, I'd go back to sit with the girls. So eventually, I was made to sit in the middle of the classroom, by myself. "You're not a girl, and you won't play with the boys, so you're just going to have to sit in the middle!" the teacher scolded me.

Here was another confrontation with a void: not being allowed to be myself. I wanted to be creative in my own way so I could discover the activities at which I was truly exceptional. Instead, I was being asked to fit into what conventional society expected of me. From that void developed one of my highest values: I learned how important it was not to let authority stop me from being true to myself. I placed an equally high value on helping other people find the means to become *their* true selves. Being forced to sit in the middle as a so-called punishment also helped me value the idea of embracing all sorts of polarities in life, which in turn assisted me later on in finding the middle path with a more gender-balanced perspective for the rest of my life's journey.

In first grade, I encountered yet another void. I was supposed to learn to read, but I showed early symptoms of dyslexia, and I couldn't make any meaning out of the letters, words, or phrases on the page.

I couldn't pronounce the words, either, so I was diagnosed with speech problems. From the regular class, I was put into the remedial class, and from the remedial class, I was put into what they called the dunce class. My parents were called in and told that I would never be able to read, write, or communicate. They were informed that I would never amount to very much or go very far in life.

From that series of voids, I eventually developed a very high value on reading, studying, learning, and teaching. And so every one of my voids created the values that continue to shape my life today. Although I was not supposed to go far in life, I went on to build a multimillion-dollar global business. Although I had difficulty reading and speaking, I became an internationally renowned writer and educator. And although I had once been called a dunce, I went on to graduate from college with honors, to teach myself numerous specialties as an expert in a number of different areas as I conducted advanced research in multiple fields, including philosophy, psychology, anthropology, physiology, chemistry, mathematics, physics, and astronomy.

Challenging as these childhood experiences seemed to be at the time, they were the essential voids that shaped my highest values. Because I had been previously blocked in my learning, I valued knowledge. Because I had been unable to communicate, I valued teaching and writing. Because I had felt trapped, I valued travel. And so I discovered this key principle: perceived *voids* create *values*. What you perceive as lacking—and want more of—determines what you value.

Significantly, this is a never-ending process. When one void is filled, another opens up, spurring you to new efforts—and new values. Indeed, some voids might never be filled. The artist hungry for self-expression, the mystic eager to know the secrets of the universe, the scientist ravenous for new knowledge, the person of service longing to help humanity—these people are driven by voids so great that their values become equally great. An entire lifetime might not be enough to fulfill their highest values.

Other voids can be filled more easily, so that the values they engender are left behind. A young man might feel a void of self-confidence, so that he values impressing others or proving to himself what he can do. Later in life, he feels more confident, and so his values shift to other areas—serving others, perhaps, or raising a family, or founding a new enterprise. A young woman feels a void of self-love, so she values relationships that feed her need to be admired. Later in life, she appreciates herself more fully, and so her values shift to other areas—deepening her romantic and family relationships, perhaps, or expressing herself, or exploring new ideas in science or business.

Thus, some of our values change throughout our lives. Others remain an essential part of who we are. Either way, however, your perceived voids determine your values—and your values shape your life. That is why understanding your highest values and organizing your life to pursue them is the secret to living an inspired and fulfilling life.

THE POWER OF VALUES

If there is something that you believe you would love to have in your life—such as a more fulfilling career, a life partner, or greater financial freedom—I can tell you that the reason you don't yet have it in that particular form is almost certainly that you don't truly value it enough. There is something else you value more, and that is where your energy, time, money, and focus have gone, whether you are aware of it or not. When you *truly* value something, you are constantly on the lookout for opportunities to fulfill that value. You'll notice people, places, things, ideas, or events to fulfill your value that another person will surely miss. You'll mobilize your energy to take advantage of those opportunities. And you'll bring all your mental, physical, and spiritual resources to bear to make sure that you fulfill what you truly seek.

Your highest values determine your *attention, retention,* and *intention*: what you notice, what you remember, and what you intend or act upon. We hear a lot these days about Attention Deficit Disorder—the difficulties some people seem to have in being attentive and focusing steadily. But all of us have some degree of Attention Deficit Disorder for the things we don't value. For the things we do highly value, we have what I call Attention Surplus Order, which does a fabulous job of filtering your perceptions. Out of all the stimuli in your environment, the ones you notice are the ones that will help you fulfill your highest values. Your highest values will lead you to notice things that another person might miss—even if you tried to point it out!

I experienced a striking example of the power of attention a few years ago when a close friend was driving us to her favorite sushi bar in Houston. We were on a block crowded with stores of all kinds, but out of that myriad of choices, my friend zeroed in on a new shoe boutique that hadn't been there the last time she drove by. She not only picked that one tiny store out of the dozens of other boutiques on that busy block, she even noticed two or three particular pairs of especially desirable shoes in the shop window.

I, on the other hand, couldn't for the life of me see that store, even when she tried to show me where it was. I didn't share her high value for shoes, and so I couldn't break through all the "noise" in the environment to see what had immediately attracted her. Her values gave her Attention Surplus Order for those shoes. My values made it virtually impossible for me to see them at all.

On the other hand, I'm interested in city planning, so I couldn't take my eyes off the high-rise condominium that was being erected on the corner. I tried to talk to my friend about the things I had noticed—the design of the building and the way it was being sited relative to the street—but I might as well have been talking about a building in China. She had driven right past that high-rise and not seen it, while I rode right past that shoe store and missed it completely. Her higher values determined her attention. My higher values determined mine. Between the two of us, which one is more likely to find fabulous shoes? Her values are perfectly aligned with that goal. If I decide I want a pair of quality shoes, I may have to momentarily realign my values to fit that goal, or link that goal to my highest values so that my Attention Surplus Order leads me where I want to go. (I will talk you through this process many times throughout the book, helping you complete it in various key areas of your life.)

Your highest values also affect what you remember, creating what I call "selective biased retention." That is, you are far more likely to retain information that you believe will help you attain your highest values and to forget information that does not relate to those values. My friend, to continue with the previous example, will probably never forget the address of that shoe store. I probably wouldn't remember it if you paid me. Her memory leads her to fulfill her higher values. My memory leads me to fulfill mine.

We all know people who say, "Oh, I can't remember anything—I have a mind like a sieve"—and then they rattle off the scores of their favorite teams, the results of their latest blood pressure test and cholesterol count, or the details of their child's latest triumph in school. They may indeed have terrible memories for the things that don't matter to them. But for what truly matters, they have selective biased retention—the ability to select and hold on to the information that supports their highest values.

Finally, your highest values create what I call "selective biased *intention*," adding an extra power to those intentions that truly align with those most important values. If you place a high value on health, you'll make sure you get to the gym, even if you have to give up some other pleasures to do so. If you place a higher value on "dressing for success," you might skip the gym in order to stop by your favorite fine clothing store. If you want to know what you truly value, look at what you make time for. Your highest values lend power to those intentions, and so they are the ones you fulfill.

Think about the power we mobilize when we bring together attention, retention, and intention to fulfill our highest values! There is really no stopping us. A mother who has as her highest value her newborn child can sleep through a freight train and yet be awakened by the whimpering of her baby. A child who is immersed in a video game may not hear you ask, "How was school today?" but immediately looks up when you say, "Would you like to come with me to see that new movie you were talking about?" All of us have had the experience of forgetting the names of random guests at a party—except for that one attractive man or woman, whose every detail is vividly etched into our memories! We've all had the experience of being too tired to accept an invitation from one person—and then jumping off the couch and getting ourselves dressed to take up the offer of somebody else. What we value most shapes how we process information, what we remember, and how we act, so that our minds, emotions, and intentions all work together to fulfill those most meaningful values.

This is why your true highest values are infinitely more powerful than any social idealisms and why it is so important not to allow social idealisms to cloud the clarity of your most inspiring values. When you are guided by social idealisms, you might try to do what you "should" or "ought to"—but if your attempts at maintaining attention, retention, and intention are not aligned with your highest values, you are likely to make only a halfhearted effort and you often will not remain focused. By contrast, when you seek to fulfill your highest values, you focus instantly on whatever helps you reach your goal and you mobilize every bit of your mind, body, and spirit to help you get there.

That's why the Values Factor is the key to achieving a fulfilling life. By becoming aware of your highest values, you mobilize your deepest power. It's an unbeatable combination.

HOW THE VALUES FACTOR CAN HELP YOU ACHIEVE YOUR GOALS

As you can see, becoming aware of your highest values exponentially expands your power to achieve anything you attempt to do. Discovering your true highest values creates a powerful synergy between your patience, your integrity, and your leadership abilities.

Knowing your highest values vastly increases your patience and perseverance. When you seek to achieve a goal that aligns with your highest values, you develop the power to wait as long as you need to, persevering in any effort required to achieve your goals.

Likewise, the Values Factor builds your integrity. Whenever you set goals that align with your highest value, you have true integrity: your words, tone, and actions all add up to one clear, unified purpose. This integrity affects others, who see and respond to it, and it also affects you, as you strengthen and deepen your single-minded, wholehearted intention.

In the same way, the Values Factor awakens your inner leader. When you are pursuing the highest values that you hold dear, you become empowered with certainty and clarity. You find yourself confident in the path that you choose to take and are inspired to lead others who may also be inspired by or along that path.

By increasing your patience, integrity, and leadership, the Values Factor helps you achieve your goals. In fact, it is highly improbable that you would achieve any goal that is *not* deeply linked to your highest values. If there is a goal in your life that you have already met or are on the road to meeting, you can be pretty sure that it reflects the things you value most.

What about the goals where you feel blocked or frustrated? Why are there some goals that you have tried and could not meet, maybe even several times, or some goals that seem so far out of reach that you can't even imagine trying for them?

Those seemingly elusive goals feel as though they're beyond your grasp either because they are truly unrealistic or because they are not really aligned with your highest values. This is a powerful point that eludes many people, so let's look at it a little more closely.

A truly unrealistic goal is one that doesn't take material reality into account. I'd be the first to agree that we can have an enormous impact upon the world around us, but that doesn't mean we can be or do anything we like with no regard for external constraints. A person who wanted to enter a highly competitive field with no training or experience might be continually frustrated in the path toward this goal—though a realistic plan for getting the necessary training and experience might achieve results. A person who consciously sets his or her romantic sights on a potential new life partner, but who is unconsciously still deeply connected to a previous relationship, might be unable to sustain that goal—though the search for a different life partner might temporarily bear fruit. Values are extraordinarily powerful, but they aren't *all*-powerful. So a certain amount of realism is in order.

What about the realistic goals that you have been trying to meet but are still not meeting? If you have a goal that frustrates you in this way, you have two choices:

1. You might discover that you don't really value the goal enough, after all, and that it is more of an idle fantasy than a true intention. Perhaps your goal is a remnant of something that once appealed to you as a child or a young adult, and you have held on to it even while your actual highest values have changed. Perhaps your goal is more driven by social idealisms or the pressure of those around you, and you know, deep down, that reaching that goal would not be genuinely fulfilling to you. Letting go of a goal that you don't really value can be an extraordinarily fulfilling experience that makes room in your life for new goals that you do value.

2. If you genuinely want to achieve a goal and find yourself unable to do so, you have another option: find a way to link your goal to your highest values.

I recently encountered a striking example of the first option: someone who readjusted his goals so that they more accurately expressed his true highest values. My friend Joshua writes and occasionally leads seminars, but for a period of his life, he was a bit frustrated that he didn't have the kind of career that I do. He had in the back of his mind the idea that he wanted to be a bestselling author and internationally renowned speaker, and whenever we spoke, I could hear that he felt some envy and regret.

So one day, when I happened to be giving a seminar in his home city, Joshua and I had a long dinner, and we were able to talk over exactly what my life was like. How did I spend each hour of my day? What did I think about? Where did my energy go? What was my weekly schedule like, and my monthly schedule, and my yearly schedule? What did I have time to do and what activities did I choose to forego in favor of what I valued more?

My friend realized that the life that I loved so much would actually be deeply unfulfilling for him. He liked the *idea* of being a bestselling author and international speaker. But when he thought about the time spent away from his family; the mental energy given to conversations with editors and speakers' bureaus and hosts on TV and radio programs; the hours spent on airplanes and in hotel rooms, he realized that if he actually had a life like mine, he would be deeply frustrated and unfulfilled. Whereas my highest values are researching, writing, traveling, and teaching—all of which are perfectly aligned with the life I lead—his highest values revolved around home, family, lots of quiet time to think and write, and long walks in the woods beside his beloved house. None of those values would be fulfilled by having a speaking and writing career like mine. In fact, that career would actively frustrate his true highest values. That was why he had not fully mobilized his resources toward achieving that career. Yet he had somehow held on to the idea that such a career was his true goal.

As soon as my friend got in touch with his *true* values, he let go of the goal that did not align with them. He gave up that nagging feeling that somehow he *should* be working harder to become a famous author or he *should* be out seeking more prestigious speaking engagements. He realized that the life he wanted was the life he had, and he was able to free up his energy for goals that really *did* fulfill his highest values: working on his new book, deepening his relationship with his wife and children, making sure to find time each week for at least one long hike.

On the other hand, I've worked with many clients who have chosen the second option: linking their unmet goals with their deepest, most important values. As a result, they have been able to achieve extraordinary progress in areas where they were formerly blocked.

For example, I once counseled an extraordinary doctor who ran into a conflict between his value of healing and his goal of providing for his family. This dedicated health professional prized healing so much that every time he got a little money, he immediately spent it to acquire knowledge that he believed would help him become a more effective doctor. He couldn't afford to re-carpet the house or get new furniture for the living room, let alone build a college fund for his children or even pay his bills on time, because every single dollar he could spare went to attending scientific seminars and buying health-related books.

After several years of this, his home was overflowing with books and he had run his family into debt. His wife was angry that they might not be able to send their two children to college, and she was upset about all the hours she'd spent negotiating with bill collectors and creditors. His children couldn't understand why their father, despite being a prominent professional, couldn't give them some of the things their friends took for granted: music lessons, trips to the amusement park, family vacations.

The doctor didn't care about unpaid bills or family vacations, but he was upset because his family was upset. He wanted to help his wife and children become more fulfilled, and he couldn't understand why he kept not meeting his financial goals.

Yet however important he thought those goals "should" be, this man kept putting his learning and his healing first. Given his high value on healing and learning and his low value on financial freedom, he was going to consistently choose books over his bank account.

Unlike my writer friend, however, this doctor was not willing to give up his goal of fiscal responsibility. He saw how much his financial chaos was frustrating his family, so he came to me for help.

The Values Factor to the rescue! I showed this dedicated man how to link his goal of financial independence to his highest value of healing. I helped him see that creating financial independence would actually free him to focus on his patients without having to worry about his wife and children. Furthermore, becoming more financially viable would give him more influence and prestige among other doctors and other health professionals, increasing the likelihood that people would listen to his opinions and follow his suggestions. He might even be able to fund research or build clinics with the fruits of his investments. With my help, he began to see more and more links between building wealth and achieving his healing mission.

The doctor and I made so many links that he began to approach his old goals in a new way. Now that his highest value was linked to his goal of financial freedom as well as to his goal of healing and learning, he brought to bear every ounce of his dedication to reaching *all* of his goals. It was as if the three goals—money, healing, and learning—had become one single goal, with each piece feeding the others and with the doctor's highest values feeding them all. Instead of halfheartedly trying to put a few dollars into a savings account, the doctor now eagerly embraced the opportunity to study the financial pages, accelerate his rate of savings, make some sound investments, and multiply his wealth for himself and his family. At my suggestion, he began charging his colleagues for the opportunity to observe him at work, linking his value of sharing his knowledge with his goal of improving his finances. He also found ways of accessing health education information for free through the library (this was in pre-Internet days!) rather than spending so much money on books.

Within a few months, to his family's great relief, my client had completely transformed his financial situation. Once this dedicated man had linked his real highest value of healing with his goal of financial independence, there was no stopping him. That is the power of the Values Factor.

MAKING THE MOST OF THIS BOOK

The value you get from this book will be in direct proportion to how deeply you engage with it. If you read this book as a passive observer, you will learn something—but you will not learn nearly as much as if you engage with it, deeply and fully, relating it to your own life, your own goals, and your own true highest values. Chapter by chapter, you will have the opportunity to discover your highest values and integrate them with your endeavors in each core area of life.

The book begins with an explanation of how to identify your highest values: a provocative thirteen-part questionnaire in which you become aware of your current values by looking at how you actually live. With what do you fill your home and work space? What occupies your time? What energizes you? Where do you spend your money? What do you talk about and think about? In which areas of your life are you most focused and organized? What inspires you? What are your most consistent long-term goals? What do you love to research and explore?

Through this process, you come to realize that your highest values are not the social idealisms to which you give lip service—such vague abstractions as honesty or integrity—but the core purposes that drive your actions and shape your life. Understanding your highest values is the key to understanding yourself, your purpose, and your inspired destiny. It is also the key to creating a life's work that will fulfill you, forging relationships that will both challenge and nourish you, and tapping into your own unique genius.

As I've said, my highest values are researching, writing, traveling, and teaching. Understanding these values has enabled me to create a life based on these values. I live on a luxury ship that enables me to travel the world even when I'm "at home," studying the laws of human potential and writing about what I've discovered. I also fly around the globe to teach others about what I've learned.

Other people have different values. Rose Kennedy's highest value was raising a family of leaders. She spent her days nurturing, educating, and inspiring her children, grooming them for the leadership she envisioned as their birthright. She would not have found my life fulfilling, any more than I would have been fulfilled by hers. Yet by understanding her own highest value and shaping her life accordingly, she both found fulfillment and was of profound service to others. Whenever I meet a parent who tells me that their highest value is caring for their children, I think of Rose Kennedy and the power she found in knowing her highest values.

Each of us has our own highest values, which we understand and express in our own unique ways. I've already told you about my client, the respected doctor, whose highest values were healing, learning more about healing, and teaching others to heal. His life faltered when he tried to build wealth and to create a fulfilling life for his family in a way that was disconnected from his highest values. His life became far more productive and fulfilling when he found a way to link his wealth-creating efforts to his highest values so that he could build wealth and security *through* healing, learning, and teaching.

Another client's highest value was dancing. Although she was middle-aged and slightly overweight, she was a graceful woman who simply loved to dance. When I met her, she felt despair about not finding work that fulfilled her—and she had absolutely no idea that at her age, she could create a life organized around her devotion to dance. By showing her the power of the Values Factor, I helped her build an international dance touring business based on the activity that she loved most. Her enterprise succeeded because it was deeply rooted in her highest values. This in turn enabled her to live her destiny, activate her genius, and create a fulfilling career.

Once you have identified your highest values, it's time to align your goals to them. I show you how to use this process in the seven core areas of life: relationships, education, career, financial life, social influence, health, and your inspired spiritual quest. I explain the way to achieve fulfillment in each of these areas: align your goals and your highest values.

This might sound simple—because it is simple. When our goals and highest values are aligned, we access resources we never even realized we had because, finally, all of our abilities, stamina, and intention are mobilized together toward creating the life that we truly love—the life that suits our unique purpose in the world. Yet for want of understanding of this simple, powerful concept, most people are living lives of quiet desperation instead of the amazing lives of inspiration that are their birthright. No matter who you are or what goals you have, understanding the Values Factor can help you create an extraordinary life that inspires and fulfills you every day.

MASTERING THE VALUES FACTOR

I feel grateful that I've been able to create such a fulfilling life, one that enables me to pursue my highest purpose. As a result, I've spent the past two and a half decades helping hundreds of thousands of people achieve *their* breakthroughs, showing them how to discover their highest values and then set their goals accordingly. Now, people all over the world are tapping into the enormous power of the Values Factor: a concrete approach to determining their highest values and using them to achieve their most meaningful goals.

People who draw upon their own highest values can live truly extraordinary lives. They access enormous inspiration and inner drive to achieve even the most daunting task; they notice opportunities that others miss; they create fulfilling relationships of all types— with life partners, family members, colleagues, friends; and they put themselves on the path to fulfilling their inspired destiny.

Knowing your highest values and applying your intentions accordingly gives you the opportunity for so many rewards in your life: everything from financial achievement, love, and more fulfilling relationships to leadership, integrity, and a deeper sense of meaning. Mastering the Values Factor can mean the difference between a life that lacks inspiration and a life that is bursting with it, between a life that feels stagnant and one that is overflowing with purpose and inner drive. Mastering the Values Factor is the key to transforming and fulfilling your life.

Identifying Your Values

Choose a job you love, and you will never
have to work a day in your life.

—CONFUCIUS

Now that you understand the importance of values, it's time to identify your own values—a process that could well be one of the most important actions you ever take. A famous proverb from the Greek tradition is eloquent testimony to the importance of identifying your values: *know thyself, be thyself, love thyself.* How can you be yourself unless you know who you are? And how can you love yourself unless you *are* truly yourself, living your life according to your own highest values? Know yourself and your highest values; live authentically based on those values; and love yourself for being a unique creature unlike any other in the universe. In other words, identifying your highest values is your first step on the road to self-knowledge, self-love, and fulfillment of your life's purpose.

If identifying your highest values is most important, setting goals and intentions according to these highest values comes second. Unless your goals and intentions align with your highest values, they have little probability of being realized. You simply won't mobilize the full power of physical, mental, and spiritual resources to bring those goals about. Knowing your highest values is not only the key to self-knowledge and self-love; it is the means by which you can accomplish any goal you set—as long as it is a true expression of your highest values. (Of course, I don't recommend setting goals that defy any of the known laws of the universe. For example, I wouldn't suggest that you attempt anything such as levitation, which would violate the law of gravity—such an effort can be obviously self-defeating!) Being able to set goals in alignment with your highest values is the power of the Values Factor: the secret to living a full and meaningful life.

PASSION VERSUS HIGHEST VALUES

Because the way we talk about our lives has such tremendous impact on how we think and how we live, I'd like to take a moment to clarify a few terms. Ever since the 1985 publication of *A Passion for Excellence* by Tom Peters and Nancy Austin, the term "passion" has become increasingly popular. People often say, "I've got to find my passion" or "I'm looking for work or a relationship that I can be passionate about." As a result, many have come to believe that the secret to an inspired life is passion.

"Passion," however, is not a synonym for our highest values. "Passion" literally means "suffering." It refers not to our most inspired or higher natures, but to our animal selves, the ungoverned, out-of-control emotions that often drive us toward immediate gratification, addiction, and other states that are by definition not aligned with our highest values. Passion often drives us to seek a kind of perpetual bliss that is unobtainable even as we strive to avoid unhappiness, challenges, discomfort, or suffering, which are ultimately unavoidable. So if you choose to live by your passion, you are not living according to your highest values. You are simply following the impulses and instincts of your animal nature, manifesting lust, greed, gluttony, sloth, and addiction—"passions" that can become significant obstacles to leading a fulfilled and inspired life. Indeed, when people live according to their lower values—when they follow other people's values or subordinate themselves to social idealisms—they often seek immediate gratification, passion, or some other type of addictive pleasure. Instead of starting on the long, rewarding journey of inner fulfillment of their highest values, they seek instant gains and outer pleasures.

Rather than being driven by passion, truly fulfilled human beings will follow their mission, inspired by their highest values and most integrated being. Just as your values are completely individual and unique to you, so is your mission the expression of your own unique contribution to the world. Discovering this mission—the contribution that only *you* can make—is the key to a life that can be meaningful beyond your wildest dreams.

If you study the lives of the greatest contributors to our world, you will readily discover that each of them danced to the beat of his or her own unique drum, following his or her own inspiration. They chose not to subordinate themselves or their highest values to others. Instead, they forged extraordinary lives in pursuit of their own inspired missions. Groundbreaking physicist Albert Einstein put it very nicely when he said ironically, "To punish me for my contempt for authority, fate made me an authority myself." In a similar vein, American philosopher Ralph Waldo Emerson noted, "Envy is ignorance, imitation is suicide."

In other words, only by being true to yourself can you maintain your integrity, achieve your own authority, and find the fulfillment that you inwardly seek. The alternative was chillingly described by Emerson's contemporary Henry David Thoreau, who wrote, "The mass of men live lives of quiet desperation. What is called resignation is confirmed desperation." Thoreau saw quite clearly that most people never tap into what really inspires them. Instead, they subordinate themselves to social idealisms (what they think they "ought" to do), the values of others whom they look up to, or their own limited beliefs about what is possible for them. They stand in sharp contrast to the people who dare to leave a legacy by creating a life based on their highest values, a life that makes a unique contribution to current and future generations of humanity.

Isn't it interesting that so many people subordinate themselves to great leaders—political, religious, and artistic leaders—and yet, the great leaders achieved their influence precisely by *not* subordinating themselves? Great leaders refuse to placate the social norm or to remain stuck in stagnant traditions or old paradigms. Instead, they embrace the challenge of giving birth to new ideas and new visions, and succeed in making significant and novel contributions to the world.

You can do exactly the same thing if you choose. You can resemble the great leaders who have left their mark on history. You can draw on your truest self—as expressed by your highest value—to make a great contribution to the world. True, you may run the risk of being ridiculed and violently opposed until your truth becomes self-evident. This was the fate of such religious leaders as Jesus, Moses, Buddha, and Mohammed, and of such political leaders as Abraham Lincoln, Martin Luther King Jr., and Elizabeth Cady Stanton. Business leaders like Walt Disney and Steve Jobs were not readily understood at first; nor were groundbreaking scientists like Galileo or Charles Darwin. Yet these are the leaders whom many respect and seek to emulate today, the leaders whose discoveries, enterprises, and visions continue to shape our world. Each man or woman's power comes from their ability to understand and fulfill their own highest values and to shape their lives accordingly.

The stakes here are very high. If you don't understand your highest values and build a life around them, you run the risk of being disempowered and overpowered by other people's expectations or commands.

How do you know whether you are living according to your true highest values? Just look at your life. That old saying "Actions speak louder than words" is especially true when it comes to values: our lives are constantly demonstrating what matters to us most.

For example, if you say you value health and well-being but haven't managed to give up smoking, then there is almost certainly something you value more than health. For example, perhaps you value the relaxation that smoking brings, and you haven't yet found anything that relaxes you as much. The relaxation may mean so much to you that you can't bring yourself to give up smoking, even though you know it is supposed to be bad for you. Or perhaps there are unconscious motives involved—perhaps your father smoked, and smoking makes you feel closer to him; or perhaps your smoking was an early attempt to defy your mother and you still value the sense of independence and autonomy that you associate with this once forbidden activity. (In the chapter on health, I'll help you sort through these issues and make more empowered decisions about your health.)

Or, if you say you value financial independence but find yourself spending rather than saving and investing, then you almost certainly value something more than financial independence. Perhaps you like the idea of saving money but value the pleasure you get from indulging in a movie, a new possession, or a much-needed vacation. Or again, you might have unconscious motives: you might associate saving with feeling restricted and tied down, while you associate spending with feeling powerful and fancy-free. (In later chapters, I'll help you sort through these issues as well.)

As I say to my clients, your life never lies. What you value most is what your life will reveal.

Unfortunately, most of us spend far too much time *not* consciously honoring our own highest values. Instead, we subordinate ourselves to other people's values—or at least, we try. Perhaps we attempt to buy into the values of the family we grew up in, the community we were raised in, or the religious institution we have always belonged to. Often, we try to have it both ways. In private, we hold fast to our true highest values. In public, though, we try our best to act as though we accept the values of those whom we view as authority figures. We make sure our parents understand that we have absorbed their values of choosing security above all else, even if privately we long for a more creative or adventurous life. We make sure that the people who go to our church or synagogue understand that we follow all the rules of our religion, even if privately we harbor doubts or disagreements. We may not even expect to bring our outer and inner selves into alignment, but this attempted outer façade and inner repression takes its toll.

Most people experience conflicts of this kind. As a result, they live out the gloomy observation of Thoreau, leading quiet lives of desperation, rather than the amazing life of inspiration that comes from knowing and living according to their own highest values. Anytime you expect yourself to live outside your own highest values, you will probably perceive your life as frustrating or even daunting as true meaning and fulfillment seem to elude you.

So let's make the Values Factor work for you by identifying your true highest values! We'll begin by uncovering the social idealisms that may have you in their grip—notions that you may have been blindly attempting to follow rather than doing the diligent work of identifying your true highest values. In order to identify our "love to's," we may first need to identify our "shoulds."

Exercise 1. Identify Your Social Idealisms

Instructions: Write down each idea you hold expressing that you "should," "have to," or are "supposed to" do something. Then write down which authority figure or life situation gave you that message.

Ideas expressing "should," "have to," or "supposed to"	Where this idea came from
I should save and invest my money.	father, wealth-building books

SIGNS OF LIVING BY SOMEONE ELSE'S VALUES

1. You hear yourself using imperative language.

- I should be doing this.
- I ought to be doing that.
- I am supposed to be doing this.
- I need to do that.
- I must do this.

2. You experience the ABCD's of negativity.

A = Anger and Aggression
B = Blame and Betrayal
C = Criticism and Challenge
D = Despair and Depression

YOUR HIGHEST VALUES OR
SOMEONE ELSE'S?

Now, let's get one thing clear. I am not for a moment suggesting that there *must* be an opposition between the values you were raised with and the values you genuinely hold. Nor am I suggesting that your values must be "selfish," as opposed to the "unselfish" values embodied in social idealisms. History is full of individuals whose apparent highest values centered on fighting for human rights, protecting the environment, improving the lives of animals, discovering new cures for deadly diseases, spreading knowledge, or making beautiful art. Likewise, many great entrepreneurs and business leaders had a vision for how to make the world a greater place through providing products and services that millions of people needed. In all of these cases, each individual made an enormous contribution to humanity—but that contribution was possible only because they lived by their own highest values.

So you don't need to blindly reject all of the values or social idealisms you were raised with. But neither can you simply assume that these values are necessarily your own. Whether your values involve building wealth or curing cancer, writing poetry or running a restaurant, raising a family or digging a garden, the key is that you identify your true highest values for yourself and then consciously craft a life that is based on fully expressing them. That is the way to mobilize your resources in service of your mission. That is the way to create the inspired and fulfilling life that can make your work feel like a treat and turn every day into a vacation. And that is the way to create deep, fulfilling, authentic relationships with your loving, intimate partner; your family; your colleagues; and your community.

How do you know whether you are living by your own values or by someone else's? There are two simple ways to tell:

1. Whenever you try to live according to someone else's values, you find yourself saying "should," "ought to," and "have to."

2. When you fail to do what you thought you "should," you experience the ABCD's of negativity—anger, blame, criticism, and despair—directed toward yourself.

Whenever I hear someone say, "I tried to do it, but I just didn't seem to get around to it," I understand that what they have "tried" to do isn't really all that important to them. What *was* truly more important to them was what they kept doing instead! That is why they kept doing it. So if you say you want to do something *but you are not doing it*, your actions reveal that this action is not really important to you.

In other words, saying, "I have to . . ." or "I should . . ." is a kind of fantasy in which you try to convince yourself that something outside of your true highest values really is important to you. Then, when you fail to do what you "should," you beat yourself up. The ABCD's of negativity are likely to follow. However, that beating yourself up is actually a gift! Why? Because it's your way of getting yourself to set authentic goals according to your *true* highest values. It may feel as though you are "sabotaging" yourself, that you can't stay focused, or that you can't stay disciplined. You might even say to yourself, "What is wrong with me? Why can't I do what I say I should do?" But whenever you try to force your mind and body to do something that does not fit who you truly are, your whole self rebels. Your apparent "failure" is really your authentic self asking to be heard. The ABCD's of negativity are the pains that reveal how out of touch you are with your true highest values.

How can you return to your true highest values? One useful step is to ask yourself what you truly love doing. Move on to Exercise 2 to learn more.

Exercise 2. Discover What You Love

To identify your true highest values, begin by asking yourself what you love to do. What activities inspire you? Which situations do you find meaningful? What relationships do you feel deeply connected to? Discovering what you love and what inspires you will help connect you to your highest values.

Instructions: Complete the statement "I love to . . ." as often as you can, each time identifying a different activity that you truly love.
  For example:

I love to . . . spend time with my children.
I love to . . . go out to dinner at a quiet restaurant with someone
    I enjoy talking to.
I love to . . . grow my business.
I love to . . . negotiate complicated deals.
I love to . . . hang out with my friends.

I love to . . .	
I love to . . .	
I love to . . .	
I love to . . .	
I love to . . .	
I love to . . .	

Now, look over what you wrote. In the box on the right, put a check next to the activities that you find *most* inspiring.

SIGNS OF LIVING BY YOUR OWN HIGHEST VALUES

1. You hear yourself using affirmative language.

- I love doing this.
- I am inspired by doing that.
- I dream of doing this.
- I feel it is my destiny to do that.
- I choose and live to do this.

2. You experience an alignment between your highest values and your actions.

- I have done exactly as I dreamed and planned.
- I am inspired by the way I am acting.
- I am enthused about what I am doing.
- I love what I am doing.
- I am grateful to be able to do what I love.

YOUR HIGHEST VALUES REVEAL YOUR IDENTITY

One of the great things about getting in touch with your highest values is that you thereby discover who you are. Whatever you value most in life ultimately determines your identity.

Think about what happens when someone asks, "Who are you?"

If you have young children and your highest value is your children, you will answer, "I'm a mother" or "I'm a father."

If owning a business represents your highest value, you will answer, "I'm an entrepreneur."

If your highest value involves writing, painting, or engaging in some other artistic activity, you might well answer, "I'm an artist," even if you earn your living as a waitress or an auto mechanic. If you're a child, and your highest value is school, you might say, "I'm a fifth-grader." But if your highest value is sports or games, you might reply, "I'm a baseball player" or "I'm a seventh-level dragon master."

If your highest value is your religion, you might identify yourself by saying, "I'm a Christian," "I'm a Muslim," or "I'm a Jew." If your highest value is your sexuality or your looks, you might answer, "I'm a beautiful woman" or "I'm a real ladies' man!" or even "I'm a great lover." If your highest value is embodied in your hobby or a vocation, you might say, "I'm a vintage records collector," "I'm a golfer," or "I'm a seasoned traveler." Whatever you most value determines who you are.

Discovering your identity is a powerful route to identifying your values. Explore Exercise 3 to dig deeper.

Exercise 3. Discover Your Identity

Instructions: Answer the following questions:

How do you identify yourself?

_____

_____

_____

What values does this reveal?

_____

_____

_____

How does your partner identify himself or herself?

_____

_____

_____

What values does this reveal?

_____

_____

_____

Think of one of your friends. How does that person identify himself or herself?

_____

_____

_____

What values does this reveal?

_____

_____

_____

Think of a colleague. How does that person identify himself or herself?

_____

_____

_____

What values does this reveal?

_____

_____

_____

AS YOU CHANGE, SO DO YOUR HIGHEST VALUES

Because your identity reflects your highest values, you can expect your identity to change as your highest values change and vice versa. What is important to you at one age or stage of life is likely to be quite different from what matters to you at another age or stage of life, as the following chart reflects:

Ages	Possible Values
0–10	playing, having fun, developing selective skills
10–20	social interaction
20–30	establishing a relationship, career, and financial foundation
30–40	establishing a family and a social and vocational identity
40–50	ensuring financial security and further education of your offspring
50–60	traveling and doing meaningful activities that have been delayed
60–70	leaving a legacy and preparing for mortality
70–80	contributing back to society and assisting the next generation
80–90	concentrating on activities that help you maintain your faculties and continued contribution

As we saw in the previous chapter, your highest values seldom remain stagnant. As you fill a void, a new void appears, generating a new value. Fulfillment of one value initiates a new dissatisfaction and a new void, which in turn drives you to new areas of fulfillment. Once you have developed your ability to earn money and build a career, you may desire to contribute more socially. Once you have built a career, you may wish to expand your influence, first within your profession and then beyond. Once you have established your influence in the present, you may wish to leave a legacy for future generations. Your highest values evolve as you grow into each new identity. The Values Factor can help you become aware of this evolution so that you can best align your goals and your highest values at every stage of your journey.

Your values in relationships evolve as well. In adolescence, you may wish to establish your ability to have romantic relationships and to explore what your sexual identity means to you. Once you have established your romantic or sexual identity, you may wish to move into deeper and more meaningful relationships that make greater demands upon you, enabling you to grow and change and build a life with your partner. Building a life with a partner might evolve into creating a family. When your children have grown up and left home, you may go on to create a new life with your partner, perhaps traveling the world, pursuing a great cause, or discovering new activities that the two of you now have time to share. Or you may rewrite your relationship to accommodate new ambitions at work, new involvement in the community, or new hobbies, avocations, or interests. Once again, being aware of the Values Factor can help you bring your goals and highest values into alignment.

Thinking about how your highest values have grown and evolved either gradually or abruptly can help you identify what they are now. Complete Exercise 4 to learn more about your constantly evolving highest values.

Exercise 4. Understand How Your Highest Values Evolve

Instructions: Complete the following chart. If you have not yet reached a given stage of life, imagine what your highest values might be at that point:

Time Period	Key Values
Childhood	1.
	2.
	3.
Adolescence	1.
	2.
	3.
Early Adulthood	1.
	2.
	3.
Thirties	1.
	2.
	3.
Forties	1.
	2.
	3.
Fifties	1.
	2.
	3.
Sixties	1.
	2.
	3.

Time Period	Key Values
Seventies and Beyond	1.
	2.
	3.

DETERMINING YOUR HIGHEST VALUES STEP BY STEP

Now it's time to take a closer look at your life to see exactly which highest values it reveals today. This is a multistep process in which you keep refining your answers until your hierarchy of values finally emerges with crystal clarity.

Step 1: Answer the Following Thirteen Questions with Three Examples for Each. For Each Answer, Choose the Three Examples That Are Most Important to You.

1. How do you fill your personal or professional space?

Have you ever noticed the way things that are really not important to you go into the trash, the attic, or the storage closet? You might believe that you value your prized baseball card collection, but if you have it packed away in the attic where you never see it, the collection is probably not as important to you as those things that you see and use every day. In fact, you usually keep the things that are important to you where you can see or touch them, either at home or at work.

What does your life demonstrate through *your* space? When you look around your home or office, do you see family photos, sports trophies, business awards, books? Do you see beautiful objects, comfortable furniture for friends to sit on, or souvenirs of favorite places you've visited? Perhaps your space is full of games, puzzles, DVDs,

CDs, or other forms of entertainment. Whatever you see around you is a very strong clue as to what you value most. Which three items do you fill your personal or professional space with most?

_____

_____

_____

2. How do you spend your time?

Here's another value determinant you can count on: people make time for things that are really important to them and run out of time for things that aren't. Even though people usually say, "I don't have time for what really I want to do," the truth is that they are too busy doing what is truly most important to them. And what they *think* they want to be doing isn't really what's most important. You find time for things that are really important to you. Somehow, you figure it out.

So how do you spend your time? I personally spend my days researching, writing, traveling, and teaching. Those are my four highest values. I find time for doing them . . . and I am too busy to ever find time for cooking, driving, and doing domestic things, which are low on my list of values. How you spend your time tells you what matters to you most. Which three actions do you truly spend your time on most?

_____

_____

_____

3. How do you spend your energy?

You have energy for the things that inspire you—the things you value most—even while you run out of energy for things that do not inspire you. That's because things that are low among your values drain you, whereas things that are high among your values energize you. In fact, when you are doing something that you value highly, you have more energy afterward than when you started because you're doing something that you love and are inspired by. So which three actions do you spend your energy on—and where do you get your energy?

_____

_____

_____

4. How do you spend your money?

Again, you find money for things that are valuable to you, but you don't want to part with your money for things that are not important to you. So your choices about spending money tell you a great deal about what you value most.

Now, at this point, you might be noticing some overlap: some similarities between what you fill your space with and how you spend your time, energy, and money. That is a great sign. It means that you have already aligned a lot of your highest values, goals, and daily activities. If you notice a lot of divergence between the answers to these first four questions, you might be writing answers that are not exactly true. Perhaps you are writing what you wish or hope your answer would be, or what you think it should be according to some external authority or social idealism. The key is to identify where or how you truly spend your money. So, what are the three items you spend most of your money on and always find money for?

_____

_____

_____

5. Where do you have the most order and organization?

We bring order and organization to things that are important to us and allow chaos and disorder with things that are low on our values. So look at where you have the greatest order and organization in your life and you'll have a true sense of what matters most to you. It could be your social calendar, your dietary regimen, your clothes and wardrobe, your business, your finances, your spiritual ritual, your cooking area, or your house.

Everyone has some item or area of life that is most organized. In my case, I see the most order and organization in my research and teaching materials, and in my itinerary for traveling. This helps me see that my values involve researching, writing, traveling, and teaching. Which three items or areas do you have most organized?

_____

_____

_____

6. Where are you most reliable, disciplined, and focused?

You don't have to be prodded from the outside to do the things that you value the most. You are inspired from within to do those things . . . and so you do them. Look at the activities, relationships, and goals for which you are disciplined, reliable, and focused—the things that nobody has to get you up to do. For me, again, that's researching, writing, traveling, and teaching. I love those activities! Which three activities are you most reliable or disciplined at doing?

_____

_____

_____

7. What do you think about, and what is your innermost dominant thought?

I'm not talking about negative self-thoughts or the things that distract you. I'm not talking about the fantasies, "shoulds," or "oughts." I'm talking about your most common thoughts about how you want your life—thoughts that you show slow or steady evidence of actually bringing to fruition. Which three things are you thinking about most?

_____

_____

_____

8. What do you visualize and realize?

Again, I'm not talking about fantasies. I'm asking what you visualize for your life that is slowly but surely coming true.

In my case, I visualize traveling the world and setting foot in every country on the face of the earth and teaching. That is what I visualize. And that is what I am realizing. Which three outcomes are you mostly visualizing and realizing?

_____

_____

_____

9. What is your internal dialogue?

What do you keep talking to yourself about the most? I am not asking about negative self-talk or self-aggrandizement. I want you to think of things you say to yourself about what you desire—internal dialogues that actually seem to be coming true and showing some fruits. Which three outcomes about how you would love your life to be do you talk to yourself about most?

_____

_____

_____

10. What do you talk about in social settings?

Okay, now here's a clue that you'll probably notice for other people as well as yourself. What are the topics that you keep wanting to bring into the conversation that nobody has to remind you to talk about? What subjects turn you into an instant extrovert?

You've probably noticed that there are topics that immediately bring you to life and start you talking . . . and others that turn you into an introvert who has nothing to say or who wants to change the subject. You can use this same insight to analyze other people's values. If you go up to somebody and they ask you about your kids, that means that either their kids or your kids are important to them. If they say, "How's business?" they value business. If they ask, "Are you seeing anyone new?" then relationships matter to them. Topics that attract you are a key to what you value. Which three topics do you keep wanting to talk to others about most?

_____

_____

_____

11. What inspires you?

What inspires you now? What has inspired you in the past? Who inspires you? What is common to the people who inspire you? Figuring out what inspires you most reveals what you value most. Which three people, actions, or outcomes inspire you most, and what is common to them?

---

12. What are the most consistent long-term goals that you have set?

What are the three long-term goals that you have focused on that you are bringing into reality? Again, I'm not talking about the fantasies that nothing is happening with. I want the dreams you are bringing into reality slowly but surely, the dreams that have been dominating your mind and your thoughts for a while—the dreams that you are bringing into daily life, step by step by step. So which are the three most important goals that you keep focusing on that are gradually coming true and appear in your reality?

---

13. What do you love to learn about most?

What topics of study inspire you the most? When you enter a bookstore, which section do you make a beeline for? Which magazines and newspapers do you subscribe to, and which sections do you turn to first? Are there nonfiction TV shows or film documentaries that you seek out? Are there topics that you find yourself thinking about or asking questions about? The three answers to these questions will help reveal your highest values.

_____

_____

_____

THE 13 QUESTIONS THAT REVEAL YOUR HIGHEST VALUES

1. How do you fill your space?

2. How do you spend your time?

3. How do you spend your energy?

4. How do you spend your money?

5. Where are you most organized?

6. Where are you most reliable?

7. What dominates your thoughts?

8. What do you visualize most?

9. What do you most often talk to yourself about?

10. What do you most often talk to others about?

11. What inspires you?

12. What goals stand out in your life and have stood the test of time?

13. What topics do you love to study, read about, or research?

Step 2: Identify the Answers That Repeat Most Often

Once you've given three answers for each of the thirteen questions, you'll see that among your thirty-nine answers there is a certain amount of repetition—perhaps even a lot of repetition. You may be expressing the same kinds of values in different ways—for example, "spending time with people I like," "having a drink with my coworkers," "going out to eat with my friends"—but if you look closely, you can see some patterns begin to emerge.

So look at the answer that is most often repeated and write beside it the number of how often it repeats. Then find the second most frequent answer, then the third, and so on, until you have ranked every single answer. This gives you a good primary indicator of what your highest values are. You can even start making decisions based on this initial hierarchy of values—and you can see how your life is already demonstrating your natural commitment to these highest values.

Step 3: Summarize and Prioritize Your Values

Based on how often your answers appear and repeat, create a list of your five most important values in priority order, with the most important value first and the least important value last:

1. _____

2. _____

3. _____

4. _____

5. _____

This list gives you a good indicator of what your hierarchy of values is, a structure that you can start building your life around and making decisions from. The hierarchy of values on this list helps you see which values your life demonstrates to be most important.

Step 4: Double-Check Your Hierarchy of Values

To ensure that you have accurately determined your hierarchy of values, ask yourself the following questions:

- When I have a choice between the first and second of the values on the list, which do I most often choose? Which one does my life most commonly demonstrate as most important?
- When I have a choice between the second and third of the values on the list, which do I most often choose? Which one does my life most commonly demonstrate as most important?
- When I have a choice between the third and fourth of the values on the list, which do I most often choose? Which one does my life most commonly demonstrate as most important?

Continue questioning in this way until you have examined every one of the values on your list. Then proceed to Step 5.

Step 5: If Necessary, Revise Your List

Write your final hierarchy of values in the space below:

1. _____

2. _____

3. _____

4. _____

5. _____

Welcome to your most important values! These highest values determine your daily perceptions, decisions, and actions. They are leading you to your current destiny and determining the evolution of your life's journey.

Step 6: Continue to Reevaluate Your Values

Because your highest values keep evolving, I suggest that you reevaluate your hierarchy of values every three months. Follow the five previous steps every three months and keep records of the evolution of your highest values along your life's journey.

LIVING YOUR HIGHEST VALUES

Now that you have a sense of your highest values, you have the opportunity and power to reshape your life to ensure that your goals, your actions, your relationships, your career, and your highest values all align. Throughout this book, you will see how awareness of your highest values enables you to create the inspired life you dream of, one that expresses your unique contribution and mission here on earth.

In the next chapter, you will take your journey one step further as you come to understand the value of challenge. Mastering the material in that chapter will enable you to proceed with a more balanced perspective, which in turn will enable you to pursue your mission with renewed dedication and inspiration.

The Value of Challenge

We are all faced with a series of great opportunities brilliantly disguised as impossible situations.

—CHARLES SWINDOLL

M ost of us have had at least brief moments of saying, "I feel empty inside. I just don't feel fulfilled."

We're probably used to thinking of those moments as "bad" times. I'd like to suggest that they are also our blessings in disguise.

One of the most powerful discoveries I ever made came in my early twenties. After a childhood and adolescence full of physical and mental challenges, I had become inspired to discover my most meaningful purpose—and, accordingly, to awaken some of my dormant powers. From being a dyslexic child in braces who could barely speak, read, or write, I went on to become one of the top students at the junior college, university, and then professional school that I attended, with a lifelong hunger for research, study, writing, and communication.

From this experience, I learned a basic truth: your hierarchy of voids determines your hierarchy of values. Whatever you perceive to be most missing becomes the most important thing in your life.

Whatever you think is most empty wants to be fulfilled. It was this realization that awakened me to the Values Factor.

Paradoxically, those people who have accomplished greatness in their lives have also experienced times of feeling great emptiness. Martin Luther King Jr. had a profound sense that justice was lacking in American life . . . and so he placed an immense value on achieving justice. Albert Einstein had a deep sense of his own ignorance . . . and so he placed an extraordinary value on achieving knowledge. Helen Keller felt the vast void of being unable to hear or see . . . and so she developed an enormous value on being able to overcome her disabilities and communicate with others. By experiencing voids and challenges, these people were inspired to accomplishments that helped change the course of human history. Your greatest voids determine your greatest values—and people who have experienced the very greatest voids are often those who achieve the most inspiring accomplishments. This is the value of challenge.

CHOOSE THE CHALLENGES
THAT INSPIRE YOU

Even minor voids and challenges can produce values and awaken the drive to accomplish meaningful acts. However, generally speaking, greater voids and challenges tend to produce both greater values and greater drives to achieve. Thus, the world's great revolutions, innovations, and transformations have all been inspired by truly challenging voids. These monumental challenges and vast voids appeared so great to various emerging leaders throughout history that they reshaped these leaders' highest values, affecting their entire lives and the lives of those they influenced.

For example, the monumental lack of justice that Martin Luther King Jr. perceived for himself and his people was the challenging void out of which King created a whole new value, inspiring him to lead a movement that would transform his nation and his world. Had King felt more fulfilled by the world as it was, he would not have felt his powerful desire to change the injustice that he perceived. He would not have been willing to make the extraordinary efforts to rally others to his point of view, inspiring them with his own vision of the justice and equality that might be possible. In fact, his profound *lack* of fulfillment was a source of his inspiration, and what moved him to inspire others. Paradoxically, King had both to help others see the inspiring possibilities that he himself could see *and* to help others share his lack of fulfillment with the world as it was. When hundreds of thousands of people of all races found their own dissatisfaction with racial injustice, they, like King, were willing to make their own extraordinary efforts to fulfill a new vision of human justice. Like King, they saw the void of justice in their world—and so they embraced the value of *justice* with a new intensity and commitment.

Our lives are filled with an unending series of perceived challenges. Some we pursue and become inspired by, others simply cause us to cringe. When we live according to our highest values, we intentionally pursue those challenges or challenging opportunities that inspire us. That is because embracing our highest values allows us to fully mobilize all of our internal resources—all of our energy, drive, and commitment; all of our attention, focus, and clarity; all of our intelligence, talent, and ability. Because our highest values are so important to us, we no longer depend upon our need for support. Instead, we become willing to embrace support and challenge equally, and this willingness frees us to surmount every perceived obstacle and rise to every perceived challenge.

By contrast, when we attempt to live according to another's highest values or according to any of our own *lower* values, we lack the inspiration that only our own highest values can provide us. Accordingly, we resist challenge and seek only support, and as a result, we frequently face unwanted challenges that cause us to despair.

The secret to living an inspired life, then, is to focus on those challenging voids that inspire us to stretch beyond our limits and create new visions, new possibilities, and new selves. Possibly our greatest creativity and innovation emerge when we are faced with these life-changing challenges. In fact, as I have consistently said, if you don't go after challenges that inspire you, you'll have to deal with challenges that don't! Likewise, if you don't fill your day with activities that inspire you, it will fill up with activities that don't.

The power of the Values Factor is that it helps us to recognize the value of challenge by helping us to see how our most important values are directly produced by our greatest and most challenging voids. Once we recognize the value of challenge, we can find inspiration in situations that previously frustrated or dispirited us. We can also learn to choose intentionally our most inspiring challenges, according to our highest values, so that we have little time for the challenges that do *not* inspire us.

The notion of an inspiring challenge may seem unusual to many of us, who are used to viewing challenges in a negative way—as dangers to be avoided or pains to be minimized. After all, most people want ease without difficulty, pleasure without pain, opportunity without challenge, and fulfillment without deprivation. Most of us have the fantasy of creating a life that is all "good" and no "bad," all positive and no negative, just as we may foolishly want marriages that are all support and no challenges, or jobs that only build our pride and never deflate it.

But the world doesn't work that way. The inspirations that lead you to your greatest fulfillment are derived from precisely those challenges that spur you on to fill a void, answer a question, solve a problem, untangle a mystery, unveil an unknown, make order out of disorder, or meet a need. Your ability to engage in this process of growth and transformation is exactly what creates worth for others and for yourself, allowing you to lead a fulfilled and inspired life.

We all have a deep-seated yearning to *know* and *understand*. This wish to transform the *unknown* into the *known* is part of a quest for knowledge that the entire human race shares. We feel it collectively and we feel it individually. Whatever is most missing in our awareness, we want to fulfill or find solutions to. And we are valuable to the world to the degree that we can help others find those solutions. In fact, every job out there—every product, service, or profession—is valuable because it helps someone to transform their challenges or fill their voids.

Again, this is the importance of the Values Factor. It enables us to perceive the potential value in every situation—even those that, at first glance, we may view as meaningless, dispiriting, or frustrating. The Values Factor helps us to see voids, challenges, and apparent obstacles as opportunities, possibilities, and sources of inspiration.

Think about it. A businessman or -woman creates a product or service that meets people's needs and thereby helps them fulfill their voids. A salesman or -woman connects customers with the products or services that will fulfill their voids or needs. A politician helps bring the value of governed order out of the void of chaos. One way or another, just about any job that we value in this society is somehow involved with helping other people transform their challenges: meet a need, answer a question, solve a problem, untangle a mystery, or create a new vision.

In this way, the "bad news" of challenging voids becomes the "good news" of fulfilling values. The "bad news" of challenges, difficulties, and obstacles becomes the "good news" of inspiration, fulfillment, and value to ourselves and others. Anytime you find a void in the world that inspires you, you have found at least one of your niches to serve! Now you can't wait to go and fulfill your life by filling other people's voids. You can solve your own challenges by helping others solve theirs—and you'll have found an incredible financial opportunity at the same time. If you can help other people solve their challenges, there's your wealth—and there's your self-worth. Now you know you're valuable to others, and you can build self-worth from that.

I can offer my own example as proof. I encountered some challenging voids growing up, including physical restriction and some significant learning problems. As a result, I dedicated my life to researching, writing, traveling, and teaching. I find these highest values profoundly fulfilling—and seldom more so than when I am helping other people to find their own freedom, genius, and authentic selves. By fulfilling and inspiring others, I fulfill and inspire myself. By turning my greatest voids into my highest values, I have created a lucrative profession that to me is also the most exhilarating mission in the world. My frustrating voids became my inspiring values. The same can be true for you if you are willing to master the Values Factor.

BALANCING CHALLENGES AND SUPPORT

I repeat: your greatest difficulties, obstacles, responsibilities, and challenges are the voids out of which you forge your highest values. By experiencing challenges and responsibilities, especially as you are growing up, you can develop a precocious independence as you discover your own ability to rise to the occasion, meet your challenges, and effectively assume your responsibilities.

On the other hand, when you experience an overabundance of support, you can develop a form of juvenile dependence upon that support. You become addicted to the feelings of ease, comfort, and security that you associated with being supported, and to your brain's chemical reaction to perceiving that you have someone to rely on and perhaps to take care of you. (In scientific terms, this experience sets off a flood of the brain chemical known as dopamine, one of the "feel-good chemicals" that is literally associated with addiction.) Then, because the universe always seeks to restore balance, your dependence upon support will cause you to attract one challenge after another until you finally succeed in freeing yourself from your dependence.

Thus, if you wish to emerge as a more mature, inspired, and fulfilled individual, you want to make the most of your perceived challenges. You want to recognize both the hidden upside of your challenges and the hidden downside of support. Challenges inspire you to grow, to strive, to achieve, and—like King, Einstein, and Keller—to become a true leader and visionary. Support, which is anything that you believe assists you in the fulfillment of your own highest values, might have its downside in that you can become dependent upon those whom you perceive as offering you support, and dependent upon support itself. Instead of taking on life's challenges, you remain juvenile.

To take a simple example, a child whose parents can always be counted upon to tie her shoes will likely never learn to tie her own shoes. She becomes addicted to their help and support, and so she does not have the stamina or drive to do the hard work of learning to tie her own shoes. A child whose parents do not always offer support is thrown back upon her own resources. If she wants the freedom of movement that comes from wearing properly tied shoes, she is inspired to take on the challenge of learning how to tie them herself. She has the opportunity to develop a precocious independence that she might never discover if she perceives that her parents are ready to support her with every little task.

Of course, if the child experiences *no* support—no one to give her food and shelter and warm clothing—she might literally die. If she has no one to teach her how to tie her shoes or to read a book or to drive a car, she will likely find herself living an unfulfilling life. At every stage of her growth and development, she needs the *right* balance of challenge and support. In fact, scientists and social scientists across many disciplines agree: the maximum growth occurs on the border of challenge and support.

Balancing these ever-present forces of challenge and support allows you to grow and function optimally. That is because both challenge and support have something to teach us about our true relationship to the world, in which we are autonomous, independent, and free, and at the same time dependent, vulnerable, and constrained. Only when we can embrace our need for both sides of the equation—both challenge and support—can we truly welcome the challenges that inspire us to fulfill our mission.

The Values Factor is key here because it becomes much more natural to welcome inspiring challenges and to embrace the balance between challenge and support when you live according to your own highest values. At this point, you might be wondering just what the various forms of balance between challenge and support might be. The answer is that this balance is always changing, depending on your age, personal history, and circumstances. Think again of Martin Luther King, Jr. He was inspired by the challenges facing his people—but he also found support from a trusted circle of advisers and from the thousands of people who eventually joined his movement. Or think of Helen Keller. She was inspired by the challenges of not being able to hear or see—but she also found support from her beloved teacher, Anne Sullivan, who taught her to sign and helped her take on new challenges, such as entering Radcliffe College and completing her studies there. Nature inherently maintains this balance.

Living by your own highest values gives you the chance to perceive your achievements and celebrate your accomplishments because you recognize that you have been true to yourself and to your mission, even if you have also encountered what initially appear to be setbacks. It is when you are living according to your highest values that you most naturally embrace the balance of challenge and support in the pursuit of your most inspiring mission. Because you are no longer addicted to support and no longer spend an inordinate amount of time and energy seeking it, you are able to serenely appreciate a balanced reality, gratefully opening your heart to life as it truly is, not as you wish it could be.

Living by other people's values, on the other hand, is virtually guaranteed to make you feel frustrated much of the time—even if things appear to be going well! That's because you can never truly live up to another person's highest values. Those external values are just not important enough to call forth your greatest and most inspiring actions. They won't inspire you to mobilize the energy, dedication, attention, and retention that you need to do a superlative job in any area—work, relationships, personal development, or spiritual growth. Only when you live by your own highest values and honor yourself accordingly can you fully realize your true potential. Only then can you welcome the essential and catalytic challenges that inspire you.

Ironically, many uninspiring challenges arise precisely *because* we are not living by our highest values. In such cases, we unconsciously attract these challenges, which are designed to wake us up and bring us back to our highest values and truest selves. These initially uninspiring challenges may appear to be extremely difficult or painful—but they are also precisely what we need to drive us back to claim our true highest values and create the lives that are most meaningful for us.

The following exercise can help you explore this question further.

Exercise 1: What's "Wrong" with Your Life?

Most of us tend to seek more ease than difficulty and therefore tend to engage in unbalanced wishful thinking. We unwisely embrace pleasure and reject pain; seek support and avoid challenge; desire acceptance and despise rejection.

This is an unbalanced perspective that engenders significantly unrealistic expectations. We convince ourselves that we *could* experience only pleasure, support, and acceptance. Then, when life inexorably presents us with its inevitable balance of pain and pleasure, challenge and support, and rejection and acceptance, we feel ungrateful. That ingratitude—which springs from our unrealistic expectations—leads us to believe that life on earth is "hell."

But we don't have to see things that way. We can choose to live according to our highest values and become willing to create a more balanced perspective. When we live with a more realistic set of expectations and embrace both sides of life's equation, we become able to open our hearts with gratitude and experience more fulfillment and inspiration. Whether we encounter pain or pleasure, acceptance or rejection, challenge or support, we continue to feel that gratitude. The hell of ingratitude loses its power over us, for we realize that our fulfillment and inspiration do not depend on circumstances but upon our own ability to embrace both sides of life.

Our first step is to get clear about what we imagine to be difficult or challenging, and about what we misperceive to be "wrong" with our lives. Here's an exercise to get you started on that process.

Instructions: In the space on the next page, write down each aspect of your life that you perceive as "out of order," "missing," "an error," "difficult," or "painful." Start from the beginning of your memory of yourself—for example, "I didn't have a mother; my brother used to tease me about being ugly; I was often picked last for the team"—and continue on into the present day—for example, "My children are a handful," "I feel anxious in public," "I feel unattractive," "I don't have enough money," and so on. Don't worry about being realistic, fair, or balanced—the goal here is to identify the apparent fears, frustrations, difficulties, and lacks that you experience both consciously and unconsciously.

Once you have completed your list, rank it in order, with "1" being the most important challenge, difficulty, void, or pain, "2" being second most important, and so on. Identify, in order, the top ten sources of pain or void in your life.

"Wrongs" or Sources of Void or Pain	Rank

THE VALUE OF CHALLENGE: RYAN'S STORY

Sometimes when we attempt to depart quite far from our own highest values, life throws us what looks like uninspiring challenges—challenges that may initially appear as unqualified tragedies. When we look at these challenges differently, however, we can begin to find the deeper meaning in them. Once we see their benefits, these challenges may suddenly appear to be inspiring opportunities. Such was the case of one of my clients, a man I counseled a few years ago whom I will call Ryan.

Ryan was a high-achieving businessman in his late thirties, a midlevel executive in an import-export firm in Southern California. He was involved with a beautiful woman who had achieved her own high-level professional and financial status as a divorce attorney. The two of them had just gotten married and were about to have their first child.

Yet despite his "happy" life façade, Ryan believed he was miserable. He had come to me because of what he considered illness—low energy, tightness and pain in his jaw, and frequent headaches. I could see right away that Ryan was a man in conflict with himself. One of his highest values was pleasing his family, employers, and other authority figures upon whom he depended. He tried to live according to their highest values as he desperately attempted to subordinate the rest of his highest values so that he could fulfill his very highest value of pleasing them.

As I spoke with Ryan about his life, Ryan's frustrations emerged. Although Ryan insisted that he was "happy" in his marriage, I discovered that his wife played the dominant role at home while Ryan withdrew emotionally, becoming increasingly passive and refusing to speak up about what bothered him. It was clear that in this relationship, neither party was fully empowered in all areas of their life. Instead, Ryan's wife had all the power at home because that was where her highest values and his lowest values lay. At the same time, when work- or finance-related decisions came up, Ryan was empowered and his wife was disempowered. For example, his wife had chosen a career involving less responsibility, prestige, and fulfillment because she expected to devote more of her energy to caring for their home and for the children they someday hoped to have. If Ryan needed to stay late at work or make other decisions to support his career, his wife picked up the slack at home to enable Ryan to do this. That's because Ryan's highest values and his wife's lowest values were in the areas of career and finance.

Ryan's disempowerment at home and in the relationship was creating its own counterbalance. Ryan withdrew and refused to participate in any dialogue, while his wife felt angered by Ryan's withdrawal.

Ryan further declared that he had never really wanted to get married. His wife had been the one to push the relationship to that level, since she desired both the financial security of a "good provider" and a husband who would enable her to quit work and have a child. At age thirty-two, she had decided that she "had to have" a baby before she turned thirty-five, and she was desperate to create the "perfect" family she thought she wanted. Ryan seemed like the perfect person to help her achieve her goals.

Ryan, on the other hand, had been relieved to find someone who would "take over" his life for him, since he claimed that he never really felt certain about who he was or what he was doing. As we talked, I found that Ryan had also never wanted to enter the business world. His true love was the violin, which he practiced faithfully two hours every day. "I don't see how I could ever make a living playing music," he told me despondently. "And I can't disappoint my parents—they've struggled so hard to put me through school. They've done everything for me. If I became a 'penniless musician,' it would kill them."

So Ryan kept attempting to subordinate his values to those of his parents and his wife. And when his wife became pregnant, he insisted that he was "happy" about it and eager to become the father, husband, and family man that everyone else seemed to want him to be. Only his difficulties—his physical symptoms—were telling a different story, signaling how Ryan's true self was rebelling against the social idealisms of "good son," "fatherhood," and "fiscal responsibility" that were dominating his life.

"Ryan," I asked him once, "is this the life you envisioned for yourself?"

His face fell. "Well, no," he said, almost in a whisper. "I thought I'd spend my whole life playing music. I mean, I knew I couldn't do that, not really. But . . ."

As the pregnancy continued, Ryan withdrew even further—and in response, his wife became ever more demanding. She had a lot of New Age beliefs and had decided she wanted a natural childbirth, at home, with Ryan as an active participant. As the pregnancy continued, she became ever more rigid in what she chose to eat, how she exercised, and how she prepared for the birth. It was as though all her concerns about her relationship with Ryan and her approaching parenthood were being channeled into efforts to control every aspect of the birth.

Meanwhile, Ryan's parents believed firmly in the latest medical technology and were appalled at the prospect of their grandchild being born "like a peasant in a mud hut," as his mother put it. They argued constantly with Ryan about his wife's decision, trying to force him to force his wife to have their baby in a hospital.

Now Ryan had a new conflict to deal with, between his parents and his wife. Note that his own highest values were partly hidden from view. They were attempting to express themselves through symptoms, but Ryan still kept attempting to live according to the highest values of his wife and family members. He was simply trying to please everyone else. As a result, he was feeling numb, he was often physically absent, and he was struggling with an illness that continued to compound. In response, both Ryan's parents and his wife became ever more dominant and demanding.

Note that everyone in the situation was facing challenges—in each case, because they were following social idealisms and focusing on other people's values rather than shaping their lives by their own highest values. Abandoning, ignoring, or suppressing their own highest values produced tremendous frustration for every individual involved. And the further away each person got from their own highest values, the more intense their uninspiring challenges became.

For example, Ryan's parents were prey to the social idealisms of "advanced medicine," "earning a good living," and "obedient son." Rather than looking at their own lives and their own highest values, they wanted to project their adopted values onto Ryan and attempt to control him—as a son, a husband, and a father. The less able they were to control Ryan, the more anxious, frustrated, and unfulfilled everyone involved seemed to become.

Likewise, Ryan's wife was prey to society's notions that "you have to have a baby by age thirty-five," "you need to marry a good provider," and "you should have the perfect natural childbirth." Subordinating herself to these external values or social idealisms, she faced increasing challenges: a husband who didn't behave as she wanted him to, in-laws who continued to pressure her, and the prospect of a birth whose outcome she could influence but not control.

Ryan himself, of course, felt completely beset by these uninspiring challenges. He felt guilty about displeasing his wife and parents, frustrated with his career, and terrified of becoming a father. He felt increasingly that his wife didn't care for him but had just wanted someone to provide her with a child, and he believed that once the baby came, he would have even less time for his music.

Then an event occurred that virtually everyone involved considered to be a tragedy. As we shall see, however, "tragedy" is often a matter of perception, and apparently tragic events often turn out to have a balance of their own.

The seemingly tragic event was that Ryan's baby was stillborn. Ryan, his wife, and his parents all appeared to be devastated. However, once we looked a little deeper, the truth turned out to be far more complex, and so did the responses of everyone involved in it.

At the time, I recognized that many people would view this event as painful beyond words. But I also saw it as the challenge sent to call every person in this situation back to his or her true self. This apparently agonizing void, it seemed to me, could become the inspiring opportunity for everyone involved to discover their truer and higher values.

Accordingly, when Ryan came to see me after his baby's death, I asked him what possible benefits he might derive from this apparent challenge. At first, the question made him so angry that he almost left our session. But although he couldn't respond that day, he promised to think about the question and to try to answer it later on.

Over time, not only Ryan but everyone in the situation began to see what this challenge had to teach them. Ryan's wife realized that she could not completely control her birth, and she had to ask herself why she had wanted this child so much and what she had been willing to do to ensure that she gave birth "on schedule." She had to face her true feelings about Ryan and to appreciate that he was not really the fantasy man she initially envisioned. She had to look at her true highest values—what really mattered to her—and to focus on those, rather than trying to build a kind of socially ideal picture-book marriage, with Ryan cast in the role of the perfect husband. Eventually, she divorced Ryan, left her law practice, became a full-time yoga instructor, and ended up having two children later in life, at ages thirty-eight and forty-one. She chose to have these children in a more balanced partnership with the owner of a large construction company who had come in to do some estimates on her yoga studio. The stillborn birth of her child had pushed her to discover her true highest values and create a life more aligned with them. She left behind the social idealisms of "traditional marriage," "good provider," "financial security," and "baby on schedule" and created an entirely new and unexpected life that inspired and fulfilled her.

Ryan, meanwhile, discovered his true highest values as he worked with me. He began to realize that he could indeed find a way to make a living as a musician. He began producing and selling tapes, charging for music lessons, and organizing his life around time for practice and study. He became a respected performer in chamber groups and small ensembles, and eventually he even performed at Carnegie Hall. After the divorce, he and his wife actually became friends, in part because of the apparently tragic events they had been through together. Just as King, Einstein, and Keller were inspired to greater growth and achievement through the voids they encountered, so were Ryan and his wife able to more maturely embrace each other as they encountered the void of their child's stillbirth. This is why I do not consider these events tragic. Out of these voids, greater values grow. To truly experience gratitude for life's balance, we would be wise to embrace both the seemingly painful challenges and the seemingly joyous support. Both are part of life, and true wisdom lies in finding fulfillment and inspiration in both.

This was an insight that Ryan and his wife were able to achieve. Although their marriage ended, they found new common ground in their quest for discovering their true highest values and shaping their lives accordingly. Because Ryan's parents were humbled in their attempt to control their son, I thought they, too, might be able to give up their social idealisms and reclaim their true highest values. Instead, they chose to ignore the potential lessons in their grandson's stillbirth and insisted on continuing as they had before. Since they persisted in trying to control Ryan, he chose to spend less time with them and to share fewer aspects of his life with them. Ryan's mother and father each developed increasingly challenging illnesses as they aged, which I viewed as the result of their bodies' efforts to call them back to their highest values and their truest and most openhearted selves. (For more on this view of illness and wellness, see Chapter 10.) How Ryan's parents will respond to their latest challenges remains to be seen.

Ryan, however, stands out in my mind as a man who eventually saw the value of his challenge. Like King, Einstein, and Keller, he chose growth and opportunity rather than defeat. His growth was not easy, and his challenges were great. Yet the value he found in these experiences was enormous. He benefited—and so did his new wife, his ex-wife, his new circle of friends, his music colleagues, his students, and all who listen to him play.

Ryan now fulfills himself through fulfilling others, honoring his highest values, and participating fully in his own life as a musician. I expect that he will go on to encounter other obstacles and challenging voids—and that he will create new values and inspiring opportunities as he does so.

In Ryan's life, his challenging voids created enormous value—as they can do, ultimately, in every life. I created Exercise 2 to give you the opportunity to think about how the challenges in your life have offered you, too, the chances to create value and inspiring opportunities.

Exercise 2: The Value of Difficulty

Now that you've identified what you perceive to be challenging voids or "wrongs" with your life, it's time to discover the benefits you have derived from those difficult challenges. This exercise can help you explore the value of difficult challenges and begin to awaken within you the power of the Values Factor.

Instructions: Review the top ten list of perceived "wrongs" or the perceived sources of challenging difficulty "void" or "pain" that you cataloged in Exercise 1 on page 66. For each "wrong," list at least five associated benefits. For example, if one of your "wrongs" is "being criticized by my parents," then the benefits might include "initiated deep self-reflection and evaluation to determine what was true"; "created more independence"; "became closer to my friends"; "forced to consider my parents' values and to communicate my values to them in terms of their own values, resulting in improved communication"; "drove me to clean my room and house when I didn't always 'feel like it'"; "made me look for what role I might have played in initiating their response"; and so on.

"Wrong"	Benefit
1.	1.
	2.
	3.
	4.
	5.
2.	1.
	2.
	3.
	4.
	5.
3.	1.
	2.
	3.
	4.
	5.
4.	1.
	2.
	3.
	4.
	5.
5.	1.
	2.
	3.
	4.
	5.

"Wrong"	Benefit
6.	1.
	2.
	3.
	4.
	5.
7.	1.
	2.
	3.
	4.
	5.
8.	1.
	2.
	3.
	4.
	5.
9.	1.
	2.
	3.
	4.
	5.
10.	1.
	2.
	3.
	4.
	5.

HOW CHALLENGES SHAPE YOUR BRAIN

Challenges don't only awaken us to our highest values. They also literally reshape our brains, primarily through our brain's glial cells. These are specialized cells in our brains that are in many cases more numerous than our nerve cells, sometimes by a factor as high as ten to one. When we are fulfilling our highest values and doing challenging work that inspires us, our glial cells support our neurons by *myelinization*: the strengthening and thickening of the myelin sheaths that surround the nerve cells in our brain and spinal cord. These sheaths, composed of protein and fatty substances, help neurons transmit impulses so that they can move more quickly and efficiently within our brains.

Further myelinization results from pursuing problems or difficulties that equally support and challenge our highest values, and that at the same time inspire us. These inspiring challenges cause new synapses to form, connecting our brain cells with one another in new and more complex ways. Accordingly our ability to think, reason, analyze, and create expands. Thus, fulfilling our highest values leads our brain to refine and elevate its internal communication, allowing it—and us—to reach a higher potential.

By the same token, when we encounter obstacles that we view one-sidedly; when we desire support that we believe we are not getting; when we feel that our growth is being blocked or stunted; when we do not feel inspired; and when we are *not* fulfilling our highest values, our brain begins to demyelinate and even degenerate. It makes fewer internal connections, diminishes nerve cells, and experiences a thinning of the myelin sheath. In short: *tackling the challenges that inspire us helps our brains, while living according to other people's values and being saddled with uninspiring challenges is a hindrance to our brains.*

The key thing here is that each of us decides what inspires us *according to our own highest values.* I cannot decide what "should" inspire you, any more than you can decide what "should" inspire me. As spouses, friends, employers, and parents, we are wise to consider this before being tempted to impose our own highest values onto others, since what inspires them might seem unfulfilling to us, and vice versa.

For example, a teenage boy who is riveted by a video game is literally remolding his brain while playing *because he is inspired by the game*. Each new level that the teenager solves spurs him to go up to another, more difficult, level. As the brain prepares for that level, the game advances, and the teenager continues, challenging his brain to master a new level of complexity. Because each new level of the game is a new type of inspiring challenge, pursuing and mastering those challenges leads to further growth in that boy's skills and in his brain.

If you, too, love video games, you will immediately resonate with this example. If, like some people, you find them uninvigorating or even boring, you might have difficulty even imagining how they might be inspiring, let alone beneficial to the brain. But I assure you that every inspiring challenge literally re-creates our brain into a more complex organ that functions on a higher level. The key is to make sure that the challenge *is* inspiring—to *us*. If a challenge is only frustrating—because it's too easy, too hard, or simply not in line with our highest values—tackling it will not initiate the same thickening of the myelin sheath, the same increase in glial cells, or the same general enhancement of brain function.

What is true for video games is true for any area of human endeavor. The dancer who strives to reach an ever-larger audience or who pushes herself to express still more profound insights through her movement, the doctor who seeks to improve the wellness of ever more patients or who pushes himself to delve ever more deeply into the mysteries of wellness and illness, the educator who develops new approaches to familiar topics or who pushes herself to a greater understanding of how people learn— all of these people are reshaping their brains as they continue to face the challenges that inspire them. All of them are growing physically as well as mentally and spiritually. All of them have come to embrace the value of inspiring challenges—and both they and the world are richer for it.

PREDATOR OR PREY?

The necessary balance between support and challenge is built into our very physiology. Our autonomic nervous system—the part of our bodies that regulates "automatic" or involuntary functions such as breathing, sleep, digestion, sexual response, and many other cellular functions—is divided into two subsystems: the *sympathetic* nervous system, which regulates the fight-or-flight response, and the *parasympathetic* nervous system, which regulates the rest-and-digest response.

These two systems fit into the food chain built right into our planet's ecosystem. A food chain must include both predators and prey—otherwise, it wouldn't work. Every creature on the food chain both eats and is eaten—is both predator and prey. We humans, too, are both predators and prey, and the two aspects of our nervous system reflect that.

Our sympathetic nervous system is designed to help us instinctively escape from predators. When we encounter a potential threat—anything from a raging tiger to an angry boss to an unmet deadline to a frustrating traffic jam—our body floods with cortisol, which cues our muscles to tense, our eyes to widen, our breathing to speed up, and our hearts to race. Our entire physiology mobilizes to fight, freeze, or run away in our efforts to avoid being "eaten."

The parasympathetic nervous system is designed to help us consume our own prey. It includes the digestive system, the sexual response, and the relaxation response—everything that enables us to consume food, reproduce our species, and rest up for another day. For optimal wellness, both the sympathetic and the parasympathetic systems must be functioning at peak efficiency and in balance. When they are in balance, we experience wellness, promoting "eustress," a scientific term that essentially means "pleasant stress" or "inspiring challenges." When our systems are imbalanced, we experience illness, generating distress—that is, uninspiring challenges.

Our emotional responses are shaped by those physical responses. Sometimes, as prey, we fear approaching threats—the parent who might berate us, the romantic partner who "consumes" us, the responsibility that will drain us. Sometimes, as predators, we fear losing that which we seek—the loved one that we wish to claim for our own, the job that brings fulfillment and prestige, the deep satisfaction of a victory or accomplishment.

In other words, challenge and support are not simply psychological phenomena. These responses operate on a physical level.

As we just saw, challenges activate the sympathetic nervous system. They oxidize and acidify our bodies, creating catabolic responses that cause us to lose weight and muscle mass as well as initiating apoptosis, or preprogrammed cell death.

Support, on the other hand, activates the parasympathetic nervous system. It also makes us more "reduced" and alkaline, creating anabolic responses that cause us to gain weight and to build muscle mass as well as initiating mitosis, or preprogrammed cell division and growth. (Like oxidation, "reduction" is a chemical process that can occur within our bodies.)

Out of the balance between these two types of responses, we achieve that optimal growth and development that is known to occur at the border between challenge and support, or at the border between disorder and order. This is a physiological concept and the way our bodies are designed to work. (For more on the

continued...

connection between the Values Factor and wellness, see Chapter 10.)

In other words, our bodies and minds are designed for a mix of both challenges and support. To grow to our highest level and to fulfill our mission, we need a balance of both. The symptoms of our illnesses, as mentioned previously, may be our bodies' way of awakening us to the importance of balance, the value in embracing both sides of life's equation equally, and the benefits of living true to our highest values. Our bodies are trying to teach us the Values Factor.

ON THE WAY, NOT *IN* THE WAY

Recently, I was speaking with Jasmine, a client who perceived that she had been hit with a series of extremely painful challenges. She had ended a long-term romantic relationship, lost one close friend to cancer, and nursed her father through a long illness that resulted in his death. Another close friend had moved to another city, and she had had a serious falling-out with a third. The end of her relationship had required her to leave a house she loved, while the economic downturn was posing serious challenges to her consulting firm and she was concerned that she might lose her business. "I feel as though the ground has been cut out from under me in just about every area of my life," she told me.

The two of us talked together about how she could turn these challenging voids into valuable and inspiring opportunities. "I could handle one or two challenges," she said, trying to laugh, "but I don't know what to do with *all* of these. I'm trying hard not to feel completely hopeless, but that *is* how I feel. I just feel completely defeated."

Jasmine was aware of how challenges that we find inspiring can help our brains grow, while challenges that we find frustrating and dispiriting can cause our brains to degenerate. "Dr. Demartini," she said to me, "I know it sounds silly, but I'm really concerned about my brain and my well-being! How do I protect them when I'm feeling so awful? And how do I find the value in all of this when I can't see a way out?"

Although Jasmine seemed to be flooded with "troubles" that she was trying to cope with, I congratulated her for seeking the most productive way of dealing with them. "The secret," I told her, "is in the way you look at your difficult challenges. If you see all of these challenges as *on* the way, rather than *in* the way, as instructive, not obstructive, your brain will stay active and continue to grow, and you will be more likely to maintain your wellness and well-being."

Jasmine thought about that for a moment. "So instead of seeing a problem as a final defeat," she said slowly, "I am now beginning to see it as a step on the way to something greater."

"Yes," I said. "When you embrace your challenges as lessons about living according to your highest values, you begin to understand what they're teaching you in a way that cues your brain to stay engaged and responsive. Your brain will adapt to these difficult challenges and learn from them—and that effort will literally help your brain to grow. And that in turn will offer you creative solutions and opportunities."

Jasmine and I continued to talk about the importance of valuing her apparent challenges. I told her that many people live in a fantasy that they can have ease without difficulty and support without challenge. Then, when they encounter difficulties and challenges, they feel frustrated, almost insulted, that life isn't working out the way they'd fantasized. Because they don't value and seek out the difficult challenges that might inspire them, they end up attracting difficult challenges that do *not* inspire them. I reminded Jasmine that maximum growth and development occur at the border of support and challenge, ease and difficulty, order and disorder—that is simply a law of nature. That is why when we live according to our highest values and embrace both support and challenge equally, we grow and develop most efficiently and fulfill our most inspired missions.

"You don't necessarily know where the border is set," I told her. "The amount of challenge that *you* think belongs in your life is not necessarily the amount of challenge that life is going to throw at you. It is all about your perceptions. Maybe you can handle more challenges than you think you can at first. Maybe there is something to learn from going through this set of difficult challenges that initially appears to be much harder and more overwhelming than you ever expected. In fact, these obstacles are not *in* your way, but simply *on* your way. Once you ask the essential questions about these challenges, discovering their accompanying benefits and opportunities, and once you welcome them and seek the inspiration that they hold, you won't miss the inspiring lessons they have to teach you. These challenges are only feedback responses guiding you to your most authentic self so that you can live more fully according to your highest values. If you don't see your challenges in this way, you may spend all your energy resisting them rather than discovering their potential value."

After I asked Jasmine specific questions that helped her discover the hidden benefits of all the challenges she was facing, she came to appreciate this approach. "I've done my best to alter my situation," she told me. "But now I have found meaning in these challenges. I have transformed my problems, and now I am actually inspired by them."

The key to finding inspiration in your difficulties is asking the right questions. It can be helpful to see how both support and challenge are necessary. Asking the right questions can awaken you to how each of your challenges is actually helping you to fulfill your highest values.

So ask yourself what is most important to you in life, and then ask what the challenges you face have taught you about what really matters. Ask as well how they are assisting you. Perhaps they have reinforced the beliefs and highest values you've held for a long time, or perhaps they have caused your beliefs and highest values to change. Perhaps the challenging obstacles you face have caused you to see new ways that you can fulfill your highest values. Check out the following exercise to think about this question further.

Exercise 3: How Challenges Have Affected Your Hierarchy of Values

Challenges hold hidden inspirations that cause you to deepen, rethink, or possibly alter the present set of values that you hold. In this exercise, you have the opportunity to explore how challenges have affected your hierarchy of values.

Instructions: Identify a recently perceived challenge that you have undergone. Think about how that challenge has affected your set of values. Did it cause you to reconsider values you had previously held and adopt *new* values? Did it cause you to reconfirm your allegiance to an old value? Did you discover that the challenge resulted from living by your highest values—or from attempting to not live by them? There are no right or wrong answers to these question, only the truth as you see it. Spend at least fifteen minutes writing about how your recent challenge affected your hierarchy of values.

THE HELL OF INGRATITUDE

Most of us are familiar with the Western and Middle Eastern religious notion of "hell" or its equivalent as an image of unhappiness, suffering, and pain. When things are seemingly not going "right" in our lives, we may say, "I'm in hell," "What a hell of a day," or "That was a hellish experience." Whatever your religious perspective, the *image* of hell is meant to indicate the ultimate in human suffering.

Yet if values come from voids and if great challenges can call us to our greatest achievements, why do we resist pain and difficult challenges? It's true that we often *seek* people, activities, and situations that support our highest values and keep us unintentionally dependent. But have you ever noticed that we also *attract* people, activities, and situations that challenge our values and make us grow?

There is a reason for this inevitable attraction—and it happens in every aspect of our lives. The life partner we "fall in love" with, the family we create, the enterprise we build, the life we design—no matter how "perfect" these are for us, how well-suited, how ideal, they are going to be accompanied by some difficult challenges. Or, if they aren't, we are going to attract those difficult challenges from somewhere else. It is a law of nature. You can't have only ease, support, and pleasure. You also must have some difficulty, challenge, and pain. There is and has to be a balance. There has to be both. Otherwise, we would never develop or grow. We would remain exactly as we are: static, smug, and secure in our present stage of development, without having fully discovered our truest, highest values. We would not experience the challenging voids that drive us to greater and greater efforts, deeper and deeper growth, higher and higher values. Without voids, without difficulties, without pains and challenges, we would never go on to achieve the greatness of which we are truly capable.

And yet, if we are less mature or possibly unawake, we want that ease without the hardship; we want that pleasure without the pain. Spiritually, we may seek what some Western and Middle Eastern religious leaders have called heaven, which many have imagined to be a place of eternal rest, pleasure, and so-called happiness—a place where no effort is required. In relationships, we want people who always support us and never challenge us. Mentally, we seek the security of knowing our ideas to be true. We like the idea of learning what comes easily and resist the idea of struggling to achieve knowledge. In our careers, we wish for achievement without setback, an unbroken story of triumph, with no bankruptcies, lost jobs, or even periods of uncertainty. Financially speaking, we want money without effort, and when we look at our social circles, we want to be surrounded by admirers only—people who think we are wonderful, not people who doubt, question, or reject us. And physically, we expect—or at least we want—what we think of as "perfect" health, not to mention a flawless appearance and endless reserves of energy, without disease, blemishes, or fatigue.

We desire these pleasures without pains, and we think of them as heaven, while their opposites—spiritual struggle, demanding relationships, mental challenges, career roadblocks, financial reverses, social rejection, imperfect health—we consider to be hell.

But life without challenge does not offer true fulfillment—it is a delusion. And life with challenge is not hell—it is a source of an inspiring and expanding reality.

In fact, we need both challenge and support. Too much support, and we have a state of perpetual infantile dependency, which can result in children who take longer to grow up and leave home, business leaders who fear to innovate, and educators who rely on old-fashioned methods of instruction and seldom ask themselves whether a new society requires new forms of teaching people.

On the other hand, too much challenge, and we have a state of precocious independence and possibly burnout. It results in children who leave home possibly too soon, taking on challenges they're not ready for; business leaders who think they can ride roughshod over the needs of others; and educators who exclude the highest values of those they teach.

What's the solution? A wise balance of challenge and support.

So I would offer two new definitions of hell:

1. Hell is anything about which we have an unbalanced perspective. Hell is what we experience anytime we want ease without difficulty, support without challenge, pleasure without pain. Hell is the futility of expecting ourselves or others to be one-sided: to be uniformly generous, honorable, and kind, with no room for selfishness, dishonor, and cruelty. Anytime we expect *anything* on this planet to be one-sided, we are setting ourselves up for a life that feels like it's in hell. As the Buddha implied, the desire for that which is unattainable and the desire to avoid that which is unavoidable is the source of human suffering.

2. Hell is ingratitude. If we can't appreciate the value of difficult challenges, how can we be grateful for the people, activities, and situations that challenge us and help us grow? If we can't see the ways that voids create values, how can we embrace the challenging voids and difficulties that we attract? How can we appreciate the greatness that these voids and difficulties make possible? When we are ungrateful, life is hell.

Even Pope John XXIII once said that hell was a state of ingratitude, while heaven was gratitude. So hell is not someplace you go. Hell is a state of mind that emerges when you try to live with unrealistic expectations such as ease without difficulty, support without challenge, pleasure without pain. If that is truly what you seek, your life will disappoint you—and it will be a living hell.

By contrast, every time you set an objective that fits your highest values, you are more likely to embrace challenge and support or pain and pleasure equally because you understand that both sides of the equation of life are part of fulfilling your highest values. Your greatest voids create your highest values. And your highest values lead you to feel grateful for the synchronous balance in life—both pain and pleasure, challenge and support—that brings you closer to fulfilling what is most meaningful. That is why the Values Factor and gratitude are so closely intertwined. Knowing your true highest values and embracing situations that challenge them as well as situations that support them is the key to developing gratitude.

THE HEAVEN OF GRATITUDE

I have asked people all over the world what they would do if they knew that they had only twenty-four hours left to live. The vast majority tell me that they would want to say, "Thank you, I love you," to the people who have contributed to their lives.

Why? Because gratitude and love are the ultimate result of all that is. They are the essence of our very existence. They are the fulfillment of our highest values. So by the time we are facing death, we realize that all of our one-sided judgments are simply symptoms of incomplete awareness. What really matters is the ultimate and balanced state of "Thank you, I love you."

It's easy to feel a transient and false form of gratitude when the events of your life support your highest values and everything appears to be easy and going well. If you want to "count your blessings" during an apparently happy time, you can usually come up with a very long list of things to be grateful for.

When true gratitude really comes in handy, though, is when your life seems to be hitting one roadblock after another and when everything around you seems to be challenging your highest values. When you are coping with a broken heart, a troubled child, a rocky marriage, or a retrenched job, you might find it nearly impossible to summon up feelings of gratitude—not only for the so-called good things in your life but also for the pain and challenges that are calling you to a deeper level of strength and understanding. Yet, paradoxically, this very challenge is what leads you to a deeper search for meaning, so that you awaken to the ever-present synchronous balance or hidden order that results in true gratitude. It is this deeper sense of true gratitude that brings poise and presence during these apparently challenging times. That's why people who imagine having only twenty-four hours to live momentarily transcend their illusory judgments involving one-sided polarities and have only one wish: to say, "Thank you, I love you," to the special people they love.

I find it interesting that the word "gratitude" is close to the words *gracias* ("thank you" in Spanish) and *grace* ("mercy" in French). If we have a perfectly balanced perspective, embracing both pain and pleasure, we achieve a state of grace. In this state, we inwardly acknowledge the inherent balance and order of life. We feel a transcendent mercy for all the "rights" and "wrongs" that we used to fixate on, and we feel gratitude for every balanced moment of support and challenge, pleasure and pain, ease and difficulty, that ever crossed our path. True gratitude momentarily dissolves the voids and fulfills the value. The moment we feel gratitude, our heart opens . . . and out comes true love. This is the ultimate expression of the Values Factor . . . and its ultimate power.

Living Your Destiny

Man is so made that when anything fires his soul,
impossibilities vanish.

—JEAN DE LA FONTAINE

M any years ago in Quebec City, I was conducting a seminar entitled the Prophecy I Experience, my seven-day program that
is the follow-up to the Breakthrough Experience. I had been talking
about pursuing work you love and being paid handsomely for it, and
one of my students had trouble seeing how this concept could ever
apply to her.

"Dr. Demartini," she said to me, "I know what I would love to do,
but I don't know how to make a living doing it. I love dancing. But
who is ever going to pay me to do that?!"

This was a large woman—a bit overweight, perhaps, but quite
graceful. I looked at her, and I could easily see that the thought of
dancing inspired her. I saw how her whole face lit up when she said
the words "I love dancing," and I was sure there must be a way for her
to viably fulfill this value that was clearly one of her highest.

So I asked her, "Why do you say no one will pay you?"

She shrugged and gestured to her body. "Just look at me," she
said. "Obviously, I can't be a professional dancer."

I said, "It sounds to me as though dancing is one of your highest
values, so no, it isn't obvious to me at all."

Now she was very uncomfortable—but she was also very interested. So she said, "I don't know what you mean. I don't know how to do what you're saying. At my age, especially, how can I be paid to be a dancer?"

Now I happened to know from some things she had said in the workshop that besides dancing, one of her highest values was traveling. This had caught my attention, since travel is also one of my highest values. So I said, "Why don't you create a touring business that revolves around dancing?"

"I don't understand," she said again. "Talk to me. What do you mean?"

"Well," I said, "you love dancing, right? You also love traveling. Those are the things you love to do."

"Yes . . ."

"All right. So why don't you organize select groups of people who love to dance to go on tour to foreign countries and learn all the great dances of each country and have an adventure?"

A little lightbulb went on inside her.

"Oh, my God!" she said. "I would love to take people to Spain and study flamenco dancing because, actually, that is something I am really great at."

"That's wonderful," I said. "Why don't you go to the Latin dance studios in the city where you live and let people know that you are offering that opportunity? Now you can offer to other people the two things you love most!"

Well, it wasn't but a short few months until she had her first gig in Spain. She took twelve people over for a week of flamenco dancing, and it was greatly received. She organized a discount on the flights and the entertainment and the whole package, she charged an extra fee to cover all the costs, and she made a net return of $4,800 from spending a week doing flamenco dancing in Spain. And from there, her business took off. To this day, she is exactly what she said she could not be—a professional dancer who travels the world, doing what she loves, and helping other people to do so, too.

Whenever I think about the Values Factor, I think of this woman, because to me, she is the perfect example of how to find your life's purpose and begin to viably live your inspired destiny. It all goes back to values. Your highest values tell you what you love and what matters most to you. And your highest value—the thing you love most and that matters to you most—is your life's purpose. Following that purpose is the greatest and most inspiring journey you could ever undertake.

SPIRITUALITY AND YOUR VALUES

One of the greatest misunderstandings I encounter is the idea that "spirituality" or "being spiritual" are somehow separate from any other aspect of human behavior. It is as though spirituality is reserved for "Sundays" and "Fridays" and "Saturdays" and not the remaining weekdays, or as though it is reserved for churches and mosques and synagogues, and not for every space we might enter. People often fail to recognize that *every* quality and action is a spiritual expression, even those that are conventionally seen as mundane, trivial, or even sinful. For as some spiritual leaders have asked, where is God *not*? If God is truly everywhere, then all places and all activities are spiritual.

Yet because of our social or religious indoctrination, many of us have come to consider some people to be more spiritual than others. This is unwise and can result in a form of tribal thinking based in exclusion, where we view ourselves and people like us as "spiritual" while we view people "outside the tribe" as "unspiritual."

In my view, though, we are all equally spiritual. All of us express our unique spirituality according to our specific hierarchy of values. Fulfilling your highest value is your life's purpose, your destiny, and your most meaningful spiritual path. For the student I met in Quebec City, her life's purpose and her inspired destiny was dancing. For the doctor I told you about in Chapter 1, his life's purpose and his inspired destiny was healing. For one person, a spiritual path might call for founding a business. For someone else, it might be raising a child. Anything that speaks to your highest value is part of your spiritual path and helping you fulfill your destiny.

This is why I asked you to identify your highest values in Chapter 2 and then to rank them in order of importance to you. Your very highest value—the value that means most to you—is your *telos*, a Greek word meaning "end in mind" or "purpose." This evolving highest value also represents your evolving purpose here on earth. It is what inspires you most—the purpose you feel grateful for simply pursuing. Your truest and wisest way of serving the world is to do the thing you love most. That is your spiritual path—and your inspired destiny.

A few years ago a woman attending the Breakthrough Experience program raised her hand and asked me the following question: "What do you do when your husband is totally dedicated to material objectives and nothing spiritual and you are focused primarily on spirituality?"

I responded by saying that was not probable and her perception was probably only a projection of her highest values onto him—a projected label. And that her husband equally had his form of inspiration or spirituality, but it was not being recognized or appreciated.

I further asked her how she defined spirituality. She stated that her meditations, yoga asanas, prayers, spiritual readings, and chantings were all her spiritual expressions.

I then asked her what exactly her husband did for a living. She stated that he owned an IT company with two hundred employees, and with clients and customers around the world.

So I said to her, "Let me get this straight: your husband is dedicated to growing a company that serves potentially millions of people globally, employs two hundred people, helps pay substantial taxes, gives families the opportunity to send their children to school, inspires employees and customers, contributes employment to society, and stimulates the economy—and you don't see that this is in any way a spiritual service to the world?"

I then asked her if she worked. She stated that no, she was not into working for material things.

I responded, "Are you sure that your husband is not being spiritual according to his highest values and you are simply being spiritual according to yours? If he was not expressing his spirituality in his fashion, would you not have to go to work and make a material income to make it possible for you to continue your present form of spirituality? Maybe each of you is both a spiritual and a material being, just expressing your spirituality and materiality according to your own highest values? He is not more or less spiritual than you— just different in his spiritual expression."

I sensed that she finally understood my point and my even more meaningful lesson of not projecting her values onto him but instead appreciating his highest values for what they were. His dedication to his company and creating a material income made her spiritual expression possible while her dedication to study and meditation exposed him to a view of the universe that he otherwise would have had no access to. She needed his income to have the time to study. He needed her study to give meaning to his economic activities. Although they did not realize it, they were each doing "half the work" that together made up a meaningful whole.

This is why I told her that it was not wise to say that she was spiritual and he was not. In fact, this woman and her husband were complementary opposites, which together made up the family balance of love. Each partner was able to do what he or she loved at least in part because of their partner's complementary opposite highest values. Family dynamics demand such complementary opposites to make up the whole of family love.

I suggest that you, too, consider the benefits of embracing your spirituality in its fullest sense rather than defining it narrowly as simply "meditation," "religious beliefs," or some other more conventionally accepted view of spirituality. If you can see more clearly how you express your spirituality according to your own highest values, you will be further empowered to move more swiftly and surely to fulfill your destiny. Whatever truly inspires you is also a form of spirituality, whether it is a business, as for the husband of the woman I just told you about, or yoga and meditation, as for the woman herself.

FULFILLING YOUR PURPOSE

As we have seen, your highest value is the thing that is most valuable to *you*. Your highest value gives rise to your evolving life purpose:

Your life purpose is the most effective and efficient pathway to fulfill the greatest amount of void with the greatest amount of value.

This is again what the ancient Greeks called the *telos*: the end you have in mind. *Telos* is the most important thing in your life, your chief aim, your purpose, and your mission.

Telos, purpose, mission: that is what we are dedicated to. That is what is most fulfilling. That is what inspires us. That is what we are most disciplined in doing and can't wait to get up in the morning to do.

The study of the *telos* is called teleology. When we are thinking about something in a teleological way, we are looking at the end—the ultimate goal—and organizing our entire lives in order to fulfill it. We are saying in effect, "*There* is my purpose, my ultimate end. What gives my life meaning is moving toward or fulfilling that end. Now, how can I envision the steps that will get me from here to there?" Keeping that evolving or ultimate goal in mind, we ask about every step we take: "How does *this* help me fulfill my purpose?" We evaluate every perception, every action, every decision, based on how it helps us reach that ultimate goal.

Thinking teleologically also means that we see every obstacle in our path as *on* the way, rather than *in* the way. When we encounter a difficulty or a challenge, we don't ask, "Why is this obstacle keeping me from achieving what is most important?" We ask, "How is this apparent obstacle *helping* me to fulfill my purpose? What missing piece of achieving my life's purpose is this apparent obstacle supplying? What help is this obstacle providing that I didn't even know I needed? How is this obstacle secretly offering me many, many benefits that will actually help me achieve my purpose in a fuller, or more complete way?" Seeing apparent obstacles in this more balanced way becomes natural—and fulfilling—once you truly understand the Values Factor.

THE BENEFITS OF LIVING OUR DESTINY

The Buddhists talk about karma—the inevitable results of all the actions you have ever taken. In a sense, karma might be seen as cause and effect. But another key Buddhist concept is dharma—wise behavior or "right" action, which moves you toward fulfillment, nirvana, or personal liberation. In a sense, dharma might be seen as "purpose."

So when we live according to that which is most important to us—when we live teleologically, with meaning and purpose—we are living with dharma and not karma. We are the purposeful driver of our destiny looking forward into the cause of our future, not looking back into the effect of our past actions. We are living with inspiration, not desperation. We are living fulfilled instead of unfulfilled. Those are the results of living our lives according to what is most important to us—structuring our lives according to the Values Factor.

Just as every one of us has a unique set of values, each of us has a unique destiny and a unique form of spirituality or spiritual journey, guided by our highest values. You are on your own completely individual spiritual path. However, if you choose not to honor your highest values and fulfill your inspired purpose, you might find yourself tending to break down, feeling unfulfilled, and living a less meaningful life.

- You will probably feel less fulfilled or inspired by your life.
- You will probably feel less grateful for your life.
- You will probably feel less empowered spiritually and you might even subordinate yourself to someone else's version of spirituality or to their labels of good and evil.
- You will probably live according to stagnant traditions instead of living according to your own unique spiritual path.
- You will probably hold unrealistic expectations and judge yourself and others unwisely.
- You will probably live with more distractions and tangents.
- You will probably be vulnerable to searching for one-sided fantasies—pleasure without pain, support without challenge, which could lead you to experience a great deal of frustration as a result.
- You will probably not equally embrace both the pains and pleasures of life.

On the other hand, when you are acting in a way that fulfills your highest value:

- You awaken your inspired mission.
- You recognize your ever-present spirituality.
- You can offer balanced service to others.
- You appreciate spirituality in a more universal and balanced way, rather than either submitting to some religion or rejecting it.

- You love and appreciate yourself and others . . . for who you all are, not for who you think you or they "should" be.

DISCOVERING YOUR DESTINY—AND GETTING PAID FOR IT

I am a firm believer in the notion that the quality of your life is based on the quality of the questions you ask. For more than forty years, I have been asking myself the question—almost daily—that I asked my client in Quebec City:

What is it that I would absolutely love to do, and how do I get handsomely paid to do it?

That is one of the greatest questions you can ask because in that way your vocation and vacation can become the same. More important, asking this type of question leads you to discover your life's purpose, which is based on your highest values—the things that matter to you most. And when you discover that evolving purpose, you are on the way to living your inspired destiny. Your highest values are there to lead you to your purpose, and your purpose is there to guide you to your destiny. This is why the Values Factor is so important. Once you have begun with the expression of your highest values—with what you truly love to do—you know you are on your most inspired path.

You are not alone. Whatever you might love to do, there are also others who would love to do the same or something similar. So if you can find a way of helping these other people do what you would love to do, you will be able to get to do what you would love and get paid for it. That is the secret of providing inspired service.

Of course, you won't get well paid unless you truly provide a quality service to people. But helping people do what they love—which is also something that you love—is the greatest and most fulfilling service you could possibly provide. You are not only fulfilling your own highest values, you are helping other people fulfill theirs. I can tell you from personal experience, there is very little on earth more satisfying than that.

So find out what you would love to do, then find a way of serving other people with it, and then get handsomely—or beautifully—paid to do it. Here is another question you can ask that will help you on this inspiring path:

> *What are the seven highest-priority action steps I can do today to move me closer toward getting paid handsomely for doing what I love to do?*

If you can keep asking that question and keep working on your answers, you will find at least one viable way of doing it. I started doing that when I was in my teens and here I am today traveling the world, doing what I love to do, and getting handsomely paid for it. I am shaping my life in alignment with my highest values, following my purpose, and living my inspired destiny. That is what I have chosen to do—and if you make the same choice, you can do that, too. The following exercise can help get you started.

Exercise 1: How Can I Get Handsomely Paid for What I Would Love to Do?

There is a reason Thoreau spoke of the vast majority of humans leading lives of "quiet desperation." Most people do not believe they can live by their highest values, find their purpose, or live their inspired destiny. Once you pursue that end, your life can begin to change from one of quiet desperation to one of amazing inspiration. The first step is to ask yourself the following three questions:

- What would I absolutely love to do?
- How can I get paid handsomely or beautifully to do it?
- What are the seven highest-priority action steps I can take today toward that end?

This exercise will walk you through that process.

Step 1: What Do I Most Love to Do?

Instructions: Make a list of all the things you most love to do. Don't worry about whether they're "practical" or try to imagine any way in which you can make a living from them—that comes later. Just think of the activities you would most love to do. Include such ordinary activities as listening to a friend's problem, planning a party, organizing a closet, giving a friend financial advice, watching a sports game, or playing with your pet. Your goal initially is not to think about potential careers but to get in touch with your highest values and the things that are most meaningful to you.

I love to . . .

1. _____

2. _____

3. _____

4. _____

5. _____

6. _____

7. _____

8. _____

9. _____

10. _____

Step 2: How Can I Get Paid Handsomely for It?

For each activity, imagine three ways that someone might pay you to do it. Let your imagination run free without yet worrying about the practical aspects of building a business or career. For example, if you love playing with your pet, you might consider a dog-walking service or a pet daycare business where people leave their animal companions while on vacation. If you love watching sports on TV, you might consider a blog where you provide commentary on games or an Internet-based fantasy-football league. Your goal for this step is to creatively envision ways of getting to spend your day doing what you love and getting paid to do it.

What I Would Love to Do	Possible Business or Career That Will Pay Me
1.	1.
	2.
	3.
2.	1.
	2.
	3.
3.	1.
	2.
	3.
4.	1.
	2.
	3.

What I Would Love to Do	Possible Business or Career That Will Pay Me
5.	1.
	2.
	3.
6.	1.
	2.
	3.
7.	1.
	2.
	3.
8.	1.
	2.
	3.
9.	1.
	2.
	3.
10.	1.
	2.
	3.

Step 3: Envision the Possibilities

Some things that you love to do have "staying power": you would be inspired to do them all day long, day after day. Other things may be inspiring only periodically. For example, you might love going to the beach, but you might not want to live at the beach. You might love traveling on vacation, but you might not necessarily want to travel several months out of the year. You might love playing with your own children after dinner, but you might not necessarily want to spend a full day playing with other people's children. So your next step is to look over the list you made in Step 2. Envision yourself doing each activity you listed as a full-time job. Then pick five businesses or careers that genuinely sound like something you would love to do. Don't worry yet about how you could create this business or career. Just ask yourself whether you would genuinely be fulfilled by doing it full-time or perhaps part-time.

My Top Five Businesses or Careers

1. _____
2. _____
3. _____
4. _____
5. _____

Step 4: What Are My Seven Highest-Priority Action Steps?

From your top five businesses or careers, pick the one that inspires you most. Ask yourself what are the seven highest-priority action steps you could take today toward that goal.

Seven Highest-Priority Action Steps

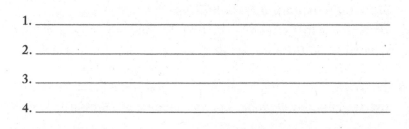

1. _____
2. _____
3. _____
4. _____

5. _____

6. _____

7. _____

If you do not yet feel inspired, repeat the exercise with your next highest choice from the list of your top five. Continue until you have developed a brief plan that inspires you. Some entrepreneurs are owners of many businesses, so your vision does not have to be limited to only one.

FREEING YOURSELF FROM DELUSION

Recently I was giving a seminar in Australia, and a woman approached me as it ended. "Dr. Demartini," she said to me, "I am so inspired by everything you have said—but I still don't know what my purpose is."

"I don't believe you," I told her. "Your life automatically demonstrates your present life's purpose. So what is your life demonstrating? What do you do every day or nearly every day? What is it that you love doing that nobody ever has to remind you to do?"

"But I don't have a career or a vocation or a mission or any of these things you talked about," she protested. "I don't run a business. I haven't even completed a college degree. All I do every day is take care of my children."

So I asked her, "Do you love taking care of your children?"

Her face lit up. "Oh, yes."

"Well, then," I asked her, "is *that* your mission? Is *that* your present life purpose? Raising a beautiful family expresses your highest value, and, at least until your children are grown, that sounds like your current inspired destiny."

She began to cry. "That's all I ever wanted to do," she said.

"I always dreamed of raising a beautiful family, and now I'm doing it. But compared with running a business or going back to school or having a great career, it doesn't seem like much."

I told this woman that her sense of inferiority and inadequacy was only because she was comparing her highest values with someone else's, injecting their values into her life and clouding over her own. I then told this woman that she reminded me of Rose Kennedy, who once said that she had dedicated her life to raising a family of world leaders.

"That was her mission," I said, "and your family is yours. Your life is clearly demonstrating that right now. Of course, if you want to change your mission, you can. But then you'll have to change your highest values. Because every single day of your life, your highest values are going to dictate your mission and inspired destiny."

My student went away inspired about the choices she had made and about the realization that the whole time she had actually been on track. Her questions reminded me of a common delusion that many people have. They see "mission," "purpose," and "values" as something outside themselves—something they have to be forced, motivated, or disciplined to do. Then they beat themselves up for thinking that they don't have what they say they want or for not doing what they think they "should."

It doesn't work like that. Your highest values will ultimately determine your actions. What you do is by definition what you consciously or unconsciously want to do. Every action you take reflects what's most important to you. If you say, "I would love to play with my kids, but I have to go to work or else I'll get fired," what you are really saying is, "It's more important to me to have a job and bring in some income and provide my family with some financial security than it is to play with my kids." If you say, "I would love to spend this afternoon reading a book and just relaxing, but I have to go to a family dinner at my parents' house," then what you are really saying is,

"I value pleasing my parents and my family and maintaining a relationship with them more than taking time for my reading or myself." What you actually do reveals what is most important to you.

So your first step in living your inspired destiny is freeing yourself from your delusions and being honest about what you're really deciding and doing. Seeing the truth clearly means not deluding yourself about what you are actually doing or what you would truly love to do.

For example, my student in Australia really wanted a beautiful family, and her actions reflected that. But she had deluded herself into thinking that she "should" have a career, run a business, or go back to school. Then she beat herself up for not living according to what she thought her destiny should be, when she was actually living by it all along. Her highest values revolved around family and children, and she was absolutely fulfilling those values.

On the other hand, sometimes we spend a lifetime attempting to subordinate our highest values to someone else's, and that is absolutely *not* fulfilling. We delude ourselves into thinking that we are living according to our highest values. But really we have attempted to subordinate our values to someone else's. We will definitely find it more fulfilling to claim our own highest values and live accordingly.

I once worked with a man who had spent his entire life up to that point trying to please his father and attempting to subordinate his second and third highest values to the highest values of his dad. Having his dad be proud of him was extremely important to him. It was apparently his highest value.

This man, whom I'll call Antonio, had gone to law school and business school, because that's what his father said he had wanted. He had married the woman his father wanted him to marry. He lived in the part of the country that his father wanted him to live in. His entire life was organized around getting his father to acknowledge him and congratulate him for his accomplishments.

Of course, most of this was unconscious. Antonio had little idea that he was living to please his father. He was so out of touch with his own second and third highest values that he didn't even realize he had subordinated them. He just kept plugging away, trying to get his dad to say, "Great job!"

Eventually, Antonio's father retired, and Antonio took over his dad's business, again trying to please his father. But his father seldom gave Antonio approval in the way that Antonio sought, and, a few years after retiring, the father died.

Suddenly, the business that Antonio was running faced the unexpected. It turned out that there were substantial outstanding debts associated with the company, a fact that came out when the company was audited. A few months later, the company went under, and Antonio was bankrupt. His wife took the kids and left him. His friends shunned him. So did the rest of his family. Antonio had already been struggling with obesity and hypertension. The added strain was too much for him, and he experienced a nearly fatal heart attack.

At this point—broke, in debt, alone, in poor health—Antonio felt close to suicide. It seemed that his whole life had come crashing down around him. Seeking help for his health problems, Antonio came to me.

After hearing his whole story, I thought for a moment. Then I said, "It sounds to me as though the day your business went bankrupt was the greatest day of your life."

"What?" Antonio stared at me. He couldn't tell whether I was joking, stupid, or just plain cruel.

"Antonio," I said, "that life you had before—was that really the life you wanted? Was it fulfilling? Was it inspiring? Did you wake up every day inspired about what you were going to get to do?"

Despite his outward display of "misery," Antonio had to laugh. "No," he said. "Of course not."

"So it was very obvious that you unconsciously didn't want to be trapped in that dynamic," I told him. "And look at you now. You're out of a relationship you didn't want to be in, with a woman you no longer have affection for, if you ever did. Because of the bankruptcy, you don't even have to pay her large sums of money, even though you were together for more than twenty years! You have a chance to start over, to do anything you would love to do. You're completely free, and you have nowhere to go but up. So what is it you would love to do?"

Antonio stared at me blankly. It had been so long since he had considered his own second and third highest values that he could barely remember what they were. Yet now that his dad had passed away, these second and third highest values were finally emerging as his very highest values.

"What would you love to do?" I asked him, just as I had asked the woman in Quebec City and the woman in Australia.

A tiny spark came into Antonio's eyes. "Ever since I can remember, I've loved repairing and fixing up fast, fancy sports cars," he said. "But I can't see how I could make a living from that."

"Why not?" I asked him. "What's stopping you?"

Slowly Antonio realized that, in fact, nothing was stopping him. With his father gone, there was no one to tell him what to do, whom to marry, or where to live. So he moved to Florida and began a business of recycling and upgrading classic cars. And he loved it! He was finally building a business around what he really loved to do, and as he claimed his present highest values, everything else in his life began to change. He stopped wearing the formal suits that had been part of his old life and began dressing in more casual clothes that made him feel more comfortable—and more confident, because now he felt like himself. He realized that his obesity had been a shield against a woman he hadn't really wanted to be with, so now he was free to lose weight, which he did. His heart health improved—and so did his romantic life. He began a fulfilling partnership with a new woman who valued Antonio for what he was, not for how much money he made.

Antonio had come to realize that his illnesses, his financial challenges, and his marital discord were all signs that he had continually attempted to live according to his own highest value—which was pleasing his dad. Yet all his efforts had been to no end, since his father seldom provided the feedback he so desired. Meanwhile, he was repressing his second and third highest values and inner truth. So his unfulfillment took its toll.

Antonio's first step, then, was to free himself from his delusion and unrealistic expectation: to realize that his primary duty was *not* to subordinate any of his values to his father's but rather to live his own unique and inspired destiny. From that point on, his life became far more fulfilling because he was finally fulfilling his own newly emerged highest values.

Remember, your highest values are most fully expressed by what you spontaneously do. If you have to look to some kind of outside motivation to get you going, the activity is not really important to you. For what you truly love, care about, or find important, you require no outside motivation whatsoever. You don't need outside motivation to eat, sleep, or jump out of the way of a runaway truck—and you don't need outside motivation to fulfill your highest values. Whatever seems most important to you is what you will spontaneously do.

Why do people fall into their delusions? Because they keep injecting the values of other people into themselves, subordinating their own higher values to those of others. Then they think they "should" be doing something that they don't really find important. Their fantasies and delusions about what their mission "should" be keep them from appreciating what their mission truly is.

DELAYED GRATIFICATION

Now, since there is no ease without difficulty, no support without challenge, your mission may sometimes require you to do something that is seemingly unpleasant, frustrating, or temporarily unfulfilling.

In fact, anything that you do in your daily life that you can't see as fulfilling your highest values will leave you feeling drained. That is why it is important to honor your most inspiring challenges, for they make you precociously independent and cause you to grow.

How do you honor your challenges? There is a simple, effective way to do so:

Link every action or experience that you find unfulfilling, that you cannot delegate, and that you feel you must do or face to your highest values.

Once you understand that an action that you might initially perceive as "unfulfilling" can actually help you fulfill your highest values, you can become more fully inspired to do it. And if you are able to view things in this way, these "unfulfilling" actions won't leave you feeling drained—they will leave you feeling fulfilled.

Now, in order to find this inspiration, you may have to expand your time horizons. For example, Jordan, who took my seminar the Breakthrough Experience in Phoenix, was frustrated by his life working as a waiter. Although Jordan worked at a high-end restaurant and made quite a decent living from tips, he had always wanted to study Web design. He had a vision of himself creating complex websites that could perform intricate tasks while remaining user-friendly and reliable. He loved the idea of using his creativity in this way, and he was enthused by the thought of all the people he could help.

So, inspired by what he discovered and decided during my seminar, he enrolled in his local public university intending to get his degree as well as to expand his knowledge of the field. Jordan was being both inspired and realistic. He realized that the kinds of jobs he wanted required the credential of a college degree as well as the actual skills needed to perform specific tasks. He was prepared to take the steps that would lead him to his goal.

Soon, though, Jordan found himself frustrated by the many

requirements for the degree that seemed irrelevant to his ultimate goal. When I came through town again, Jordan refreshed his knowledge by attending my seminar a second time, and he came up to speak to me afterward.

"I don't mind taking classes that relate to what I want to learn," he told me. "In fact, I love them! But why do I have to take all these *other* classes that don't relate—English for non-majors, a basic math class, and something about history? I am inspired by my design classes and frustrated by all the others. Help!"

I gave Jordan two suggestions:

1. Link every subject you are studying at school to your highest values and ultimate goal. If you can see ways in which these topics are part of reaching your goal, you will be inspired to do well in every course, and the information you are learning will stick.

2. Widen your time frame. If your ultimate goal is just one day away, your inspiration will easily sustain you for that one day. But if a key step toward meeting your goal takes four years (as it did in Jordan's case), you need to stretch out your horizons so that four years feels like a manageable time period. Focusing on the links between your immediate actions and your ultimate goal is one way to do this. Breaking your long-term goal down into a series of more manageable short-term steps and then linking them is another option. (I explain exactly how to do this in later chapters, and I offer several exercises to walk you through it.)

Either way, here is the secret of not giving up on whatever it takes to reach your goal, achieve your purpose, fulfill your mission, and live your destiny:

Link whatever you see as being in the way to being on the way. Then chunk down your necessary action steps into more manageable bites.

Throughout this book, I'll provide more specific suggestions for linking your short-term actions to your long-term goal, particularly in Chapters 7 and 8. Meanwhile, I'd like to share with you the key part of this message: if your actions are aligned with your highest values, you automatically "walk your talk," so that you tackle ever greater challenges over increasingly large amounts of time and space. The process of pursuing your mission and living your destiny makes your brain become ever more capable and causes the magnitude of space and time in your mind to expand.

If, on the other hand, you are attempting to live according to someone else's highest values, you are likely to feel unfulfilled. You will end up seeking immediate gratification, your space and time horizons will shrink, and you'll begin thinking in terms of your immediate passions rather than your inspired mission. Living by your highest values expands your outreach and enables you to live your more expanded destiny. Subordinating your highest values limits your reach and keeps you from the fulfilling your most meaningful destiny, which you deserve.

WHAT COMPLAINING REALLY MEANS

A few weeks ago, I was giving a seminar in South Africa, and I had the opportunity to speak with the wife of a high-achieving entrepreneur.

"Dr. Demartini," she told me, "I love everything you said about mission and fulfillment. I have only one question: how do I convince my husband that *he* should find something more fulfilling to do?"

I had actually met her husband, whom I knew to be one of the most driven and ambitious entrepreneurs in South Africa. I was surprised at this perspective on a man who to me had seemed to be living an extremely fulfilling life.

"What makes you think he is not fulfilled?" I asked her.

"Oh," she said, "he's always complaining about something. He complains about his long hours, about how other people aren't working up to his standards, about how he has to do all sorts of things himself that he prefers to delegate, about how long everything takes to get to the level of quality that he requires. I don't think he has stopped complaining since the day I married him! I always thought that was just his way, but now that I've taken your seminar, I wonder if it means that he is leading an uninspired life and maybe he would love to do something different."

I shook my head. "I seldom pay attention to people's complaints," I told her. "I primarily look at their actions. Because no matter what people say, they won't continue to do what they do if they don't see more advantages than disadvantages in doing so. People may not be aware of what they perceive as advantages. They may even see advantages in seemingly self-destructive behavior, such as overeating or smoking. But, if a person is undertaking a behavior, he or she believes *on some level* that this behavior will be of benefit in achieving his or her highest values." (For some examples of how this principle operates in the field of wellness, see Chapter 10.)

The woman nodded, and I continued. "So, having said that, how does your husband spend his time? What is a typical day, week, month, and year for him?"

The woman told me that her husband typically bounded out of bed at six in the morning, worked out, ate a healthy breakfast, and headed for his computer. There he conducted business for a couple of hours before heading to the office, where he usually remained until eight or nine at night, sometimes longer. On weekends, he worked from home, usually at least six hours a day, but sometimes longer.

"Most years, I can get him to take a two-week vacation," she told me. "But some years, he says there's a crisis somewhere, and he can't afford to take even that."

"I don't know if your husband is fulfilling his highest values or not," I told her. "I don't know if he is living his destiny, or if he is driven by something else—maybe attempting to subordinate his own values to his mother's or trying to win approval from his father. Without talking to him, I couldn't say. But I can tell you that his complaining is irrelevant. Clearly, your husband is doing exactly what he prefers to do and is working exactly as hard as he wants to work. The complaining just means that he hasn't yet seen how the thing he is complaining about is actually serving him. On some level, he knows that all his hard work is serving some higher purpose in his life, or he wouldn't do it. But he hasn't become conscious of *how* some of his daily actions and business challenges are serving him, so he complains. He may simply be comparing his present actions and career position to a fantasy of what he feels it should or could be."

"Well," said the woman, "I can tell you that *I* am getting tired of all that complaining! I am getting tired of seldom seeing my husband and rarely getting to go on vacation with him!"

"Your complaining about him means just as little as his complaining about work," I told her. "You are still with your husband—you have not yet left him or divorced him—so I have to believe that you are still getting more advantages than disadvantages from the relationship. Otherwise, you would have left!"

Sometimes people complain because they don't see how certain actions are serving them—whether their own actions or those of other people in their lives—especially when they compare reality with the fantasies they develop based on injected values or social idealism. Sometimes they prefer the security of something they know to an unknown that might be more fulfilling but perhaps is also more frightening. Sometimes they haven't yet seen an alternative, or they can only imagine a less fulfilling alternative and haven't yet managed to envision a more meaningful one.

For example, a woman says that she wants to lose weight. Yet she continues to overeat. Why?

Perhaps as a child when she was at a healthy weight, her mother insisted on dressing her up in girly clothes that did not fit the woman's own sense of her personality and spirit, and she was only allowed to choose her own look when she was too overweight for her mother to even attempt to impose a different one. Perhaps as a teenager when she was at a healthy weight, she received unwanted attention from men that she did not know how to handle and perhaps as a result engaged in sexual activities that she later felt violated by or conflicted about. Perhaps as a woman when she was at a healthy weight, she was treated with less professional respect at work. Or perhaps she was never at a healthy weight but feared all these outcomes for herself because of what she saw happening to her mother, her sisters, or her women friends. If the woman is not aware of her negative or painful associations with being at a healthy weight, she will pursue her highest values—say, independence, self-respect, sexual autonomy, or professional achievement—by overeating, even though she does not realize this is why she "must" overeat. Once she becomes aware of these associations, she is free to pursue her highest values in other ways and overeating loses its compulsive power.

So, if you find yourself frequently complaining about your circumstances, I suggest you do what I do:

Look at your actions, not your words.
Consider all of your possible alternatives.
Decide whether you prefer one of the possible alternatives to your current choice.
If you choose to continue as you have been, look for ways to link your current situation to your highest values.

Exercise 2 can help you with this process.

Exercise 2: How Can I Rethink Something That Frustrates Me?

Our actions, more than just our words, reveal our true highest values and our true decisions. If something in your life frustrates you and you have not yet acted to change it, consider how you can either act differently or link the frustrating circumstances to your highest values. This exercise will help you learn to do that.

Step 1: What Frustrates Me

Instructions: Make a list of all the things that currently frustrate you. Don't worry about whether there are "justifiable reasons" for these problems or not. Simply list the frustrations.

I am frustrated by. . .

_____

_____

_____

_____

_____

_____

When you have finished listing your frustrations, put a star by the three *most* frustrating situations.

Step 2: Consider the Alternatives

For each of your top three frustrations, imagine six viable alternative actions. These don't have to be limited only to alternatives that you would actually choose. Just imagine what possible viable alternative actions you could take if you *didn't* participate in the situation as you currently do. For example, if you have a demanding parent who requires help and visits that you find frustrating, your alternatives might include:

1. Meet with this parent to discuss your frustrations and attempt to negotiate a reasonable solution with him or her.

2. Hire an aide for your parent (get another job or work longer hours if necessary to afford it).

3. Organize a reasonable and viable regular schedule for communication and visits and stop responding to this parent's random, nonemergency calls.

4. Negotiate a limit—only one visit every two weeks.

5. Unilaterally implement a limit—only one visit every two weeks.

You might not prefer some of these options—you might only realistically choose one of them—but it's important to identify any possible alternatives before simply rejecting your parent and remaining frustrated.

Step 3: Choose or Reject a Viable Alternative

Seriously consider whether you prefer any of the viable alternatives you have envisioned to your current situation. If so, list the seven highest-priority action steps you could take today to implement that alternative. If not, move on to Step 4.

Step 4: Link Your Situation to Your Highest Values

List Ten Ways That Your Current Situation and Your Participation in It Helps to Fulfill Your Highest Values:

1. _____

2. _____

3. _____

4. _____

5. _____

6. _____

7. _____

8. _____

9. _____

10. _____

If you see no realistic or viable alternatives, then it is wise to keep repeatedly asking yourself, "How specifically is my current situation helping me to fulfill my present highest values?" By repeatedly linking benefits to apparent difficulties in this manner, you will reduce the intensity of your frustration.

GETTING HONEST ABOUT YOUR DESTINY

So many people I work with are not willing to be honest about what their true highest values actually are. Instead, they inject what I call social idealisms or imperatives into their life: what they think their values should be, what the world expects their values to be—anything other than what their life actually demonstrates. This is self-defeating, because proclaiming social idealisms instead of your true highest values simply sets up fantasies that cloud the issue and won't help you create an inspired or fulfilling life. Anytime you expect yourself to live outside your true highest values, you will set yourself up for the ABCD's of negativity: aggression and anger with yourself; feelings of self-betrayal and self-blame; self-criticism and feelings of self challenge; self-deprecation and depression.

I see this in corporate mission statements frequently. Companies create and write these artificial statements that have nothing to do with their actual leader's highest values or their true missions. They just lay out social idealisms for the sake of marketing. The problem is, employees and customers can't rally around these mission statements because they don't really mean anything to people. You have to look at what you really, truly value to lead a company. It is congruency that brings leadership.

Many years ago, I worked with a gentleman who was the founder of a company. He had a nice mission statement that sounded great for marketing, but to me, it was just empty social idealisms: "To build the number one forestry and paper company in Australia that cares about the environment and the customer and sells or shares quality paper with people throughout the world."

Then I asked him what drove him to build this company. How did he get started?

He told me an amazing story about being a poor kid who couldn't even afford to buy his own pads of paper when he was in school—he had to fish paper out of the trash can so he would have something to write on. Years later, he had gone on to found a paper company. His mission for creating paper and for making it affordable to other poor children had built a multimillion-dollar business.

In other words, this man's mission was inspired by his highest values. Living in alignment with his highest values had given him the power to achieve his mission—the power of the Values Factor. But because this man preferred to fill his mission statement with empty words like "trust," "integrity," and "service"—words that sound great but don't really always express a person's true highest values—

he was depriving both himself and his company of the power contained in his true highest values.

When I conduct my thirteen-step value determination process with people around the world, "integrity" seldom shows up as an individual's highest value. Integrity is a state of being that automatically occurs when you set intentions and goals that match your true highest values. Integrity is not something you strive for—it's something you live with, something that emerges automatically when you live congruently with your highest values and when you awaken your natural-born inner leader.

Your values, as we have seen, are driven by your voids. They are an attempt to fill up what is perceived as missing or to solve what is perceived to be unknown. As Aristotle's teachings implied, your perceived emptiness drives your fulfillment. Your void drives your value. Yet a lot of social idealisms cloud the clarity of what is truly driving people.

For instance, one of the social idealisms that is commonly injected and parroted is, "It is more blessed to give than to receive." This religious idealism might initially sound nice, altruistic, and kind, but once you stop and actually investigate the statement a bit deeper, you can see that it is an imbalanced statement. If you are blessed by giving to another person then that implies that they would be cursed by receiving, since they are receiving and not fairly giving back. Their receiving without giving could also rob them of accountability, responsibility, dignity, and productivity and set them up for feelings of obligation and dependency. Wiser and more sustainable relationships demand fair exchanges, not giving something for nothing or receiving something for nothing, both of which result in incomplete and unfair transactions. When you live congruently with your true highest values, you are more likely to honor yourself and others equally and maintain fair and equitable exchanges, not initiate one-sided, incomplete transactions. Our truest nature is neither altruistic nor narcissistic: it is a perfect balance of both.

Such social idealisms become even more distracting when they lead a person to subordinate their highest values to someone else's. If we see someone that seems more empowered than we are, we might subordinate ourselves to that other person, minimizing our highest values and adopting theirs. We tend to think that we should be somehow different from who we are. This clouds our minds and makes us self-defeat and beat ourselves up. It creates seemingly insolvable moral dilemmas. And all because we keep minimizing ourselves to our exaggerations of others.

In the Breakthrough Experience, I show people that whatever they see in others is inside themselves. Yet if you are too humble to admit that what you see in others is inside you, too, you will keep minimizing yourself. As I said in the movie *The Secret*, until the voice and the vision that you hold on the inside is louder than all opinions and injections that you bring in from the outside, you are not going to master your life.

Yet many times people just don't honor their magnificence and their own unique set of values. They don't recognize where they have the power in their life. As a result, they cloud their clarity. They don't feel inspired and fulfilled by their lives and their destiny—they just feel lost.

The specific techniques that I teach in the Breakthrough Experience—particularly the Demartini Method—can help with that. When you learn this approach in my seminar programs, you discover that you hold everything you admire in others within yourself, right here, right now. You don't need to keep minimizing yourself and subordinating your highest values to someone else's. You can claim your own highest values and live your own inspired destiny.

You can achieve the same goal through applying the Values Factor. Once you focus on your highest values, you will feel the inner drive and inspiration you need to pursue your highest values and fulfill your destiny. That is the secret to an inspired and fulfilling life.

Deepening Your Love

Where there is love there is life.

—MAHATMA GANDHI

The Values Factor has the potential to enrich every aspect of your life. But it is especially powerful when it comes to your relationships. If you are seeking deeper, richer, and more meaningful relationships—whether you're attempting to find a life partner, starting a new romantic relationship, enlivening your marriage, enriching your friendships, or empowering your dealings with colleagues, business partners, and customers—the Values Factor is the key to your fulfillment. Knowing your highest values and being aware of the highest values of others is the crucial starting point for an inspired, fulfilling relationship of any type.

Understanding the Values Factor means that you can communicate your own highest values in terms of the highest values of the people who are important to you at home, in your personal life, and at work. The more you can communicate the connection between your highest values and those of others, the more fulfilling, nurturing, and durable those relationships will be. Even more significantly, when you approach relationships in this way, you immeasurably enhance your own ability to grow.

This growth proceeds in a number of ways. First, you learn to truly appreciate other people's highest values—not simply to "tolerate" or "accept" them, nor even to "sacrifice" yourself for them. "Tolerance," "acceptance," and "sacrifice" all imply that the other person's values and corresponding traits are unpleasant or, at the very least, unimportant to you, but out of the so-called kindness of your heart you will grudgingly allow those traits to exist. What we want from our partners, and what our partners want from us, is not lukewarm tolerance, grudging acceptance, or unwilling sacrifice but open-hearted appreciation for who we are. This full-hearted appreciation is the quality that makes a relationship blossom, allowing each person to find greater fulfillment both within the relationship and in his or her life generally. Appreciation is one of the most powerful relationship tools that exists.

Second, to more fully communicate via another person's highest values, you will be required to fully understand both theirs and your own. Relationships of all types push us to understand, clarify, and claim our own highest values, and to come to terms with who we truly are.

Finally, when you come to know others more fully and engage with them more deeply and authentically, you are brought slowly but surely to the realization that every quality you admire *or* resent in another is a quality that exists within *you*. We are so often tempted to project both admirable and frustrating qualities on the people in our lives. "I admire the way he makes decisions quickly . . . but I could never be that decisive," we might say. Or, "I hate the way she is always so emotional and irrational . . . because I am always logical and rational!" We don't realize that these qualities we have projected onto other people are qualities we have as well—that we are *also* decisive or emotional or irrational. Moreover, we don't realize that the qualities we have labeled "good" also have their drawbacks, while the qualities we have labeled "bad" also have their benefits. Learning to recognize every quality in ourselves and then seeing the equal benefits and drawbacks of each quality is tremendously important for our growth and our communication with others. Relationships help us with this process like nothing else on earth!

The closer and more intimate a relationship, the more potential it has to help us grow. In our spouses and our children, we are especially likely to see our own so-called best and worst qualities—and especially likely to have intense emotional responses to those qualities. With our romantic partners, spouses, and children, we are likely to infatuate deeply with what we perceive as their "best" qualities (those traits that we perceive to support our highest values) and become enraged, hurt, or extremely frustrated with what we perceive as their "worst" (those qualities that we perceive to challenge our highest values). Intimate relationships give us our most powerful opportunity to see that the "best" and the "worst" are within us—to the exact same degree that we perceive them in anyone else. And as we engage more deeply in our relationships, we are offered chance after chance to discover that there are benefits to every "bad" quality and drawbacks to every "good" one, so that we can finally move beyond these labels to a deeper reality and a fuller understanding.

Arriving at a deeper understanding can sometimes be challenging—but the benefits are enormous! Wisdom flows from understanding that every trait has two sides and is ultimately neither "good" nor "bad" until someone unwisely labels it so. After all, every human trait must have its purpose and must serve us in some way as human beings. Otherwise it would become extinct. But because the universe is constantly manifesting balance, any trait you might at first admire is likely to have associated with it an aspect that you also despise, just as any trait that you at first despise is likely to be associated with an aspect that you also admire.

For example, say you admire someone for being highly intelligent.

Perhaps as you get to know this person better, you realize that he or she is also argumentative, authoritarian, self-righteous, or a bit of a know-it-all. Perhaps you are frustrated by someone who takes forever to get ready, a quality you despise. But perhaps this trait has another aspect that you admire, such as she puts themselves together with great style, looks beautiful or handsome, or has eye-catching magnetism. You can't have one aspect without the other, and unconditional love involves embracing both. In fact, that is the huge benefit of transcending our labels of "good" and "bad": our newfound ability to experience moments of unconditional love.

Life offers us many ways to learn these lessons—but relationships are one of the best schools I know. And the Values Factor is one of the best ways I know of for creating fulfilling, enriching relationships of all types.

THREE TYPES OF RELATIONSHIPS

There are three primary ways to conduct a relationship, each with an entirely different outcome. The terms for each relationship may look similar but they are worlds apart, so examine them closely: you might have a *careless*, a *careful*, or a *caring* relationship.

A *careless* relationship is one in which you project your own highest values onto the other person, judging them by your highest values and not considering or honoring their highest values. In this relationship dynamic, you care less about the other person than you do about yourself. You expect the other person to conform to your highest values, which you believe to be right, and whenever there is a conflict—as there inevitably is—you are certain that their values are simply wrong or at least less important than yours. Obviously, this leads to all sorts of challenges, ranging from hurt feelings and inadvertent betrayals to exploitation and actions perceived as abuse.

A *careful* relationship is when you think in terms of your partner's highest values without considering your own. In this case, you are overly concerned that the other person's highest values be supported, even as you minimize or disregard your own highest values. This type of relationship might be called "walking on eggshells." This approach likewise creates many problems, from passive-aggressive retaliation to self-exploitation and so-called depression.

Ironically, both the careless and the careful relationships are one-sided approaches that effectively ignore either the other person or yourself. In the careless relationship, you think primarily of yourself, with little regard for what the other person needs. In the careful relationship, you think primarily of the other person, but you aren't really engaging *with* the other person. You are just imagining what he or she wants and shaping your own behavior accordingly. If either you or your partner is walking on eggshells, the two of you never really get to know each other, let alone fulfill each other. You're just trying to stay out of trouble and keep the peace, which is not an effective way to achieve true intimacy or communion.

The third type of relationship is a *caring* relationship, in which you communicate your highest values in terms of the other person's. In a caring relationship, both people are actively engaged, with themselves and with each other. Each of you thinks about both yourself and the other, expressing both your love for yourself and your love for the other person. In fact, the definition of caring is knowing someone well enough to be aware of their highest values and then caring enough to express your highest values in terms of theirs.

For example, I once counseled a woman who was frustrated that her husband was away from home so often. It turned out he was working a job that required long hours and lots of travel, but as this woman experienced it, her husband was not emotionally available, especially since, when he *was* around, he was often preoccupied, short-tempered, or simply exhausted.

I asked this woman if she had any idea *why* her husband spent so much time and energy on his job.

"Oh, it's all he thinks about," she replied. "He just never has time for me."

"Yes," I replied, "but do you know *why* the job is so important to him? What highest value is he expressing by working that job to such a great extent?"

The woman admitted she didn't know, but she agreed to start a conversation with her husband about the topic. She agreed not to be critical or demanding, but simply to try to understand how her husband's work life expressed his highest values.

To her astonishment, she discovered that her husband's highest value was providing for his family. She was even more surprised to discover that the reason he had been working so hard was because he had previously talked to her about starting their own family in the next few years and he was preparing financially. This woman had been worried that a man who was so preoccupied with work wouldn't make a good husband and father. She hadn't realized that his way of *becoming* a good husband and father was to work hard and build financial security.

This woman placed a very high value upon communication with her partner, and she had been frustrated that she couldn't talk to him about the various events of her recent days. When she understood his highest values, she could express *her* highest values in terms of *his* highest values. But her husband did not place as high a value on communication about such daily events as she did, so simply saying, "I want you to talk to me" or "Won't you listen to me?" didn't really register.

Once she understood that his highest value was producing income and providing for his family, she was able to communicate in a different way. She could say, "Honey, I love and appreciate how you have provided for me financially and how you have achieved so much at work. I would really love to share with you how your dedication to work has been helping me and giving me many opportunities to do so many wonderful things. I would also love to share with you all of the activities I have been able to do recently and receive your feedback or opinion concerning some of them. What time would work for you?" Expressing what she valued—communication—in terms of what *he* valued—working and providing income for his family—enabled both partners to get what they wanted, without either partner having to minimize or disregard their own highest values.

Understanding her husband's values meant this woman was also able to view his hard work as his own form of communication. Instead of seeing her husband's absence as withdrawal, she was able to see it as an expression of his love for her—because that was how *he* saw it. Understanding her husband's point of view actually made her feel more grateful for him. The more grateful she felt, the more appreciated her husband felt. This in turn gave him more energy to think about what his wife might appreciate and what might help her feel more fulfilled.

One of the big sore spots in this couple's marriage had been the husband's wish for quiet time after work. When the husband came home each day, he felt a bit tired and wanted to sit quietly by himself and wind down. He experienced his wife's desire to talk to him as just one more demand. She experienced his quietness as a refusal to communicate. But when she understood her husband's highest values, she was able to see that giving her husband some "quiet time" after work was a form of communication just as powerful as talking with him—maybe even more so. By giving him that time, she was fulfilling her value on communication—not by talking with him, but by leaving him alone! And this initial quiet time made him more receptive to talking to her later in the evenings.

Meanwhile, her husband came to see that even though he had spent his whole day at work providing for his wife materially—his highest value—he could also spend some time *after* work fulfilling her highest value by listening to and talking with her. So through understanding the Values Factor, both partners changed their perspective and their behavior without ever having to minimize their own highest values. The wife didn't have to give up her highest value of communicating about her daily activities, and the husband didn't have to give up his highest value of providing for his family. Instead, they simply learned to express their own highest values in terms of the other person's. Their relationship became far more fulfilling as a result. Mastering the Values Factor enabled both partners to express their own highest values while also respecting their partner's highest values.

Many of us have grown up with fantasies of "a completely supportive relationship" in which there are few challenges or conflicts because "when people love each other, anything is acceptable." To a great extent, this is an unrealistic fantasy that leads inevitably to confusion and to feelings of frustration and unfulfillment. We might even experience the illusions of "betrayal" and "aggression." Since maximum growth and development in life demand a balance of both support and challenge, learning how to embrace these two complementary sides equally and simultaneously is important in every area of life, from international law to business to relationships.

The most effective approach to relationship communication and negotiation is based upon communicating your own highest values in terms of your partner's highest values. Whatever you need, want, or expect from a partner in terms of your own highest values seems obvious to you, but will often not seem so obvious to your partner. So whatever your boundaries or expectations are in your relationship, finding a way to communicate and negotiate them in terms of your partner's values—not just your own—will enable the two of you to create a more fulfilling and inspiring relationship.

We often have many illusions in this regard, because whenever we find a quality in our partner—or in anyone else—that seems to support our highest values, we tend to get lax and drop our normal rules and boundaries. To take a trivial example, suppose you have begun dating someone with whom you are infatuated because they seem to support your highest values. They mention that they are a little short of cash, and without thinking twice, you offer to lend them some money to tide them over. Weeks go by, and the other person makes no mention of repaying the loan. Meanwhile, you see the person enjoying expensive dinners and buying some costly new items for their home. You become upset and confront them. According to your values, the money was intended to pay bills and was supposed to be paid back as soon as possible. According to their values, the money was for them to continue to enjoy their extravagant lifestyle and could be paid back whenever it happened to be convenient. Because the two of you did not communicate according to each other's highest values, each of you assumed that the other person shared *your* highest values, instead of recognizing that each of you has *their own* highest values.

However, if the same situation had arisen with someone who challenged your highest values, you would never have behaved in that way. Suppose a challenging coworker were in exactly the same situation. You might offer to lend that person money, but you would be far more likely to defend yourself and "tax" your rules, making it clear exactly what you wanted and expected, and making sure that the other person understood your rules and agreed to accept them.

Nations and companies behave in exactly the same way as we do in our relationships. We all set up more rigid rules when our highest values feel highly challenged or threatened. And so, if we discover that a beloved friend or partner has significantly different values in a particular area, or if we feel that some aspect of their behavior challenges our highest values, we might be especially careful to set up clear rules and boundaries with them.

This response might not fit in with fantasies of a "completely supportive" relationship, but in real life, it is often a useful temporary response, since rules and space give you some breathing room to fulfill your own highest values when you have felt you have been excessively challenged. It also provides you time to learn how to appreciate the other person's highest values and actions and even to assist in fulfilling them.

In our money example, suppose you continue to be involved with the person whose money values are so different from your own. Early in your relationship, you might need very clear boundaries and rules around money. Perhaps you maintain separate bank accounts and only share money with very specific terms and conditions about how it is to be used and when it is to be paid back. You feel challenged by each other's attitudes around money, so clear rules and boundaries give you some breathing room to each pursue your own highest values in that area. You continue to save and handle your money carefully. The other person continues to enjoy their extravagant lifestyle. You may feel that the other person is "careless" and they may feel that you are "uptight," but your rules and boundaries have given you the space to handle these challenges.

Eventually, as you become closer, you might come to understand each other more fully. You might loosen up your requirements, understanding that any money you give this other person is not likely to be paid back. But you can appreciate the beneficial aspects of their "extravagance" and "carelessness," such as spontaneity, sense of style, and openness to different experiences. Likewise, the other person might realize how important fiscal responsibility is to you and change some aspects of their behavior around money, at least where you are concerned. If you come to share a checking account, for example, they might go out of their way to record each expenditure and account for every purchase, keeping your joint accounts neat and tidy even though their own personal checking account is a bit of a mess. Each of you acts not out of "should" and "must," but out of a genuine appreciation of each other's highest values. In fact, that is the secret to a caring relationship: creating communication that is based on a mutual appreciation of each other's highest values—a respectful dialogue that allow both partners' highest values to flourish.

Many of us are prone to the fantasy of a partner who would be exactly like us—who would share our highest values completely and always support our every need. But if any two people are exactly the same, one of them is unnecessary! The purpose of a relationship is not to support us one hundred percent, but rather to teach us to love the parts of ourselves we've disowned. A fulfilling relationship will manifest a respectful balance of support and challenge. Learning how to appreciate your partner's similarities and differences—beginning with his or her highest values—is crucial for a caring relationship.

The secret to a fulfilling relationship—in any sphere—is to remember that each of us filters love through *our own* highest values. When our partners, family members, or friends express their love for us, they often do so by manifesting or expressing through *their* highest values, not ours—and that may make it difficult sometimes to see how much they love us. A father who has a high value on education will express his love by purchasing his child a book full of valuable information. Maybe the child doesn't like to read—maybe he likes to play computer games instead. So the father is expressing his love by following his own highest values, not his son's. But the love is real—the child may simply not fully understand it.

Likewise, a mother who values beauty will show her love by helping her daughters or sons become more physically appealing. Her children may not experience this as love—they might experience it as control, criticism, or disregard. But the mother is simply manifesting her own highest values and expressing her love through them.

When parents master their skill of communicating what they value most in terms of what their children value most, a new level of relationship communication within the family emerges. Parents and children become closer as each comes to appreciate the other's values.

So the key to fulfilling relationships is the Values Factor, which enables us to understand, embrace, and honor the value systems of our loved ones. Then, instead of communicating only in terms of what *we* most value, we are able to communicate also in terms of what *they* most value. Knowing the other person's highest values will also help us realize that we are truly surrounded by love in forms we sometimes don't even recognize. As soon as we understand *how* other people express their love, we can appreciate that expression, even if it comes in a form that we ourselves might not initially value or choose. Knowing that we are loved goes a long way toward making *any* relationship more fulfilling, because we are filled with gratitude and appreciation that is likely to fulfill both us and our partners. That is why love and communication go hand in hand. That is also why the Values Factor is so helpful in achieving fulfilling relationships.

The following exercise can help you and your relationship partner communicate in a caring way. You can also use this exercise with a friend, a business partner, a family member, or anyone with whom you wish to enhance the quality of your relationship.

Exercise 1: Communicating About Values with Your Partner

This simple exercise is one of the most powerful I know. It may take a couple of hours—but it can pay off in a lifetime of communication and caring. The more links you make between your highest values and your partner's, the more you will appreciate what you are doing for them and what they are doing for you. The more you appreciate each other's highest values, the less you will have alternating monologues and the more you will have real communicative dialogues.

Remember, everybody wants to be loved and appreciated for who they are—not for the fantasy that you might be projecting onto them. When you emphasize your highest values over theirs, you will be careless and you will care less about their values than yours. When you emphasize their highest values over yours, you will be carefully walking on eggshells. But when you honor equally your highest values and theirs, and when you communicate what is important to you in terms of what is important to them, you will grow in your relationship, appreciating and loving each other more deeply. That is the secret to a lasting and fulfilling relationship.

Instructions:

1. You and your relationship partner each update your own list of values, identifying the top three. Make sure these are current highest values that your lives are actually demonstrating.

2. Each of you asks, "How is my dedicating my life to my first top value helping you fulfill your top three values?" Each of you must answer this question at least fifty times.

3. Then ask, "How is my dedicating my life to my second value helping you fulfill your top three values?" Each of you answers this question at least fifty times.

4. Next ask, "How is my dedicating my life to my third value helping you fulfill your top three values?" Each of you answers this question at least fifty times.

5. Then ask, "How is my partner dedicating their life to their highest value serving me in fulfilling my three highest values?" Each of you must answer this question at least fifty times.

6. Next ask, "How is my partner dedicating their life to their second highest value serving me in fulfilling my three highest values?" Each of you must answer this question at least fifty times.

7. Finally, ask, "How is my partner dedicating their life to their third highest value serving me in fulfilling my three highest values?" Each of you must answer this question at least fifty times.

Note: It is wise to update this exercise every quarter to keep your communication refreshed!

HOW THE VALUES FACTOR CAN TRANSFORM YOUR RELATIONSHIPS

When You Don't Understand Your Own or Others' Highest Values...

- You are more likely to have volatility in your relationships.
- You are more likely to have unrealistic expectations of yourself or others.
- You are more likely to have difficulty communicating with loved ones.
- You are more likely to minimize or exaggerate yourself.
- You are more likely to depend upon or even be addicted to a particular person or relationship, or to be completely independent from or even isolated from others.
- You are more likely to have others push you around or bully you, or to be the one who pushes or bullies in turn.
- You are more likely to settle for less than what you would truly love.
- Your relationships will likely be more vulnerable to anger and frustration.
- You are more likely to be careless or careful rather than caring.
- You are more likely to be a follower than leader of the family.
- You are more likely to compare yourself to others or envy others rather than to awaken your inner leader.

When You Understand and Acknowledge Your Own and Others' Highest Values...

- You can select a partner who offers you a wiser balance of challenge and support.
- You can more wisely recognize or select your intimate partner

through a realistic process of selection rather than seeking a fantasy.

- You can more effectively communicate with your partner based on understanding and appreciating their highest values.

- You can develop realistic expectations and standards in a relationship.

- You can awaken or reawaken sexual intimacy in an atmosphere involving a true understanding of trust and meaningful communication.

- You can break through the illusion that some have labeled "betrayal" and understand how to handle such an illusion effectively. You come to see that if you feel betrayed, that is less because of what others have done to you than because of what you have done to yourself by unwisely expecting others to live in your highest values and not their own. Either of you might also feel betrayed if you feel that your partner has provided you less value than any of your other options. For example, "I expected you to make me feel appreciated, but you are often critical of the way I like to spend time watching sports on TV. I have a better time watching sports with my friends than I do hearing you criticize me—so I feel betrayed by the way you have failed to meet my expectations for building up my self-esteem." Or, "I expected you to make me feel loved and secure—but when you spend much of the weekend playing golf, I feel betrayed. I get more value out of spending time with my friends talking about our week, watching TV, and maybe going to a movie or out to dinner. So I feel betrayed that I have married someone who did not meet my expectations for alleviating my loneliness." If you can break through these illusions, you can see that your partner has not betrayed you; they have simply not met the unrealistic

continued...

> expectations you have projected onto them. You are more
> likely to create a lasting and fulfilling relationship.
> - You can raise children together with an appreciation that you,
>   your partner, and each of your children has his or her own set
>   of highest values.
> - You can manage family dynamics among several individuals,
>   each of whom has their own set of highest values.

LETTING GO OF FANTASIES AND CELEBRATING REALITY

Virtually all of us have grown up with various fantasies about relationships. We believe that we can find the so-called perfect life partner who will nurture us and never challenge us. We believe that we can create families that are havens from conflict rather than the war zones that they also become. We believe that we can find friends who will never disappoint us and that we can work with colleagues or business partners who will always see things our way.

Oh, sure, we pay lip service to relationships that include "challenges," "conflicts," "disappointments," or "disagreements." But when we imagine these difficulties, we picture minor differences of opinion, not the soul-wrenching, heart-splitting, mind-blowing divergence of values that important relationships inevitably include.

If relationships include such significant challenges to our highest values, then how do we deepen our feelings and engage in fulfilling, inspiring relationships? *The secret is to see a balanced equation: the drawbacks to every benefit and the benefit to every drawback.*

Let me give you an example. When Evan came to see me for counseling, his major complaint was "blahness" in his marriage, which had just entered its tenth year.

"We almost never have sex anymore," Evan told me. "And when

we do, I won't lie to you—it's nothing special. Carly doesn't do anything *wrong* exactly, but I feel that we're just in this rut where nothing great or inspiring ever happens. Everything is just . . . blah."

I thought for a second. Then I asked him, "Who are you comparing your wife to?"

Evan was shocked. Clearly, regardless of whatever else he had expected me to say, this question pushed his thinking into a whole new direction.

"I don't understand," he said.

"Well," I said, "in order to have the perception of your wife that you just shared with me, with all those drawbacks, all that blahness, you would have to be comparing her with someone else—someone that you think she is *supposed* to be."

Eventually, we traced his comparison back to somebody he had met at Club Med, a vacation resort where he'd gone for a three-day weekend with a buddy more than ten years earlier. He actually arrived a few hours before his buddy, and while he was checking in, he saw a young woman wearing hot pants and a little crop top. She had a well-built body, and he immediately went "Whoo!" and started talking with her and flirting with her.

Pretty soon they had made a date to meet out at the bar by the pool, and the next thing he knew, they had gone up to his room. There they spent the next three days just exploring each other's bodies and reveling in each other's company. They had a hot tub, they had food delivered to the room, and all in all, they had everything they needed for a passionate three-day sexual experience.

Evan was actually dating someone else at the time, and he didn't want his buddy to know about this little fling. So when his buddy arrived and knocked on Evan's door, Evan just didn't answer. He and his new friend spent that three whole days together, and then, at the end of the weekend, Evan went home.

Well, of course, for three days, you can put on a pretty good façade. You can be anything you want to be—and you can be anything the other person wants you to be, or wants to believe that you are. But nobody can do that for ten years, can they?

So when Evan left the resort, he went back into his life, but that three-day fling had had a powerful effect on him. First, he had undermined his relationship with his buddy, who was naturally offended that Evan had avoided him for the entire three days that they were supposed to spend together. That friendship was never the same and eventually the two men lost touch.

Second, and even more disrupting, Evan had undermined his apparently unfulfilling relationship with his girlfriend, which completely exploded. Evan hadn't planned to tell this girlfriend about his fling, but soon he found himself comparing his girlfriend with his three-day "fantasy woman." He began finding all sorts of things wrong with the current girlfriend, and eventually, the truth came out. The girlfriend left Evan very bitterly, and Evan felt extremely sad, guilty, and, eventually, lonely as well.

Evan dated a few other people—without any mention of the "fantasy woman"—and finally met a woman whom he felt very serious about. The two of them got married, but privately, he consistently compared his wife to the fantasy woman with whom he had spent those three days. He just couldn't help it. Those three days had been the most exciting three days of Evan's sexual life. It set the model for what he thought sex and passion and pleasure were supposed to be. Whenever Evan's life seemed dull and blah, the memory of those three days could always make him smile. So Evan never really let go of that fantasy.

Now, can any wife compare to a fantasy of three days? No! Just as no man can compare to a woman's fantasy of three days with *her* dream guy. No one anywhere in the world can win against fantasies. It's just not possible.

Of course, if Evan had stayed with his fantasy woman for much longer than three days, the fantasy would have eroded. Alongside the pleasures, inevitably, some resentments would have come up until the playing field was leveled. Then the memory of his infatuation would not have remained such a fantasy. He would have had just another relationship, maybe more or less fulfilling, but either way, a more level playing field.

Instead, Evan had now been married for ten years, and he was unconsciously comparing his wife to this fantasy. So he was never satisfied with the level of romance, excitement, or sexuality in his relationship.

As soon as we identified that this "three-day fantasy woman" was the person with whom he was unconsciously comparing his wife, we had the following conversation:

> **John:** What were the drawbacks to the Club Med woman that you slept in with for three days?
> **Evan:** There were no drawbacks! Everything was perfect! It was the greatest three days of my life . . .
> **John:** No, no, everybody has two sides. So what were her drawbacks?

I had to make him look at the drawbacks because he was blinded by the infatuation of his past. Whenever you are blinded by an infatuation in the past, you automatically generate the possibility of an unfulfilling nightmare in the future. So I just kept asking him, "What were the drawbacks?"

After several minutes, Evan finally answered me.

> **Evan:** Well, she did have kind of a whiny voice.
> **John:** What else?
> **Evan:** Her hair was kind of thin and she had to wash it like twice a day.
> **John:** What else?
> **Evan:** She really didn't have an attractive smile.
> **John:** What else?

Evan: She had an oddly shaped butt.
John: What else?
Evan: She had short, stubby legs.
John: What else?
Evan: She really wasn't ambitious.

As we accumulated more and more drawbacks—nearly sixty—for his fantasy woman, Evan finally broke through his infatuation and in turn began to have more appreciation for his wife. It takes a balanced mind to liberate us from our fantasies and their corresponding reciprocal nightmares. Evan's fantasy was of the "perfect woman," but that fantasy had the nightmare side of finding his real-life wife "blah." As he discovered, dissolving and then letting go of the fantasy also allowed him to let go of the nightmare. But it sometimes takes many dozens of drawbacks or benefits to balance the equation and dissolve both nightmare and fantasy.

Once we had broken through Evan's infatuation, I asked him, "What are the benefits to your wife?"

Evan: She is stable, and she is taking care of the kids. She is quite beautiful . . .
John: What else?
Evan: I love the way she laughs when she's watching television.
John: What else?
Evan: I love to watch her in the kitchen, since she can do many cooking tasks seemingly at once.

We kept going on about the benefits of his wife until he finally was able to balance the drawbacks of the fantasy woman with the benefits of his wife. When we achieved that balance, tears came to Evan's eyes—tears of appreciation. Tears of appreciation occur when we recognize the order and the perfection of what is happening in our life at that moment. Once I brought that fantasy woman down off the pedestal, Evan started naturally appreciating his wife. In fact, he felt affection and love that he had not felt for ten years—because he had unwisely been comparing her to the fantasy. True love comes when the mind is balanced and the heart opens.

When people compare their lives or partners to fantasies, there is no way their actual lives or partners can win. Their feelings of blah or depression result from them comparing their current and balanced realities to fantasies that they remain partly addicted to. People do this with their spouses, of course, comparing them to past girlfriends and boyfriends, and they also do it with friends, colleagues, business partners, even children—anyone whom they are in any way infatuated with. They might fantasize that another person is more powerful socially. They might fantasize that another person has more wealth, more attractive physical features, more business savvy, or more spiritual awareness. Those fantasies can be addictive . . . and then *your* life and the people in your life can become unappreciated by comparison.

Why? Because once you minimize yourself in relation to anybody else or put another person on a pedestal, you will inject that person's values into your life and compare yourself and your loved ones to that person. And once you've developed that kind of fantasy, there is no way you will fully appreciate yourself or others for who they are. How can you? You are comparing yourself and others to somebody who has got a different set of values, and you have unwisely decided that those injected values are somehow "better." *Of course* the other person will be more fulfilled when they live according to *their* own highest values! We *all* feel more fulfilled when we live according to our highest values, because our highest values express what is most important to us and what we are most committed to realizing and manifesting.

However, nobody can *ever* feel fulfilled when they attempt to live according to *someone else's* highest values. It simply can't be done. Asking yourself or anyone else to measure up to another person's highest values causes all kinds of turmoil and confusion in relationships. This is called "baggage," and it is very unfulfilling. Neither you nor anyone else will ever completely live up to another person's highest values. So the minute you make that comparison, you inevitably become disappointed.

For Evan, once I took his fantasy woman off her pedestal and I took his wife out of the pit, his love and his intimacy for his wife rose up in him. He felt a glow—not of passionate fantasy but of deep appreciation and love. In most relationships, there is an oscillating transition between an animal-like passionate sexual infatuation and an eye-to-eye, heart-to-heart, open, mystical and "mission-full" love. Although some people's relationships are always dominated by animal passion, most relationships continue to oscillate between both. When you have a balanced mind, and your heart is open, and you don't put the other person above you or below you, and you put them in your heart, and you have reflective awareness, a mystical form of love opens up within you, which you experience for moments or even for extended periods of time—until the next transition or change in your life. Then you are likely to return to a temporary animal passion form of infatuation until you have worked through the new challenges of your next stage of life. However, you are unlikely ever to experience the more meaningful "mission-full" love as long as you are run by your more primitive animal passions and dominated by your impulses, instincts, infatuations, and resentments based on the fantasies or nightmares of your future or your past.

That type of infatuation and resentment can interfere with friendships, family connections, business partnerships, and any other type of relationship that matters to you. As long as your true vision is blocked by a fantasy, you will not be able to appreciate either yourself or the person you're relating to, because you won't be seeing clearly and your heart will not be open. Check out the following exercise as a way to explore this question further.

Exercise 2: Freeing Yourself from Fantasies and Resentment

If fantasies, infatuations, or resentments of any type are clouding your vision, you'll have trouble opening your heart to relationships in the present. Use this exercise to liberate yourself from your baggage so you can fully appreciate your current relationships of all types.

Instructions:

1. Think of a person from the past that you were once infatuated with or perhaps that you are still infatuated with. Complete the following chart by listing five character traits that you admire or are infatuated with most about this person—traits that you perceive to be highly supportive to your highest values. Then, next to each of these five supportive character traits, list at least five hidden drawbacks to help begin to calm down your infatuation:

Infatuated Character Trait	Hidden Drawbacks to Each Trait
1.	1.
	2.
	3.
	4.
	5.
2.	1.
	2.
	3.
	4.
	5.

Infatuated Character Trait	Hidden Drawbacks to Each Trait
3.	1.
	2.
	3.
	4.
	5.
4.	1.
	2.
	3.
	4.
	5.
5.	1.
	2.
	3.
	4.
	5.

2. Think of a person from your past whom you have been very angry with or disappointed by, particularly a person who you feel has affected your view of what a relationship—with a spouse, friend, family member, or colleague—might be. Complete the following chart by listing five of this person's character traits that you most despise or feel resentful about—traits that you perceive to be highly challenging to your highest values. Then, next to each of these five resented character traits, list at least five hidden benefits that you can think of to help begin to calm your resentment:

Resented Character Trait	Hidden Benefits to Each Trait
1.	1.
	2.
	3.
	4.
	5.
2.	1.
	2.
	3.
	4.
	5.
3.	1.
	2.
	3.
	4.
	5.
4.	1.
	2.
	3.
	4.
	5.
5.	1.
	2.
	3.
	4.
	5.

For further information on how to dissolve emotional baggage and empower your life, please consider logging on to drdemartini .com/baggage for a free inspiring audio presentation, *How to Leave Your Baggage Behind*, or consider learning the Demartini Method by attending the Breakthrough Experience.

RELATIONSHIPS EXIST TO HELP US GROW

As we have seen, you and every other individual on this planet live with a unique set of values. And your highest value underlies your identity. That highest value expresses what is most important to you, what is most meaningful, and what you are most inspired by and dedicated to.

Now, just as you don't share fingerprints or retinal patterns with any other person, you never share complete sets of values. Maybe you have some values in common in some general way with other people, but because your values are fingerprint-specific, nobody else will have the exact same viewpoints on life. Nor will anyone have the same voids driving their values—those are also specific to you. So whomever you are relating to, you are living by your values and they are living by theirs. Every decision that either of you makes will be based on what each of you perceives will fulfill your highest values most.

If you're not aware of the Values Factor, this basic truth can get you into trouble. You might find yourself expecting each other to essentially share the same values. But to expect any human being to live outside their highest values and inside yours is a delusion. You can't do it, and neither can anyone you love—not your parents, not your children, not your friends, not your business colleagues, and certainly not your husband, your wife, or your life partner. Anytime you expect anyone to live outside their values—either you or anyone else—you will end up with what I call the ABCD's of negativity: anger and aggression, blame and feelings of betrayal, criticism and challenge, despair and depression—negative feelings directed toward yourself, them, or both.

Nor can you achieve a fulfilling relationship if you view either your highest values or the other person's highest values as more important. Either putting yourself up or putting yourself down is going to lead to communication problems.

For example, if you believe that your highest values are more important than the other person's, you will become a little self-righteous and will begin to think that you have more to offer than them. You will tend to talk down to them, carelessly, because you *care less* about their values than your own. You will think that you are right, because you value your own highest values more than theirs and you believe your own values are right! And so you will expect them to live in your highest values and not their own.

However, they won't do it! They will do what every human being does: make decisions according to their *own* highest values. The instant you project your unrealistic expectations onto them, you will probably begin to feel betrayed by how they are failing to meet those expectations. Yet the other person never actually betrayed you. You betrayed *yourself* by expecting another person to live according to your highest values.

What if you play the role of the underdog and minimize yourself relative to someone else and put them on a pedestal? Once again, you will end up with the ABCD's of negativity—but this time directed primarily toward yourself. In this case, rather than projecting your highest values onto the other person, you will tend to inject *their* highest values into *your* life and attempt to live according to their highest values. But you have still created a frustrating moral dilemma because now you are making decisions according to your own highest values while attempting to live according to somebody else's.

Inevitably, this disjuncture creates problems, both in terms of how you view yourself and perhaps also in terms of how you actually behave. Soon you will find yourself thinking, "What is wrong with me?

Why can't I stay focused? Why can't I be disciplined? Why do I keep making mistakes? Why can't I continue doing what I *think I should* be doing according to these *other* highest values?" And of course, the answer is the same: "You are making decisions based on *your* highest values, so naturally you are not going to do a great job of living up to *their* highest values." The irony is that you became infatuated with this other person in the first place because you believed they predominately supported *your* highest values. Now you are beating yourself up because you can't live up to *their* highest values!

When we become infatuated with somebody, we often tend to sacrifice what is really important to us—our highest value or *telos*—until we build up enough resentment to set ourselves free and take them off the pedestal and get our life or highest values back. When we take the other person off the pedestal, we often reverse our original stance and throw them down into the pit. Now, instead of trying to live by *their* highest values, we try to get them to live according to *our* highest values. Then *they* become resentful and eventually they set themselves free and take *us* off the pedestal, and try to get *their* life back. It's a vicious cycle, but actually a necessary cycle, revolving until both parties are equal and playing together on a level field!

Every one of us wants to be loved and appreciated for who we are—for our identity, for our highest values, for what matters most to us. And we want the people in our lives to love us and appreciate us according to our highest values—to show their love and express their appreciation in the ways that mean the most to us. The woman I told you about earlier wanted her husband to express his love for her by talking to her about her day. The husband wanted his wife to express her love for him by letting him have some quiet time after work. If I want you to express your love through *my* values, and you want me to express my love through *your* values, that is a recipe for frustration—unless we understand the Values Factor and have fully completed the cross-linking of our highest values.

Certainly, we will find it more fulfilling to communicate our love and what is most important to us in terms of the other person's highest values. What will almost certainly *not* be fulfilling is to sacrifice what is most important to us and attempt to live solely in terms of the other person's highest values. Trying to live outside your highest values or expecting your loved ones to live outside theirs is a recipe for frustration. The recipe for fulfillment—for deepening your love and developing lasting and fulfilling relationships in all spheres of your life—is to make room for an exchange of both challenge and support . . . for both the other person's highest values and your own.

INFATUATION OR GROWTH?

So let's go back to the reason we're all looking for fulfilling relationships, whether with a life partner, friend, family member, or workmate. Initially, we might seek relationships with others because we believe that they will support our highest values. Our fantasy is that they will offer us only support and no challenges. When we believe that this fantasy might be coming true, we become infatuated.

However, this fantasy is unobtainable. No human being on earth can offer another person perpetual support without challenges. It just can't be done. That would be like attempting to find a one-sided magnet. And receiving both support and challenge together is a wiser outcome anyway! If we only ever received support, we'd become juvenilely dependent on the person giving it to us. So our innermost being, in its wisdom, helps us attract somebody into our lives to challenge our highest values, so we can be set free from juvenile dependency.

As we saw in the previous chapter, optimal human growth and development occurs at the border of support and challenge. This has been biologically demonstrated in almost every species, just as the food chain needs both predator and prey. We need support, which is like food. We also need challenges, which are like predators, who keep us on our toes. In order to continue to grow and evolve as a species, we must have both.

So even while we *search* for people who *support* our highest values, we *attract* people who *challenge* our highest values.

Thus, the purpose of any relationship—including a marriage—is to make sure we get both support *and* challenge. Our need for both support and challenge, ease and difficulty, and ultimately growth is so strong that we will inevitably get both, one way or another. If on some level you feel that your relationship is providing too much support, you will include other people in the relationship dynamic to make sure you get enough challenges. In a relationship you perceive to be too supportive, you may become bored and seek stimulation outside the relationship in the form of an affair. Or perhaps your marriage will be challenged by a disapproving in-law, a needy friend, or an overly demanding boss.

Likewise, in a too-challenging marriage, you might seek support from an illicit romantic partner, a soothing parent or sibling, a loving friend, a therapist, or a nurturing work situation. You will insist on receiving the balancing support from somewhere, and if you don't seem to receive it in the marriage, you will find it somewhere else. One way or another, if your support-challenge quotient is seemingly unbalanced, somebody is already in your life to make sure that you get both sides and to break you free from your addiction to one-sidedness.

This addiction can be very powerful. Many of us fantasize that our perfect relationship will always support us and never challenge us; will always be nice and never mean; will always give and never take; will always be kind and never cruel; will always be peaceful and never warlike; will always be positive and never negative. But this is delusional! And eventually your infatuation will cause you to sacrifice yourself and your own highest values, which will ultimately make you resentful, which in turn will cause you to do whatever you need to do to get your partner to challenge you. So our inner wisdom is readily at hand to make sure that we all grow.

That is the wonderful thing about marriage or any other important relationship: it enables us to grow—and perhaps even forces us to do so. We are required to gain some perspective on our own highest values, realizing that they are not the only values in the world and that other people have different higher values. We also are destined to discover qualities in ourselves that we didn't know we had—both seemingly positive and seemingly negative. And all the while, our inner wisdom is requiring us to live at the border between challenge and support, where maximum growth is not only possible but necessary.

LEARNING THE ART OF COMMUNICATION

Whenever two people are in a relationship, you are going to have two different values systems. As a result, there will be times when the two people please each other . . . and times when they displease each other!

How can two different people create a fulfilling relationship? One way is to master the art of communication: learning how to communicate what *you* value most in terms of the *other person's* highest values.

This was a process that I underwent with my late wife. She used to want to dine at fine restaurants such as New York City's Le Cirque, where meals are pricey, to say the least. To add to the expense, she generally wanted to invite another couple to join us as our guests. There I'd be, eating pricey gourmet food that was often a bit too rich for my taste, having conversations that I sometimes didn't find all that inspiring, watching everyone else drinking too much and getting loud and sometimes a bit obnoxious while I didn't drink at all. Finally, I spoke up and shared my partly repressed feelings.

"Honey, eating and drinking rich and pricey meals each night just doesn't fulfill my highest values," I told my wife. "I don't live to eat—I eat to live! I like to eat moderately and generally a bit more quickly. And I work hard for my money and prefer to spend it on more meaningful and lasting activities or experiences. I don't enjoy spending a thousand dollars a night just on food and wine. That lifestyle doesn't exactly match what is most important to me."

My wife nodded, just listening. I appreciated the deep, focused attention that she was giving me, and I appreciated even more her commitment to understanding my highest values.

"But," I continued, "if I can have some additional reasons to *justify* going out to dinner, then maybe it would be fine on occasion. So if you want me to go out to fancy dinners with your friends, then let's figure out how to make it worth both our whiles!"

My wife smiled. She understood perfectly that I was inviting her to find a way that we could both fulfill our values, and, typically, she was up to the challenge.

"Honey," she told me a few nights later, "I've contacted my girlfriend whose husband is the head of this large corporation, and I'm almost certain that if he got to know you, he'd want you to speak to his management team and maybe even bring you in as a consultant. What do you think about us taking him out to dinner along with his wife? I really like her, so she and I could talk about personal things while you pursued a potential business opportunity. That way, our restaurant tab isn't just frivolous spending—it is a potential investment!"

"Now you're talking! Thank you," I replied. "If this is what those fancy dinners are going to be like, I don't mind going out in this fashion more frequently. The rest of you can order gourmet food and wine, while I simply eat some fish and a light salad!"

She was smiling and so was I. Instead of her giving up something she truly loved, and instead of me having to be a bit frustrated through a boring, expensive evening, my resourceful wife had found a win-win. Expressing her highest values in terms of *my* highest values allowed us both to feel inspired and fulfilled.

I had my own version of creating a win-win. At first when I used to travel on business, my wife would sometimes feel lonely and frustrated that I was gone. She understood that my work was important, but she sometimes felt disheartened to see me go—and I preferred not to see her unfulfilled.

Soon I figured out how to associate my absences with something she valued. "Honey," I'd say, "I'm off on a trip to Africa and Australia, and I'll be gone about ten days. I'll be earning quite a bit of money, so why don't I meet you in Venice when my seminars are over? You organize the trip, and I'll meet you there!" Now my wife was able to appreciate my absences—because she associated them with our special rendezvous. Basically, each of us could do whatever we wanted—as long as we communicated it to the other person in such a way that both of us felt more fulfilled.

After a while, we became pretty proficient and smooth at it! And if you master the art of communication in terms of the Values Factor, you can reap the same rewards. Just remember to communicate your own highest values in terms of the other person's highest values. That way, you both become more fulfilled. You can explore this idea further in the following exercise.

Exercise 3: Communicating Your Values in Terms of Your Partner's

In any relationship—romantic, or not—the art of communication is to express your highest values in terms of the other person's highest values. Mastering this skill will allow you to achieve greater depth, inspiration, and fulfillment in all your relationships. This linking exercise can help you get there.

Instructions: Think of something that you love and want to do that your partner resists. Answer the following questions:

1. Which higher value(s) of yours does this activity or goal express?

1. _____

2. _____

3._____

2. Which higher value(s) of your partner's seem to be challenged by this activity or goal?

1. _____

2. _____

3. _____

3. Now link your activity or goal to your partner's highest values by asking, "How specifically does the action or goal I would love to do help my partner fulfill his or her highest values? Don't stop answering that question until you see clearly ten ways that your action or goal will help your partner fulfill what is most important to them. Everything is linkable. You just have to be creative. Once you make the links, your ability to communicate what you would love to do will be more fluent and effective.

The Action or Goal You Love	Links	Your Partner's Highest Values
	1.	
	2.	
	3.	
	4.	
	5.	

The Action or Goal You Love	Links	Your Partner's Highest Values
	6.	
	7.	
	8.	
	9.	
	10.	

OWNING YOURSELF TO FIND YOUR LIFE PARTNER

As we have seen, many people have a lot of fantasies about what a life partner is and how to find one. So I would love to share an important fact with you: *nobody is missing their life partner.* All of the character traits of your life partner are with you throughout your life. When you perceive that you are missing your life partner, it is because you have a somewhat incomplete understanding of what a life partner is.

As we have seen, we typically fantasize that our life partner is going to be a one-sided person who will provide support without challenge. And, as we have also seen, this is an unrealistic expectation. If you are still living with this illusion, you are missing the simple fact that everything you want in your life—every quality that you might desire or expect from a life partner—is already in your life in both a supportive and a challenging form.

Of course, your life partner's traits may not all be amalgamated into one single person. You might be getting those qualities from several people: friends, colleagues, family members. But whether the traits and qualities of your life partner are distributed among many people in your life or exist as one single person, you still already have your life partner right now, in some form, somewhere in your life.

I frequently hear about life partners from the people I teach and counsel. I usually respond by asking them to list the qualities that they're looking for in a life partner. Then I ask them, "Who in your life is already presently providing that?" One hundred percent of the time, *somebody* in their life—whether one person or many—is providing those traits. It might be somebody at work: a colleague, business partner, or even a customer. It might be a friend or neighbor. It might be a parent, brother, sister, or even a pet. Very often it is a combination of all of those. But it is absolutely certain that *somebody* is providing the traits that they seek. Sometimes they must look broadly and scan all the other people in their life in order to put this puzzle together.

Now, here's the wonderful point that emerges from looking clearly and honestly at this issue: once someone realizes that all the traits they are searching for are already present in their life, they don't feel destitute or desperate or depressed. They feel fulfilled, because they have realized, "I have my life partner"—whether in one or many forms. They also realize that it is their set of values that determines their life partner's ever-evolving form.

Why might you diversify your life-partner qualities among many different people rather than partnering with one single life partner? The answer is simple: to protect yourself from the pains or challenges that you expect to experience based on your previous one-on-one relationships.

Remember, the pains and challenges that you believe you have experienced are in a sense illusory because they are based on your fantasy of total pleasure and support. But because you have these unrealistic expectations, you see "normal life" as painful and challenging, instead of simply "the way things are." So perhaps you've accumulated memories that cause you to dread a life-partner relationship, even though you *say* you are looking for your life partner. In that case, you might fulfill those life-partner qualities from many people, because you believe that will enable you to avoid the pain of getting those qualities from just one person. Instead of making yourself vulnerable to one person who will inevitably challenge your highest values and seem to betray you and disappoint you by not meeting your unrealistic expectations, you satisfy your loneliness with friends, your need for companionship with coworkers, and your need for sexual involvement with more casual partners who somehow seem to never work out. Unconsciously, you protect yourself from what you view as betrayal, disappointment, and pain by avoiding a life-partner relationship, instead of entering into such a relationship and learning to embrace both the positive and the negative aspects of your partner's traits.

Recently a woman in one of my seminars was kind enough to drive me down to Los Angeles from Ojai, California. On the trip, she said to me, "Dr. Demartini, I don't want to pester you, but I've got to pick your brain. I am trying to find a man to be in a long-term relationship with, but no matter what I do, I don't seem to be able to find or attract him."

So I suggested that maybe she was fooling herself. Possibly deep inside, I suggested, she was associating so many challenges to her highest values and so many painful memories with being with only one man that she was unconsciously avoiding the very outcome she claimed to be searching for.

She then insisted, "But I *am* looking for a life partner. I desperately want a man in my life!"

I said, "If that were actually true, you would have probably already spotted him and attracted him."

"Dr. Demartini," she said, "how can you say that? You don't even know me."

"Well," I said, "Let's look into this desire of yours a little further." So I asked her to list all the traits that she was looking for in her life-partner relationship. Then I asked her to look at everybody in her life that was providing those qualities. Then I made sure she saw that she was not only surrounded by and receiving one hundred percent of those qualities, she was getting them in exactly the quantity she desired.

Well, it was just mind-blowing for her to realize that nothing was missing in her life—that her life partner was actually *not* missing, because her life was already full of all the life-partner qualities that she desired—just not in the form of the single man that she had been fantasizing about.

So then I asked her about her past relationships. I said, "Can you see that in every relationship, you received *some* of your life partner qualities, but you also had what you assumed to be painful or challenging emotional baggage along with the relationship? It seems you don't want to go through that challenging stuff again. You are afraid to go back into a single relationship because then you might have to deal with all that stuff that became overly challenging in your previous relationships."

"I do see that," she said slowly.

"So what you have done," I continued, "is to find some of those life-partner qualities in a person at work so you can get the same traits without having to go home with them. And you have your tennis partner. And you have a dog that is cuddling up to you, and you have a woman friend that you can call on the phone—you have all these life-partner pieces in your life without having to go through a lot of frustrating parts and possibly dealing with screaming and arguing at night, with flirtation that you don't enjoy, or excessively working things through with a partner, and so on."

This was all a revelation to her. So I continued, "Every one of the previous relationships that you have had is associated with more challenge than support, or more pain than pleasure. And now you are avoiding those misperceived, one-sided pains while striving to get the same supportive or pleasurable traits that you value from all those relationships."

Then I took her through the Demartini Method, which I teach in the Breakthrough Experience, and I showed her how to take each one of those so-called challenging pains that she had in those relationships and find out how each served her so that she could balance out her relationship equation. For any trait in someone else that she perceived had ever caused her pain, I showed her how to find that trait in herself and to find out how *that* trait had equally served her. I asked her, "If that trait that you perceived was causing you pain hadn't been there in your relationship, what would have been the drawback to you? Why was it a benefit, ultimately, to have had that 'painful' trait in your relationship?"

Well, by the time we were in Los Angeles, she had nothing but gratitude for her first relationship, nothing but gratitude for her second relationship, nothing but thank-you for all five relationships she had previously been in. And when we had reached our destination, she had let go of her previously unconscious baggage—and then, she realized, she was ready to have a new relationship with one person because now she was ready to more fully embrace the two sides that every relationship brings.

And guess what? In a few weeks, she had found a man whom she now recognized as her life partner, and, all of a sudden, she had a man in her life! We often say we want one thing, but underneath, our true highest values dictate what we create. For this woman to attract the life partner she *thought* she wanted, she had to release her emotional baggage so that her now-readjusted set of values could align her with her relationship goal.

Two concepts come into play here: Attention Surplus Order (which I explained in Chapter 1) and Intention Surplus Order. Together, these factors mean that we each have the special ability to perceive and act on opportunities that fulfill our highest values. If we truly have a high value on being in a relationship, we will perceive and act upon opportunities to be in such a relationship. If we associate our previous relationships with a series of challenging pains that we don't want to experience again, we will *not* perceive or act upon the ever-present opportunities to be in a relationship. That is why some people can easily go out and find relationships while other people can sit there for months and months, seemingly alone.

But in fact, *both* people are finding relationships—in fact, *both* people have found their life partners. One person has found their life partner mainly in one individual. The other person has found their life partner diversified among many people. Both are living according to their highest values. Consciously or unconsciously, each is creating the life they want.

The concept of a life partner ultimately represents the way either one or many people contribute all human character traits to enrich our lives—traits that we find both supportive and challenging. All of those traits are necessary to maximize our evolution and growth. We can experience our deepest and fullest love when we learn to appreciate them all.

RECOGNIZING LOVE

Once I went through the Oxford English Dictionary and found 4,628 words that referred to character traits that might be found in human behavior. I looked at each trait, and I asked myself, "Who do I know who has that trait to the most extreme possible state?" I thought of various people, and for each one I asked myself, "Where and when have I displayed that exact same trait, or perhaps a similar trait, to the exact same degree?" If I initially thought that trait was negative, I asked, "What are the benefits of it?" If I thought it was positive, I asked, "What are the drawbacks of it?" My intention was to own and balance out my judgment on all possible human traits.

But here is the important part: whichever words or traits I found in the dictionary, I also discovered when I looked honestly that I had them all! I could not find one single trait in one of the biggest dictionaries in the world that I myself had not demonstrated at some point in my life. If you filmed me during some moments, you would see me as a villain. In other moments, you would see me as a hero. That is true for me, and that is true for all of us.

Do you realize what this means? No matter what anybody says about you, it is all true. It just might not be true in the exact manner that they are expressing it. And so, when you actually own, appreciate, and love all parts of yourself, you can more fully love your life partner.

But if you don't love all parts of yourself, what happens? Any part of you that you try to run from, you will keep running into. In fact, the whole purpose of relationships is to bring into your life anything that you keep trying to get rid of. Because the magnificent world of nature is trying to teach you how to love the parts of yourself that you have been having difficulty loving.

This is why both support and challenge are part of any relationship. The more you are addicted to support, the more disheartening challenges you are going to attract. The more you are addicted to ease, the more difficulty you are going to attract. But then, finally, you embrace both support and challenge, both ease and difficulty—you welcome them both equally, and then they melt into love, because that is what love really is—a synthesis and synchronicity of all complementary opposites.

When I worked with that woman who was driving me to Los Angeles, she could not immediately see any benefits to all the so-called painful relationships she had had. So I had to prompt her a little bit, but finally she got it. And when we were through, she was in tears of gratitude for each person she had been involved with, just the way they were. She felt love for all the relationships she had been with, because she was finally able to see the benefits as well as the drawbacks to any so-called bad thing that had happened. She was able to appreciate the value in every trait that each former partner had had—and so, she was able to appreciate the same trait in herself.

What does this teach us? It shows us that the innermost essence of our being—what some have called our soul—is unconditional. S-O-U-L spells it out: spirit of unconditional love. The moment you are in an unconditional state where there are no evaluations and judgments, you say, "Thank you." Because gratitude is all you feel.

As long as you unrealistically seek a one-sided partner who will always support you and never challenge you—someone whose traits you always experience as positive and never negative—the person you attempt to love, who is actually two-sided, will have to awaken you to the truth and to the inherent balance that a real-life relationship will always provide. You will be challenged to give up your hidden agendas, such as "I expect my partner to make me feel less lonely" or "I expect my partner to make me feel better about the way I always disappointed my mother," so that you can view your partner not as a one-sided person whose "job" is to meet your expectations, but as a two-sided person with both "positive" and "negative" traits whose job is to fulfill their own highest values in life.

Your goal, then, is to view your partner *synchronously*: to see both their "positive" and "negative" traits *at the same time*, to experience both their challenge and support to your highest values *at the same time*, rather than to feel first infatuated by their seeming support of your highest values and then challenged by their seeming betrayal of your expectations. And when you are finally able to love someone from a synchronously balanced and unconditional perspective—loving them not for how they meet your conditions or expectations, but simply for who they are—transformation occurs. The moment you love somebody just as they are, they turn into the person whom you love. That is the true secret to inspiring and fulfilling relationships.

So if you still have baggage about any of your past relationships, you just haven't gone as far as you can go. Just keep going further until you have a tear of gratitude for who that person is. Then in the end, all you will have is, "Thank you, I love you."

Love and gratitude are the essence of our existence. They are the secret of an inspired and fulfilling life and they are what emerge most when you live congruently with your highest values. They are byproducts of the Values Factor.

Activating Your Genius

I am always doing that which I cannot do, in order
that I may learn how to do it.

—PABLO PICASSO

A few years ago, I was teaching an evening seminar program in
Dallas. As the program began, I asked the room a familiar
question: "Who here has a job that requires them to do something
that they are not particularly inspired by?"

Well, of course, hands were flying up all around the room! I
scanned the audience to find someone who I felt would genuinely
benefit from the experience of working with me at the front of the
room. I noticed an eager woman who appeared to be in her early
thirties. She looked determined and her hand went flying up first. I
had the impression that she was very committed to living an inspired
life, but that somewhere along the way she had begun to give up on
the belief that such a life was possible for her.

So I invited this woman, whose name was Marisa, up onto the
stage. Marisa told me she had risen quickly up the corporate ladder,
and she was already a junior vice president in a local finance company.

"What in your job do you not love doing?" I asked her.

"I hate doing the paperwork on contracts!" she replied immediately. "Oh, my God, I hate that *so much*! And it is my designated responsibility, so I am not allowed to delegate it."

The whole room laughed sympathetically. I could see that everyone was thinking of some part of their jobs that they were equally uninspired by and seemingly stuck with.

"I don't just dislike it," she confessed, taking courage from the room's support. "I'm *terrible* at it. I am just bored and terrible at understanding the legal jargon of contracts, and every time I work with them, I feel so stupid and frustrated. I've tried to become proficient at this, but it is just no use. Contracts are something I don't love and I can't seem to do them well, no matter how hard I try."

"Let's see what we can do," I told her. "First, let's look at your hierarchy of values."

Within a few minutes, using the values-determining process that I shared with you in Chapter 2, we had figured out what was most important in Marisa's life—what her highest values were. This woman wanted to be wealthy via saving and investing money. She was a single mother—she had two children in middle school—and her dream was to be able to send her kids to the best colleges and even to pay for their graduate education if they chose to go further. She wanted to create enough family wealth to support her children in any endeavor that interested them—to enable them to start their own businesses, if they so desired, to spend some time traveling, or to do whatever they wanted to do. And her goal was also to be financially independent by the time she was fifty, so that she could experience her own freedom and at the same time pursue some of the earlier dreams that she had put aside for the greater value of building her family wealth.

Now, the beautiful thing about Marisa's goals was that she was actually meeting them! She was saving money, investing it wisely, and meeting all of the financial steps that she had laid out for herself. She had risen quickly in her company, she had the respect of her colleagues, and she believed she was well on her way to achieving her ultimate goal of starting her own mutual fund and money management firm.

The only problem, she told me, was her client contracts. And I could see, when she told me about them, that there were really two problems. One was that she had to spend several hours each week doing work that did not inspire her. The other, deeper problem was that Marisa, normally confident and empowered, reverted to an insecure woman whenever she thought about those contracts. She told me that she considered herself proficient at the rest of her job—even excellent at it. But she also made it clear that dealing with the contracts made her feel "dumb."

"So what we need to do here," I told her, "is activate your contract genius."

"Well, good luck with that," she told me, rolling her eyes. "Because when it comes to those contracts, I can tell you one thing: I am absolutely *not* a genius."

So then we started the process of linking her task of understanding, negotiating, and writing large corporate client contracts, which she assumed she was not great at, to her deepest, most meaningful, highest values. I began by asking Marisa how doing the contracts was going to help her fulfill her highest value: establishing wealth for herself and her family.

"I *hate* doing those contracts!" she repeated. "I wish it wasn't part of my job."

"Yes, but that's not answering my question—that's dodging it. Let me ask you again: how is doing those contracts going to help you fulfill your highest value—building wealth?"

Eventually it came out that when Marisa was working on the contracts she was getting the opportunity to work with major decision-makers in some of the nation's biggest companies. She began to see that working on the contracts gave her the opportunity to meet with potential clients for her future firm, as well as the chance to learn a great deal about business and finance and their legalities from the heavy hitters she was working with. She understood that every time she was doing paperwork on a contract, she was laying the groundwork for personal interaction with some of the top people in the business world—people who ran companies that could become her future clients.

As she thought about it further, Marisa began to realize that these contracts that she had disliked so much were also giving her the opportunity to make contacts for her children. Perhaps some of the people she met in this way were alumni of the schools her children would someday want to attend. Or maybe they would become her children's future employers, investors, or mentors. The network of personal relationships that she had an opportunity to develop through this frustrating task actually began to look like a terrific opportunity.

As soon as Marisa was able to make more than a dozen links between her difficult duty of working with those contracts and her highest and most important value, her whole attitude shifted. You could see it happening right before your eyes. The insecure woman vanished and the confident, empowered woman took over. Instead of feeling defeated by this task that had made her feel dumb, Marisa now felt inspired to master this new area of knowledge so that she could avail herself of the all the opportunities it could bring her. Because the task was a path to fulfilling something she truly valued, she began to welcome the challenge rather than seeking to avoid the assumed pain. When I asked her whether thinking about the contracts still made her feel dumb, she shook her head impatiently and said, "I don't care how I once felt. I am inspired by doing the contracts now, because they are important to me—and I can't wait to figure them out!"

The Values Factor had enabled Marisa to link her challenging intellectual task to her highest values, thereby changing her relative Attention Deficit Disorder into its reciprocal Attention Surplus Order. As you recall, our highest values determine what we attend to and what we ignore or cannot even notice. We have some form of Attention Deficit Disorder for anything associated with our lower values, while we become highly attentive to anything associated with our highest values, organizing our perception and attention to focus on those things.

Thus, by applying the Values Factor, Marisa had transformed a boring task of desperation into an amazing opportunity for inspiration. Most important, she had activated her genius, opening up new possibilities for using her mind and her talents that she had never before suspected. In fact, that's the very definition of "genius": one who can see how uninspiring challenges are also inspiring opportunities.

GENIUS WITH AND WITHOUT THE VALUES FACTOR

If you do not link your mentally challenging activities or topics to your highest values . . .

- You might not awaken your hidden genius.
- You might not give birth to your greatest creativity and innovation.
- You might not maintain focus and will become easily scattered.
- You might not enhance the physical wellness and adaptability of your brain and its cells.
- You might be labeled a person with Attention Deficit Disorder.
- You might become vulnerable to depressive and bipolar states.
- You might not activate your full inspired drive and ambition.
- You might frequently require outside motivation.

- You might believe you have a poor memory and forget things easily.
- You might become more introverted, hesitant, and likely to procrastinate.

When you link your mentally challenging activities or topics with your highest values . . .

- You awaken your genius.
- You keep your brain growing and take advantage of its neuroplasticity—its ability to develop new capacities and deeper connections. You become capable of learning at remarkable rates.
- You retain knowledge longer and more accurately.
- You break through educational labels to define your own individual genius.
- You become a more creative and confident thinker.
- You become more vitalized.
- You experience a calm, focused, and centered mind.

AWAKEN YOUR HIDDEN POTENTIAL FOR GENIUS

Inside everyone, there is a genius. But unless you can see your hidden potential for genius, you probably won't ever awaken it. The key to awakening your inborn genius is to understand your highest values. That is where your unique genius lies.

As we have seen, every human lives by a set of values. Whichever of your values is highest calls forth your greatest creative potential. This truth expressed by the Values Factor applies to every human being, no matter how old or young. None of us has to be encouraged, reminded, or motivated to live a life of service when we are living congruently with our highest value. When it comes to our highest value, we are automatically disciplined, reliable, and focused—because we are inspired from within to fulfill what is most meaningful to us. That is how we activate the Values Factor.

By contrast, whatever is lower on your scale of values inspires you less. For lower-value tasks, you tend to hesitate, procrastinate, and feel frustrated. Although your highest value is so compelling that you can scarcely keep yourself from pursuing it, your lowest value is so uninspiring that you can barely bring yourself to do it.

By the same token, whatever is highest on your scale of values, you tend to bring order and organization to. So if you are a young boy who loves computer games and considers that your highest value, then you will have all your computer games stacked up nicely, organized according to topic, level of difficulty, or whatever system makes most sense to you. If you are a woman who loves clothes and makeup, you will have your closet and your makeup table arranged by color and style. This is all in stark contrast to whatever is lowest on your scale of values. There you may well be disordered, disorganized—a mess.

So your first step in activating your genius is to identify your highest values, because nobody ever has to get you up in the morning to pursue those values. Nobody has to get the ten-year-old boy to sit in front of that computer game. He automatically gets up and turns it on, begins to play, and absorbs whatever he learns. Maybe you have to motivate him to go to bed at night or to put his clothes away, but you don't ever have to motivate him to pursue his highest values. He is inspired from within to fulfill his ability to excel at computer games and to do what he feels called to do.

Likewise, nobody ever has to motivate a woman who loves clothes and makeup to go shopping or to put her whole heart and soul into getting dressed and ready for the day. She is inspired from within to update her wardrobe or to choose just the right shade of lipstick. Like all of us, she seeks automatically to fulfill the highest values that inspire her.

When you pursue your highest values, you do feel inspired—and fulfilled. You will pursue those values regardless of how much pain and aggravation they cost you, regardless of how you are challenged or reprimanded. By contrast, when your lowest values are involved, you will likely hesitate and procrastinate, regardless of how many pleasurable rewards you promise yourself, regardless of how you are supported or praised. True inspiration comes only from within, as we pursue those values that mean the most to us.

Certainly our values evolve and change. But we will consistently relate to them in the same way: we are inspired by our highest values even while we remain uninterested in whatever relates to our lowest values.

Moreover, our highest values indirectly dictate the activities within the sensory and motor cortices of our brain. Our values literally affect what we perceive and how we move. If a mother's highest value is on her children and she enters a mall, what will leap out at her will be children's clothes, children's educational material, children's toys. She will filter her reality according to her values, noticing anything that supports her highest values and not noticing anything that doesn't. She will move toward the objects that fulfill her highest values and away from the objects that don't.

By the same token, if her brother is an entrepreneur who is not as interested in children and he enters the same mall, he will be virtually blind to what his sister notices. What will leap out at him instead are all the factors that might determine whether the mall is a wise investment: foot traffic, vacancy rates, the age and condition of the property. His interest in these issues will inspire him to move toward the parts of the mall that enable him to gather the information that fulfills his highest values. Meanwhile, if you asked his sister about those aspects of the mall, she would be as blind to them as her brother was to all the children's stores and products.

Basically, anything that fulfills your highest values, you awaken to. Anything that does not fulfill your highest values or simply doesn't engage them, you will tend to ignore or shut down to. Your brain's glial cells and inner reticular activating system will help assure you of this. Your glial cells are specialized cells that help your brain remodel its sensory and motor nerve structures and functions.

Both the act of perception *and* the actions you take as a result create a transformation within your brain; perception and action each affect your brain separately, and together they have an even more powerful effect. This has to do with the neuroplasticity of your sensory and motor nerves, which change in response to the demands that are made on them. So by perceiving the things that fulfill your highest values and by taking corresponding actions in a manner that will fulfill your highest values—buying something at a children's store or walking over to a vacant shop to find out more about the mall's overall profitability—you literally reshape your brain to become more effective in fulfilling your highest values.

This is true whether it happens consciously or unconsciously. If you truly have as one of your highest values a desire to feed your children more nutritious food, you might find yourself noticing all sorts of places that sell healthier food, stumbling upon cookbooks with healthy recipes, and discovering TV shows specializing in healthy cooking for children. You would literally be reshaping your brain to notice these things. But if you unconsciously felt the need to eat healthier food for yourself, you might have the same experience without understanding why or how it happened. Either way, your highest value—say, to support your children's health or to support your own health—would be driving your attention and intention and shaping your brain. Both your perceptions and your actions would have this effect.

This is why the Values Factor is the key to awakening your genius, on any topic that you choose, for once you link a topic to your highest values, you awaken a greater potential within your brain for enhanced perceptual awareness and creative genius. In the example we just considered, discovering the high value you placed on your own or your children's health will awaken your creative genius in the field of nutrition. You will suddenly find yourself able to master complex knowledge about how food supports or challenges your body or your children's bodies. You will remember arcane facts about vitamins, nutrients, and anatomy. You will become something of an expert in the various properties of different foods and supplements, and you will perhaps surprise yourself with how much you know and remember about biology, chemistry, and neurology, even if these fields defeated you in school. Perhaps you could not master your science classes when you had not linked them to your highest values, but linking science or nutrition to your health or your children's health opens up a whole new ability within you that you never suspected.

Once you understand how powerfully the Values Factor operates within you, you will see that the secret to awakening your genius is simply to link any topic you'd love to excel at to your highest values. Once something is linked to your highest values, you will awaken what I have called your Attention Surplus Order. Your senses will become more acutely attentive to and aware of anything that might help you fulfill your highest values. Accordingly, you will mobilize your attention; you will bring order and organization to the topic; and you will be inspired to learn everything you can.

You will also experience Intention Surplus Order: a high probability of doing what you intend, and a reliable, disciplined, focused approach. In addition, you will experience Retention Surplus Order, which means that if a piece of information is associated with your highest values, you will remember it. Anything linked to your highest values you will tend to store in your long-term memory. Anything linked to your lower values you will tend to store in your short-term memory—if you remember it at all.

Thus, if you ask that boy who loves computer games what he remembers from his day at school, he might very well say he doesn't know. But if you asked him about his computer games, he will almost certainly be able to give you a long dissertation on the games he loves most. He will remember each of the different characters; he has mastered all the plays; and he can perform at an inspired and heightened level because he is efficiently mobilizing his motor functions and his sensory awareness in the service of what matters most to him. He may be a C student at school, but he is an absolute genius at computer games. And if he believed that any class at school could help him with what matters most to him—excelling at computer games—he would become an absolute genius at those particular classes as well.

This, then, is the secret to awakening your genius. Once you link the particular field at which you'd love to excel to your highest values, there will be no stopping you. There is no stopping *anyone* in the pursuit of his or her highest values. That is the power of the Values Factor. You can explore that power further in the exercise that follows.

Exercise 1. Activate Your Genius by Connecting to Your Highest Values

When we can link an area of knowledge or study to our highest values, we activate our genius. In this exercise, you can practice activating your genius by strengthening the links between something that you would love to learn and your highest values.

Instructions:

1. Identify a skill, topic, or type of information that you would love to master. Write it down in the far left column that follows.

2. Recall your three highest values as you identified them in Chapter 2. Write your three highest values in the far right column that follows.

3. Find at least twenty ways in which you will fulfill your three highest values by studying and mastering the skill, topic, or type of information that you have identified. Write these ways in the middle column that follows.

Skill, topic, or type of information	Twenty ways in which this skill, topic, or type of information can help you fulfill your three highest values	Your three highest values
1.	1.	1.
	2.	2.
	3.	3.
	4.	
	5.	
	6.	
	7.	
	8.	
	9.	
	10.	
	11.	
	12.	
	13.	
	14.	
	15.	
	16.	
	17.	
	18.	
	19.	
	20.	

ALLISON AWAKENS HER GENIUS

I remember once when I was doing a Value Determining seminar in Melbourne, Australia, I spoke afterward with a sixteen-year-old whose mother brought her to me because she was having so much trouble in school.

"Allison is a bright girl," her mother told me. "But she is getting terrible grades. She's not participating. She's bored all the time. She doesn't seem to have any motivation!"

"I don't believe that motivation is the key," I told the mother. "Motivation is an external force that gets you to do something that you may inwardly feel uninspired to do, like those parents who reward their children by giving them money in exchange for higher grades. That might work for a short time or in a limited way, but it doesn't truly awaken anyone's genius or lead to a real and lasting life of learning. I believe less in motivation from without and more in inspiration from within."

I could see that the mother didn't fully understand, but I agreed to work with her daughter. My first step was to determine her daughter's values. After going through the process I shared with you in Chapter 2, we found that Allison's number-one highest value was riding horses. She had a great love for horses and she lived to ride them. She had a real talent for working with horses, and her dream was to become a professional rider who competed in high-level competitions.

Many parents are baffled by what their children love, but Allison's mother was actually fine with her daughter's commitment to riding. She knew that riding was a great sport and she actively supported her daughter's interest in it. She simply wanted her daughter to have the security of a college education, and she knew that couldn't happen unless her daughter's high school grades improved.

Allison, though, couldn't understand why she should spend any time on anything that didn't involve horses. Her entire school day was a torture to her because she perceived it as one long obstacle keeping her from the stables and the riding ring.

"So," I said when Allison and I had finished determining her highest value, "riding horses is currently your most inspiring mission in life."

"Yes, exactly!" Allison said. She was relieved that, like her mother, I supported her mission. But she also expected that, like her mother, I would try to "motivate" her into being interested in school. She didn't yet realize that nothing was further from my mind.

"Fine," I said. "Now that we know your mission, let's look at your schoolwork and see what challenges you are facing."

Allison told me that she was taking six classes in the coming year: math, sociology, history, English, biology, and art.

"Fine," I said again. "Let's find out how each of these classes is going to help you become great at doing what you love with horses."

I knew that if we could just connect each of Allison's classes with her life's mission, we would awaken her openness to and genius for each of those classes. After all, Allison was already a genius with horses. She already had Attention Surplus Order for everything that had to do with the creatures she loved so much. She knew how to feed them and groom them. She knew how to guide them with subtle tugs on the reins or by shifting her weight or altering the position of her feet. She studied the techniques her riding instructors taught her and brought all her focus and concentration to every competition she entered. Her highest value had awakened her genius in the stables and the riding ring. Now we were going to awaken it in the classroom and the library—not through motivation, but through inspiration.

"What kind of riding inspires you most?" I asked her.

Allison lit up as she described the barrel races that meant the most to her—races in which a rider has to guide her mount in a clover leaf pattern around barrels placed in her path.

"Now," I asked her, "how could your math class help you be a master horse rider?" We began to explore the ways that Allison could benefit from this class by understanding the angles that were needed to navigate around the barrels. After making nearly twenty links, Allison finally began to see a strong connection between the math she would be studying and her ability to find the most efficient way of speeding along the track or arena. She also saw that knowing math could help her with the complex system of scorekeeping used to rate the riders, and with tracking her own performance.

Then we looked at sociology and how that might help her. "Sociology is the study of people in different societies," I reminded her. "So wouldn't it be helpful to you if you could understand what the different values are of each set of judges in each city and country where you plan to compete, as well as those of the breeder, trainer, and audiences?"

Allison began to see that there might be substantial differences between competing in, say, Britain and America. In Britain, perhaps the judges would be looking for more dignity and professionalism among the riders. In America, the judges might be more inclined to prefer riders who smiled and showed off their own individual styles.

"That's so curious," Allison said as we discussed this possibility. "I'm going to be way more prepared by studying the material in these classes, aren't I? If sociology can help me find distinctions among different judges and audiences, well then, that's going to help me later on."

It wasn't all that easy to find links between Allison's schoolwork and her mission, but the two of us continued to talk for nearly three hours until we had found dozens of ways that each one of Allison's courses was absolutely vital to pursuing her mission and fulfilling her highest values. When we finished our conversation, Allison was absolutely inspired. And indeed, her mother reported to me by e-mail that in the following month, Allison became a dedicated student who was now at the top of some of her classes. Once her schoolwork had been linked to her mission, there was no stopping her. The key was helping her to discover *from within* how each of her classes would help her fulfill what was most important to her—her highest value. Once we had done that, out came her hidden genius.

My experience with Allison was yet another example of a principle I have observed for a long time: *everybody wants to learn.* They just want to learn what's most meaningful, purposeful, and inspiring to them—that is, whatever has been thoroughly linked to their highest values. If people can see the connections between any topic whatsoever and their highest values, their genius can be awakened. They immediately manifest creativity, innovation, a thirst for knowledge, and a capacity to learn. If people are unable to see the connections, their ability to assimilate, absorb, and retain information goes way down. That is why the Values Factor is such a powerful way to activate your genius.

DISABLED OR MISLABELED?

If there is no stopping a person who is pursuing their highest values, there is no moving a person who is being asked to pursue something they do *not* find valuable. Lower down on the values scale is where you start having less focus, poorer memory, and hesitation or Attention Deficit Disorder, as well as what I call Retention Deficit Disorder and Intention Deficit Disorder. These are the children that are labeled "bad" or "slow" or perhaps even diagnosed with a learning disability such as ADD. These are the adults written off as "stupid," "lazy," "distracted," or "not too bright."

In my opinion, these labels are of little use and can even impede the awakening of true genius. The vast majority of children that are diagnosed with ADD have been misdiagnosed. If you follow these children throughout their day, you will almost certainly find an aspect of their lives where they are highly focused, calm, remember things, and commit themselves fully. Perhaps their area of interest is indeed computer games. Perhaps it's sports, or television, or socializing. Perhaps it's something that their surrounding adult world doesn't value. But for whatever is highest among those children's values, they will have Attention Surplus Order, Retention Surplus Order, and Intention Surplus Order. These children often have extremely concentrated highest values.

I have yet to meet a child who didn't have Attention Surplus Order somewhere in some area. If you are reading this book as a young person, just know that you have an amazing capacity. Your learning capacity and your genius are not missing. They may simply be concentrated in an area that other people do not yet value. Your genius may not be what everybody else expected, but you do have it. Don't ever question it. Don't ever let anybody tell you *don't* have this special genius—not even yourself.

By the same token, the adults who are written off as "slow" or "stupid" are likewise often being mislabeled. They are people who have never figured out how to link their life's demands with their highest values. These may be people who have a unique genius for fixing cars, soothing children, or amusing their friends with funny stories. Or perhaps their genius lies in collecting souvenirs, stretching a paycheck to last through the month, or finding the best item on a restaurant menu. Sometimes people's genius has a wide scope, and sometimes it is confined to a narrow area, but each of us has our own unique genius. And when we learn how to link our essential daily actions to our highest values, we can then activate that hidden genius in any area we choose. Once again, the Values Factor is the secret.

HIDDEN GENIUS

I have seen so many people whose genius lay out of sight, just waiting to be discovered. Once I was filming for a reality TV show in the

Hollywood area, and one of the guests was a forty-two-year-old man who had been diagnosed when he was seven years old, much as I was: he had been told that he was a slow learner, had learning problems, was dyslexic, and probably wouldn't amount to anything. I sat with him for an hour and forty-five minutes, asking him a set of questions that nobody had ever asked him. I wanted to know, "In what area do you have an amazing memory? In what area do you learn things amazingly quickly? In what area do you retain information well?"

As you can imagine, his first response was skepticism and maybe a little sadness or even anger. "I *don't* have an amazing memory," he told me. "I *can't* learn things quickly. I *don't* retain information well."

But I knew that was not the full truth. "My certainty exceeds your doubt," I answered him. "I am going to keep asking you these questions, again and again, until you discover the hidden genius, the hidden awareness that you have which you have been denying."

Like so many people, he wanted to insist on his perceived limitations—on what "everyone had always told him" that he couldn't do. So he resisted me for about ten minutes. But I was relentless, because I knew that if I could get him to realize the abilities that he had, his life would change. Given the TV show format, I had only about two hours to get this job done. But I had certainty about him and about my approach, so I persevered.

Eventually, I asked him, "How long have you had this so-called memory problem?" He said, "As long as I can remember . . . since my early childhood." I thought that his answer was very revealing: he had an amazing memory for what he could not remember! So I just kept pursuing the questions that I knew would help him break through.

Finally, as I continued to ask him in what area he had an amazing memory, he recalled a significant incident from his past. It was actually fairly ironic, because what he remembered—with great vividness and completeness—was what his teacher had told him he couldn't do. So in that way, he was still running his story—insisting on his limitations.

And I was still not buying it. I told him, "You will only remember what your teacher said if it is part of your highest values—if you are using those words to your greatest advantage. So you are getting some kinds of secondary gains out of playing that role. It is doing something for you. At the very least, it has gotten you out of doing certain things."

He started to argue, but I just said, "So in what other area do you have a great memory?"

Well, once he had unlocked one area of great memory, he had far less trouble unlocking a second, so he began telling me about certain sports trivia—information about teams, athletes, maneuvers. I kept at him for an hour and forty-five minutes—one example after another showing that he had an extraordinary memory—until finally the tears came out of his eyes and he broke through thirty-five years' worth of programming. Because for all those years he had believed that he had a learning problem when, in fact, he didn't. What he had was a highly concentrated value system that didn't match his teachers' or his parents', that didn't fit *their* highest values, that didn't conform to society's norms. But now he was discovering his hidden genius, and as he was crying, he hugged me, seeing new possibilities for what he could now do with his life.

How had this man's genius become so well-hidden? He had subordinated himself to outside influences and authorities, accepting their beliefs about him instead of asking a new set of questions and unveiling the ingenious power that he had inside. So if, like him, you doubt your own genius in any way, return to Exercise 1 on page 176 and find a way to link any area of learning you wish to master to your own highest values. Also ask yourself where you are already demonstrating your great mental genius. That is how to use the Values Factor to make your hidden genius become visible.

YOUR HIGHEST VALUES ACTIVATE YOUR GENIUS—AND YOUR CONFIDENCE

I am no exception to these principles I am describing. I too have Attention Surplus Order for my highest values, notably the study of human behavior. I have Attention Deficit Disorder for all the things that I don't feel are currently related to my highest values, such as cake decorating, shoe shopping, technology issues, and watching television. Once I learned to read at age eighteen, any interest I might have had in watching television plummeted, and now I only watch very selectively, when certain shows are on. The same is true for many forms of information technology: I might rely upon a computer or iPhone, but I have little interest in understanding how they are assembled.

To illustrate how society's values don't always match our own, I'd like you to imagine a culture in which, say, television watching was the most prestigious activity you could imagine. Now imagine me—who seldom, if ever, watches television—at a TV watching convention.

Picture it: twenty-five thousand people are there to learn how to improve their TV watching skills. They're discussing the merits of different types of couches, evaluating the relative properties of remotes, and arguing about the best way to skip over the commercials. TV watching specialists are lecturing on such topics as "How to Increase Your Weekly Viewing Time" and "Meals You Can Eat in Front of the Television." Annual awards are being given for expertise in TV watching, and people are eagerly waiting to find out who the winners are.

In the real world, I am a respected figure with a thriving career. Tens of thousands of people come each year to hear me speak, and hundreds of thousands more buy my books, tapes, and other products. I am considered a person of intelligence, and my abilities are widely appreciated. This all reflects the amount of time, energy, and commitment I have devoted to learning about many fields of human behavior, and to developing my skills in researching, writing, and teaching.

But if I were to go to that hypothetical TV watching convention, I would probably be labeled "TV-watching-learning disabled"—a slow learner with low retention. In that context, I would go immediately to the bottom of the class. And since TV watching doesn't interest me, I would probably *stay* at the bottom of the class—unless I found a way to link TV watching to my highest values.

Likewise, in a society that does not know how to value everyone's hidden genius, many people are mistakenly labeled as learning-disabled or even dunces. But the truth is that we are all potential geniuses in the area of our own highest values. There we are inevitably inspired, disciplined, reliable, and empowered. Anywhere else, we are far less likely to manifest those qualities. But whenever our highest values are involved, we are capable of extraordinary mental and physical achievements.

Imagine saying to your ten-year-old son, "I would love for you to play this particular computer game that you love and give me a report on it. And after you give your report, I'm going to give you a test."

Would that boy be hesitating and procrastinating? Not if he loves that particular game! He would say, "Cool!" and he would play it ten times, four hours straight, until he had thoroughly mastered it all.

Anytime you set a goal that is congruent with your highest values, you are likely to achieve that goal and "walk your talk." Your confidence in yourself rises, and you *know* you can do whatever it takes to pursue the values that mean the most to you. However, anytime you set a goal that does *not* fit your highest values, you tend to "limp your life." You procrastinate, you disown your goal, you avoid identifying with it, and you may even start to doubt yourself, because you are judging yourself critically for "failing" to achieve goals that you don't really care about. Remember the ABCD's of negativity: anger and aggression, blame and betrayal, criticism and challenge, and despair and depression.

FINDING THE HIDDEN GENIUS IN YOUR CHILDREN

Many parents don't see the genius in their children because they are not looking for that genius in the places where that it might actually appear. Instead of looking to see what their children truly value most, these parents are often more focused on projecting their own highest values. But children are not designed to live solely by our expectations and projections. Like every other human being on this earth, children will pursue whatever they value most—and that is where their hidden genius will manifest.

A few years ago I gave a talk to a group of some two hundred educators, teachers, and parents in a Connecticut suburb. In the audience was a woman with her twelve-year-old son, and during the question-and-answer session she put up her hand up and said, "What do you do when you have a son who is learning-disabled, lazy, unmotivated, shy . . ." She went on to put five or six labels on that boy, right while he was sitting next to her. The school counselor was sitting on the other side of the boy, and as the mother spoke, the counselor appeared almost to preen, because she was the one who had given that boy his diagnostic labels.

I vividly remembered my own experience of being labeled learning-disabled and a dunce when I was in school, so I know very well how disheartening and misleading some of those labels can be. I walked right over to the child and shook his hand and asked him his name. Then I said to the mother that there was no such thing as the child she was describing. That ruffled the feathers of the counselor, while the mother said, "I *know* this is all true about my son because I live with him, and I see that he is all those things, and now that he has been tested, we have the facts to prove it!"

I was not overly surprised to observe how much the boy's mother and his counselor wanted to label this child. I have seen this scenario quite often. *Labels are simply unrealistic expectations that people with one set of values project onto other people that they don't know how to effectively communicate with.* That is true for just about any label you can imagine, and it is especially true for the labels that we project onto children, because the children usually can't talk back and challenge those labels and demand that we take their highest values seriously.

But I wanted to show the whole room of educators how misleading and untrue these labels can be. So I said to the boy, "Do you mind if I ask you some questions?"

He was maybe a little embarrassed, but he had liked that I had shaken his hand and taken him seriously, so he said, "Uh, okay."

"Thank you," I said. "Now, where, or in what specific area of your life, are you smarter, faster, and more skilled and greater in performance than anybody else you know? What do you excel at?"

"Um . . . computer games?" he said uncertainly.

"Great!" I said. "What kind of computer games?"

"Um . . . ice hockey?" he said, still uncertain.

"Okay," I said. "So you are more skilled at computer ice hockey than your buddies?"

"Yes," said the boy, a little more confidently now.

"You can beat them at the game every time or nearly every time?"

"Well . . . almost every time."

"So you excel there?"

"Yes!" the boy said, very confident now. "Yes! I excel there."

I looked at his mother. "Now, ma'am, have you ever tested your son on computer ice hockey?"

"What kind of a question is that?" the mother said. "Of course I haven't."

I looked at his counselor. "And you, ma'am, have you ever tested this student on computer ice hockey?"

"Of course I haven't," she said as well.

"And would you both say," I continued, "that you are both illiterate in that area? If either of *you* were taking a test on computer ice hockey, would you fail? If I gave you a test on that game right now, would you be labeled unmotivated, learning-disabled, slow learners, distracted?"

Well, of course, they had to agree. So I returned my attention to the boy.

"So," I said, "you are great at computer ice hockey. And do you read magazines about real-life ice hockey?"

"Yes," he said.

"Yes," the mother repeated. "He has got those magazines all over his room. That's why he doesn't do well in school! That is all he wants to put his head into."

"Now," I asked the boy, "do you know the name of any professional ice hockey players?"

"Duh!" he said. "Sure I do."

"Fine," I said. "Please stand up and tell me some of the names of the greatest ice hockey players in the world."

The boy rattled off thirteen names, and he would have kept going if I hadn't stopped him.

"Do you know what teams they are on?" I asked.

"Yes!" he said, and rattled off the thirteen names again, telling which team each one belonged to.

"Great," I said. "Do you know what uniform numbers they have?"

"Sure!" he said, and rattled off the names and numbers.

"Now," I said, "what about their scores and goals and fouls and all that?"

"Sure," he said again. "Do you want me to tell you about them? I even know some of their girlfriends' names!"

By this point, the counselor was starting to pay close attention, and the mother's attitude had begun to change. She was looking at her son as though she had never seen him before. I told them, "Look, this boy does *not* have a learning problem. He has a problem learning what doesn't inspire him, which is the same problem we all have. *You* don't know about ice hockey because you aren't interested in it. He knows all about ice hockey because he *is* interested in it. He currently has a highly concentrated value system and he is intensely focused on his highest value: computer ice hockey."

The mother and the counselor were starting to nod, and so were the other parents and educators in the room.

"Every child absolutely loves to learn," I said. "They have an innate desire to learn whatever will help them fulfill their highest values or whatever is most meaningful to them. That is true for this boy, and it is true for all of us. So once you start educating this boy in a way that he becomes interested in the content, you have already broken through one of the greatest mysteries of awakening his genius. Children want to find the order in the mysterious chaos that they are trying to solve in their daily lives. That is why children ask so many questions."

I turned back to the boy. I said, "You have a bunch of classes in school. What classes are you having the most difficulty with?"

"Uh, math," he replied.

"Okay," I said. "Can you see how studying mathematics is going to help you become a great computer ice hockey player?"

"No," he said.

"So you can't see any relationship?"

"No."

"So you don't want to go that class?"

"No."

I turned to the audience. "What about all of you? How many of you want to take a class in computer ice hockey?"

Well, of course, no hands went up. "Right," I said. "Who wants to go to a class that has zero importance to you? Just because you have the right as an adult to say no to it, you forget what it's like to be a child who does *not* have the right to say no. But if I could force you to take an ice hockey class, would you agree that you would be bored, frustrated, get up and leave the class if you could, maybe get sick to your stomach or do whatever you could to find ways to get out of that class?"

All around the room, heads were nodding. I returned my attention to the boy.

"So you are having difficulty with math?" I said again.

"Yes," he said.

"Well, I have a question for you. When you play ice hockey, is it on an ice hockey rink?"

"Yes."

"Is the rink rectangular?"

"Yes."

"So, rectangles—now we're talking about math. Does the rectangle have in the corner circular areas so you can play in the corners?"

"Yes."

"Would you say those areas are semicircles? And are semicircles part of geometry and math?"

"Yes!" the boy said. He was almost starting to get excited.

"And you have little rectangular netted goals at each end of the rink?"

"Yes!"

"So is that mathematics? Is there a certain ratio to make up the size and the width of each of the goals?"

"Yes!"

"And here's some more math for you. What is the number of people on each team? How many starting players and how many second-string? What's the ratio of starters to second string? Isn't that a math question?"

"Yes!"

"Here's another math question: when the hockey stick hits the puck, what's the best angle for getting optimal speed and control?"

"I'm not sure."

"But that is a math question?"

"Sure!" the boy said. "I can see that."

"So would you agree that learning mathematics will help with the ratios you need to master the game? And help you keep score?"

"Yes!" said the boy. He was smiling now.

"And would math help you figure out the ratio of goals to fouls? Will knowing all these things help determine whether you become a superstar or not?"

"Yes!"

"And that determines how much money you make? And *that* is measured by mathematics?"

"Yes!"

"So is there *any* part of ice hockey that is *not* mathematics?"

"I don't see anything," the boy said.

"So maybe if you learned more about mathematics, it would give you an advantage in ice hockey over somebody that didn't know any math?"

"Yes!" said the boy. "Sure. I can see that."

"So how would you like to beat your buddies more often by having that knowledge?"

"Yeah!" the boy said. "I would *love* that."

So in front of the group—right in front of that counselor—he turned to his mother and said, "Can you get me a book that explains what he is talking about and has all that information in there?"

In other words, within fourteen minutes, I had him asking his mother to buy him a math book. The counselor was starting to write notes on this case, and the mother was starting to get her heart filled. I said, "Your son doesn't have a learning problem. It was just that his teachers and counselors didn't know how to awaken his genius.

Please consider recognizing his inner genius, because false labels could affect his confidence in thinking."

If you have children and would like to help activate their genius, the following exercise can help you do so—while helping you to view your child in a new way.

Exercise 2: Activate Your Child's Genius

Often, we don't recognize that our children have their own unique genius—which they mobilize in pursuit of their own unique highest values. It is wise to recognize that our children have their own genius and then to help them activate it by linking new skills and information to their highest values. This exercise can help you do that.

Instructions:

1. Identify some skill or area of study that your child is uninspired by, not great at, not highly interested in, or not extremely skilled at, but that you believe is essential to his or her social development. Write this skill or area of study in the far left column that follows. Note: Make sure you are completing this exercise with an open mind. Avoid judging your child's interests and simply note them.

2. Perform the Values Determination process on pages 47-57 in Chapter 2 on your child. Identify their three highest values. Write your child's three highest values in the far right column that follows.

3. Find at least twenty ways to link the skill or area of study that your child is uninspired by, not great at, not highly interested in, or not extremely skilled at to his or her three highest values. Write at least twenty ways in the middle column that follows.

Area that your child is uninspired by, is not great at, not interested in, or not skilled at	Twenty ways in which this uninspired something or class that your child is not great at, not interested in, and not skilled at can help your child fulfill his or her three highest values	Your child's three highest values
1.	1.	1.
	2.	2.
	3.	3.
	4.	
	5.	
	6.	
	7.	
	8.	
	9.	
	10.	
	11.	
	12.	
	13.	
	14.	
	15.	
	16.	
	17.	
	18.	
	19.	
	20.	

UNDERSTANDING WHY YOU
HAVE CHILDREN

I can't end this chapter without adding a few words for the parents out there who may be particularly concerned with activating the genius of their children. If you think, as parents, that you were given children to govern, control, and direct, you haven't learned why children are in your life. Your children come through you, not to you. They are here to teach you, just as much as you are here to teach them.

Do you want to know why? You and your spouse have a set of values. When you support each other's highest values, you get infatuated with each other. When you challenge each other's highest values, you become resentful of each other. When you become infatuated with each other, you become blind to each other's downsides, or the aspects of each other's traits that you dislike. When you are resentful of each other, you are blind to the upsides, the aspects of each other's traits that you like. Whatever upsides or downsides you or your partner disowns or represses, or becomes blind to, your children will own or express. Tell me what you would *always* want your children to do and they will probably repress it. Tell me what you would *never* want your children do to—and they will probably specialize in it! Having worked with thousands of families over the years, there is one thing I have noticed time and again: family dynamics demand that all repressed or disowned values get expressed somehow within the family or extended family. In other words, whatever you and your partner repress or disown, rest assured: either your children or another family member will almost certainly express those values.

You think you are caring for your children for *their* sake. But really, they are manifesting those disowned traits you find difficult—for *your* sake. They are expressing values that you do not value, and you are being forced to open your heart a little wider and open your mind a little further and appreciate them and their highest values. If you can acknowledge and appreciate that your children's values are just as important as yours, you will have learned a great deal about how to love another human being *and* about how to love yourself.

So what I recommend is that you perform the same exercise with your children that I suggested you perform with your partner on page 134 in the previous chapter. Ask yourself how your children's highest values are serving you, and answer that question forty or fifty or sixty times until you have tears of gratitude in your eyes for everything about your children's highest values—including their computer games! Then ask yourself how what you are dedicated to serves them, and answer *that* question forty or fifty or sixty times. In that way you will start a dialogue, instead of an alternating monologue, and you will learn the art of communicating in *their* highest values what you know is helpful to them in their lives. Otherwise you or some specialists may end up unwisely projecting some form of Oppositional Defiant Disorder label onto the very children you love.

Can you see how instead of labeling your children, you could actually explore what your children are inspired by and deeply interested in? You could learn how to keep up-to-date with what your children's highest values are so that there is no gap between the generations and so your children are now participating in their own inspired learning because they would truly *love* to learn. And now they associate parents who care for them with the learning process . . . and so they become open to more of the things you may have to offer.

EMBRACING YOUR UNIQUE GENIUS

Now that you see the relationship between activating your genius and knowing your highest values, you can appreciate the genius—whether hidden or fully realized—that lies within each of us. Just as each of us has a unique set of highest values, each of us has our own unique genius, unlike that of any other human on this planet. After all, if you had the same type of genius as anyone else, the universe would not need both of you!

That is why knowing your highest values and activating your genius are two crucial aspects of appreciating your own unique contribution—the contribution that you and only you can make. Appreciating the Values Factor can therefore help you to activate your unique genius and to appreciate the genius of others.

Fulfilling Your Career

Just don't give up trying to do what you really want
to do. Where there is love and inspiration, I don't
think you can go wrong.

—ELLA FITZGERALD

If you asked most people how they would describe their jobs, "inspired" or "fulfilling" would not be the words that come to mind. Most people measure their workweeks by the Monday-morning blues, Wednesday hump day, thank God it's Friday, and then finally the week-friggin'-end. Most people are not usually at work because they love to be there or are thrilled to have the experience. They're doing a job so they can make enough money to get away from it on weekends.

I have chosen not to live that way. To me, every day is a more like a holiday because I'm doing something I love to do. I understand that the work world is a very desperate existence for all too many people, so I love inspiring and empowering my students who want to turn that equation around. I would love for you to be able to go to *your* daily work as eagerly as you'd head off for vacation. I believe you deserve to have the same fulfillment that I have been able to have doing what I love.

Does that sound inspiring to you? There is a very simple way to achieve that level of fulfillment. All you have to do is determine your highest, most inspiring values. Then you can align your work "duties" or job description with those values, prioritize your duties, and gradually delegate your lower-priority duties away. Alternately, you can reorganize your life in such a way that you can go and fulfill the career that you love. Whether your decision is to change your perceptions of your current job, to find a new career, or both, the Values Factor can help you turn a quiet job of desperation into an amazing career of inspiration.

Think of some activity that you really love to do, an activity that no one has to remind you to do, an activity you are inspired by: something that, by now, you will be able to recognize as representing an expression of one of your highest values. Think about what gets you started on this beloved activity and what keeps you going as you do it. Then ask yourself what causes you to *stop* doing it—how you know when a session is over—and how you prepare yourself to start it up again the next time.

If you are thinking of an activity that really inspires you—something that you love and that represents your highest values—you can probably see that you're a real self-starter in this activity. No one has to convince you, remind you, or motivate you to begin this activity—you yourself can't wait to get started. No one has to talk you into continuing—you keep yourself going until, for whatever reason, it's time to stop. No one has to remind you to make time for this activity in the future—you set yourself up for doing it again.

Now, here is the key question: Do you conduct your career in the same way? Do you have work that you can't wait to get started on, love to keep doing, and stop only when you've reached a natural or appropriate stopping place? Do you set yourself up to start work again with the same level of inspiration? Do you feel as energized and inspired by what you do for a living as by this beloved activity you have been thinking of?

If the answer is *yes*—and especially if the beloved activity *is* what you do for a living—congratulations! Your career is already expressing your highest values.

If the answer is *no*—if you feel uninspired by the activities you get paid to do—then you're in for a treat. Because in this chapter, I'm going to show you how to do two things that will transform your entire relationship to your career:

1. How to link your daily work more closely with your highest values—whatever that work is.

2. How to consider a career change that will allow your daily work to spontaneously align more closely with your highest values.

Perhaps, as the result of reading this chapter, you'll choose to start transforming your career path, exploring other opportunities within your field, or even moving to a whole new field. Or perhaps you'll instead alter your perception of your career, and as a result, decide to stay where you are, temporarily or permanently. Either way, you can begin immediately to link your daily work more closely with your highest values. If you choose to do so, you'll be rewarded by an immediate surge of inspiration, productivity, and effectiveness.

THE VALUES FACTOR IN YOUR CAREER

When your daily work is not aligned with your highest values . . .

- You will probably be a worker more than a business leader.
- You will probably remain less inspired and unfulfilled at work.
- You will probably need reminding to get your job done.
- You will probably receive fewer promotions.
- You will probably frustrate other coworkers and be less popular and respected at work.

- You will probably get less done in a day.
- You will probably require more vacations and breaks to survive.
- You will probably be less innovative and will contribute less at work.

When your daily work does align with your highest values . . .

- You will become more of a leader.
- You will become more inspired and engaged at work.
- You will be a self-starter, getting your job done without reminders or prodding.
- You will feel more fulfilled at work.
- You will probably receive more promotions.
- You will inspire other coworkers.
- You will be more popular and respected at work.
- You will get more done in a day.
- You will require fewer vacations and breaks to thrive.
- You will be more innovative and will contribute more at work.

THE VALUES FACTOR AT WORK

My own business career started when I was four years old. I used to shine my father's shoes to earn extra money. I actually enjoyed the work as well as the pay. I felt proud of providing a service that my father needed, and I enjoyed taking scuffed, worn-looking shoes and making them appear shiny and new again. I was an enterprising young man, and while I didn't plan on shining shoes for the rest of my life, I really enjoyed knowing that it was in my power to earn money.

Even more important than the money, however, was the knowledge that I had been of service. I was aware that my father did a great deal for me, and even at a young age, I loved knowing that I had been of service to him.

When I was nine, I moved up from shoe-shining for my dad to starting my own small business. I enrolled the neighborhood kids into my own landscaping company, where I had them all mowing, edging, sweeping, raking, weeding, and clipping hedges. I went around to all our neighbors, sold the deals, and took home a tidy profit.

I enjoyed my fledgling company even more than I liked shining my dad's shoes. I got a lot of satisfaction out of making my neighbors' yards more attractive, and I liked rounding up the local kids and making sure each one got the job he could do best. Once again, I appreciated earning the money—and I also appreciated saving it. And once again, I was even more fulfilled knowing that I had been of service to all the people in my neighborhood—to the kids I hired, who needed their own spending money, and to my neighbors, who needed their yards fixed up.

However, neither of my early work experiences provided me with the long-term inspiration that could sustain a life's work. At a young age, I understood that, like most people, I needed to earn my own living, but I didn't realize until I had begun my professional teaching career that life is far more inspiring and fulfilling when your vocation is your vacation. So from the time I was in my early twenties, I was inspired to do what I loved and get paid handsomely for it, which, as we saw in Chapter 3, is one of the secrets to a fulfilling life.

As you learned in Chapter 1, I did not have a very auspicious start in life. Even though I was quite vocationally resourceful as a young boy, during that same early period, I had also been told that I would never be able to read, write, or communicate—that I would never go very far or amount to anything because of my learning difficulties. At least partly as a result, I soon became a high school dropout. As a teenager, I ended up roaming the streets, hitchhiking around, taking on odd jobs, and eventually living in a tent in a Hawaiian jungle, where I nearly died. I remember sitting there, so sick I could barely endure it, facing the bottom of the tent and thinking to myself, "If I live through this, I want to do something more with my life."

I know that if a person can start there and can go on to do whatever they love to do, then anybody reading this book can do what they love to do. I am certain that this is possible. *Do what you love and get paid handsomely for it*—that is one of the secrets to an inspiring and fulfilling life.

So it doesn't matter where you start, it doesn't matter what you have gone through, and it doesn't matter what you are going through. All that matters is identifying who you really are and what is truly inspiring to you—in other words, your highest values. Recognize your most meaningful dream and your most inspiring vision, and then take the action steps to make them both come true. This underlies the power of the Values Factor.

MAKE YOUR MISSION A PRIORITY

Mary Kay Ash, founder of Mary Kay cosmetics, once gave me some excellent advice for creating a fulfilling and inspiring career. She told me that I would be wise to every day write down the six or seven highest-priority action steps that I could do that day to help me fulfill my most inspiring mission or dream vision on earth. She told me not to write down too many steps, or I might feel overwhelmed; then they would just accumulate and I would feel as though I wasn't getting everything done.

"Just write six or seven, and get them done, and thank yourself," she said. "If you think you can get an extra two done, you can add them, but make sure you get every single action step done each day. Otherwise you have a goal overrun and feel unfulfilled because you can't complete the goals. But when you do complete them, reward yourself."

So I did this day after day after day until I had filled nearly

730 three-by-five-inch index cards with my six or seven steps for the day.

For instance, one day, I might write on a single index card:

1. Research the greatest writings and quotable sayings from the most creative and inspired minds on earth;

2. Rewrite their most meaningful thoughts, organized alphabetically by their last name, and compile them into seminar manuals and sellable books;

3. Share these books with my ever-growing number of students;

4. Travel whatever distance I need to be able to commercially share these newest ideas with receptive students from around the world;

5. Document what served the most people most efficiently;

6. Compile a list of experiences and accomplishments that I am most grateful for.

I then looked back at the cards to sort through all the duplicates. I wanted to see which action steps kept repeating time after time so I could discover which were to be my highest-priority action steps of all. Sorting through two years' worth of cards, I discovered that my four highest values were repeatedly revealed in these daily action steps. Time and again, the kinds of actions I was taking fell into four categories: research, write, travel, and teach. These types of actions represented my highest values. They are on the front cover of my 1,400 page *State of the Mission* book that I carry with me every day. This book is my workbook, in which I continue to identify and refine my personal mission, list ways to accomplish my current goals, and express my ongoing gratitude for the people I know and the things that befall me. As my life continues to evolve, so does my mission book, reflecting the path by which I fulfill my now inspired journey.

Once I knew what my very highest priorities and values were, I made a momentous decision. I vowed to delegate away any task that was lower on my list of daily priorities, that would lower my hourly income and ultimate self-worth, and that did not truly inspire me, so that I would be free to do only what inspires me and what I do best.

This decision was not determined by a fear of hard work. As you've already seen, I have been working pretty diligently since I was four years old. But when I realized what inspired me most, I also realized that the way to become a true master at those four activities was to focus on them completely. If I delegated everything else to other people, then I would be doing only what inspired me most. I would be loving what I did, doing what I loved, and becoming a master at it all. I would be living a fully inspired and fulfilled life— and I would be providing the world with more of the service of which I was capable.

When you are doing something that inspires you, you throw yourself into it fully, with all the power of your Attention Surplus Order, Intention Surplus Order, and Retention Surplus Order. You work in such a sustained and focused way at your inspiring vocation that you become a master of it. And the way to maintain that sustained focus is to let go of every task that does *not* inspire you so that you devote all your time and energy to the tasks that *do* inspire you, the tasks that are on top of your list rather than down toward the bottom, or, as I like to put it, the ABC's, not the XYZ's.

So today I research, write, travel, and teach. Those are the things I love so much that I can't wait to get up in the morning to do them. Whenever I finish any one of those activities, I go right on to the next.

Those are the activities that inspire me most. Now, what about you? I put a lot of energy into discovering what I most love and am most inspired by—the activities that most fully express my highest values. Now I am asking you to find out which activities inspire *you* and express *your* highest values.

LINKING YOUR VALUES TO YOUR JOB

In Chapter 4, I provided you with an exercise intended to help you discover the path of your inspired destiny. That exercise opened up the possibility that you might want to find another vocation or profession. But there is another possibility, which is that your current job already has the potential to inspire and fulfill you. Even if your ultimate goal is to found your own business or start a new career, you will benefit enormously from deriving the maximum fulfillment from your current situation. (For more on building wealth, see Chapter 8. For more on founding and leading an enterprise or another organization, see Chapter 9.)

Many people are uninspired by their jobs and wish they didn't have to do them. They don't see how their jobs help them pursue their mission and fulfill their highest values. So they require incentives, time off, sick leave, and all kinds of outside reminders and motivational systems to get them to do the tasks that they are uninspired by.

If you are one of these people, you probably find yourself frustrated by the work you do. In this case, the main problem for you is not that you "have to" do something you don't love doing or that you didn't happen to be born independently wealthy and free of the "need" to earn a living. The problem probably isn't with your bank account, your credentials, or even with your job itself. The problem is that you are not seeing how your present job is helping you fulfill your highest values. And you are injecting somebody else's values into your life and trying to live by them. As we have seen throughout this book, this is almost always a recipe for frustration and desperation. When you live according to your own highest values, you are reliable, determined, and focused. When you live according to someone else's highest values, you frequently struggle to complete even the simplest tasks. And then you are often frustrated, beat yourself up, and despair of ever turning your life around.

How can you tell when you're living by somebody else's values? As we also saw earlier, a reliable clue is when you hear yourself saying "should," "ought to," "have to," *and* "need to." For example, you might be saying:

I *should* keep this job.
I *have* to go to work now.
I *ought to* work harder.
I *need to* meet this friggin' deadline.
I *have got to* go to work.

This way of talking about your work reveals that you are subordinating yourself to external influences and giving power to other people and are definitely not inspired. You disown your job and disempower the part of you that works at it. As a result, you erode your certainty, your confidence, your accomplishments—and your career opportunities.

By contrast, if you link your daily job duties to your highest values, you can then begin to be more inspired and to live more by your own highest values. That is how to build your certainty, your confidence, and your accomplishments, because whenever you live congruently with your highest values, you are far more likely to accomplish what you set out for. You don't limp your life—instead, you walk your talk.

So ask yourself: "How, specifically, is doing my current job duties going to help me fulfill my highest values?" This is a crucial question for both you and your employer. If you can't see how your present job fulfills your highest values, you are going to be frustrated, uninspired, and possibly even a deadweight at that job. You are going to be "overhead" instead of "getting ahead." People who can see the light at the end of the tunnel as they fulfill their highest values are the ones getting ahead. People who can't see that light are "overhead," because they are shrinking, not shining; gravitating, not radiating. They don't see the light; they are in the darkness.

One of my many tasks as a business consultant is to help companies inspire their employees by linking their employees' job descriptions and the company's mission or vision statement with their employees' highest values. I recommend that companies ask every single employee to determine their highest values and then to ask how each of their job duties within their job description helps them fulfill those values. Employees also look at how serving the company's mission, vision, and primary objectives helps them fulfill their own highest values and purpose.

Every time I assist companies in undertaking this method, I am amazed at the results. Perhaps some employees have been questioning their jobs, but when they use this method, they realize that they are not actually in the "wrong" job. Tears of deep appreciation come out of their eyes. They see that their job is actually giving them an opportunity to fulfill their missions, their purpose, and their highest values, even if it is simply a stepping stone to something even more meaningful.

Perhaps they felt in some way that they were at this job because of a "mistake," or because they felt "trapped by necessity." However, once they link their job description or their individual job responsibilities to their highest values, they see that there were no mistakes: only stepping stones *on* the way, not *in* the way, to their more fulfilling career. They discover that, after all, they are at this job at this moment in their life to fulfill their highest values or most meaningful mission. And all of a sudden, they feel gratitude for that job, because that job is where they are meeting their highest values.

Now they can't wait to get up in the morning and go and be of service in that same job. They feel more enthused and grateful, they love their job again, and they become inspired by the company vision.

I have seen company managers use my method in as little as three hours to transform employees who were unproductive into those who were amazingly productive. Because these newly inspired employees now see their jobs as fulfilling their highest values, they become engaged, disciplined, focused, and reliable; they are filled with gratitude and enthusiasm; and they have Attention Surplus Order, Intention Surplus Order, and Retention Surplus Order.

If you are in a leadership position in your work, I'll show you how to use this method with your employees in Chapter 9. But no matter where you are or what your position is, I suggest you begin by undergoing this method for yourself, using the exercise I provide below. Once you complete this method, you too will be re-inspired by your career. Suddenly, you'll be eager to get up in the morning and go to work and serve again. You won't want to miss work or take a sick day. You'll be more inspired at work because now you see that this is also "your" company again. Suddenly, you are into wellness and not illness; inspiration instead of desperation; productivity instead of unproductivity. Since your identity revolves around your highest values, when you feel you are fulfilling those values through your job responsibilities, you feel that your company is now partly yours instead of simply the company you work for.

Does that sound like a way that you'd love to feel about *your* job? Then move on to the exercise that will help you link your current job duties with your highest values, and discover the power of the Values Factor.

Exercise 1: Discovering the Fulfillment in Your Job

As we have seen throughout this book, fulfillment comes from pursuing your highest values. This exercise will help you see how to link your current job duties and the mission or vision of your company with your own three highest values, which is guaranteed to make your job far more fulfilling. (Note: If you are in a leadership position at work or in any organization, you will find in Chapter 9 a version of this exercise that you can conduct with those whom you may be responsible to govern or manage.)

Instructions:

STEP 1: Write a detailed description of everything you do at work. Break down your job into separate tasks or responsibilities, and list each abbreviated responsibility in the far left Column A of the form that follows. Make sure that every part of your job is included in the description.

STEP 2: List your company's mission or vision statement. If your company does not have a formal mission or vision statement, create one: write a few sentences that summarize the most important values and goals of your company. Then write out an abbreviated form of your company's mission or vision statement in the far left Column E of the form that follows. For example, Microsoft's mission statement is: "To enable people and business throughout the world to realize their full potential. We work to achieve our mission through technology that transforms the way people work, play and communicate." Walmart's mission statement is: "To lower the world's cost of living."

STEP 3: Check the exercise you completed in Chapter 2 and recall your three highest values. List them in middle Column C of the form that follows.

STEP 4: Link your job description to your three highest values. For every duty, task, or responsibility within your job description, write ten to thirty ways that performing that task will help you fulfill your three highest values (your purpose). Write these abbreviated answers in Column B of the form that follows. Ask yourself, "How,

EMPLOYER OR EMPLOYEE PRODUCTIVITY, INSPIRATION, AND LOYALTY PROCEDURAL FORM

Column A	Column B	Column C	Column D	Column E
Job Responsibilities	How Column A Helps Fulfill Column C	Employee Highest Values or Purpose	How Column E Helps Fulfill Column C	Company or Employer Mission and Vision

specifically, will fulfilling my individual job responsibilities help me to fulfill my three highest values and purpose?" Answer this question ten to thirty times in Column B for each responsibility.

STEP 5: Link your company's mission or vision statement to your three highest values. Ask yourself, "How specifically will fulfilling my company's mission/vision help me fulfill my three highest values and purpose?" Answer this question ten to thirty times in Column D.

THE UNIVERSAL LAWS OF BUSINESS

As we have seen, the secret to an inspiring and fulfilling life is doing what you love and loving what you do, and getting handsomely or beautifully paid for it. In this way, your vocation can become your vacation and, as has been said about Warren Buffett, you can go "tap-dancing to work." The way you know you are having a fulfilling life is the degree to which you can't wait to get up and do the work that you are inspired by.

To some extent, you can solve this problem by finding inspiring and fulfilling work—either by linking your current job duties to your highest values or by finding a whole other type of work that fulfills your highest values and serves your mission. But there is still another step to take. Setting your own agenda and filling your day with high-priority, inspiring tasks is the only way to gain true control over your time. If you don't set your own high-priority agenda in this way, your day will automatically fill up with low-priority, uninspiring tasks. This observation is a variation of a business principle known as Cyril Northcote Parkinson's Law: Work expands to fill the time allotted.

This is not just a business law, but also a law of life. If you don't fill up your day with high-priority, inspiring tasks, your day will fill up with many frustrating, low-priority tasks or distractions. These low-priority tasks will frustrate you enough to eventually get you back onto high priorities again!

You may already have noticed this in your own life. I certainly saw it when I was in professional practice as a chiropractor years ago. If I had a gap between patients, even if it was only ten or fifteen minutes, the patients before or after would come in to fill up that time with describing a new symptom, complaining about an old problem, or asking questions. Or perhaps a salesperson would get into the office, or someone would call with a personal question for me or one of my staff. Sometimes there would even be a technical problem, such as a jammed photocopier or a broken printer, or maybe my staff would misplace a file or lose a patient's contact information.

However, when I had a seamless, nonstop, intense schedule, I noticed that we didn't have time for all those unexpected challenges and problems; nor did we seem to attract them. Because our day was full of inspiring high-priority actions, there simply wasn't room for uninspiring low-priority distractions.

From this experience, I realized that either you are filling your day with inspiration or you are attracting desperation. Either you are filling your mind's garden with flowers, or your mind is filling up with weeds.

So there is a very great reason for Parkinson's Law. Your biological, sociological, and even economic world rewards you for living according to your highest values or priorities. Everyone whose life is organized around their highest values grows, including you, every person around you, every organism, and every business.

Now, I believe the universe is filled with an expression of intelligence. I believe that it demonstrates through natural laws a high degree of regularity and a mathematical order and elegance. And I believe that the universe in general and the world in specific are helping both living organisms and living organizations evolve through the balance of support and challenge.

Therefore, when you focus only on inspiring, high-priority tasks, you are aligning yourself with the wisdom of nature: the law of efficiency or least action. This law states that whatever is accomplished will be done by the least action possible. Nature "enforces" that law to make sure that every individual is constantly giving maximum and efficient service and helping their organization to grow. Top performance of a top priority leads to the greatest efficiency.

To put it another way: whoever sets the prioritized agenda, rules. If you don't set the agenda, other people will rule. So your job is to set a prioritized agenda every day.

How do you make sure that your agenda is entirely full of high-priority items? Figure out exactly what is most inspiring and what is your particular specialty—the work that you are most qualified to do, the work that makes the greatest contribution, the work that provides you and your company the greatest competitive advantage and profitability. By definition, this high-priority work will be both most inspiring and your greatest service. Then, delegate all your other tasks—every task of a lower priority, requiring less mastery, involving less specialization—to someone who would love to do those very tasks.

This is the way both to fill your life with inspiration and to help an organization grow. Now you become the visionary able to move forward on your inspired vision of service while the "detail people" stabilize the business organization and manage your teams through further delegation.

If you are the visionary entrepreneur founding the company, you have the opportunity to manifest your highest values throughout the enterprise. You have the chance to hire people who help you pursue your mission and fulfill your highest values—people who at the same time are pursuing their own mission and fulfilling their own highest values. If you are an employee, you have ideally chosen to work for a company whose highest values you can embrace or align with and whose mission and vision you can share. Either way, you can take responsibility for your own time by setting your own agenda, filling up your day with inspiring, high-priority activities, and delegating uninspiring activities to somebody else who would love to tackle them.

PARETO'S LAW

Another business principle that dovetails with Parkinson's law is known as Vilfredo Pareto's Principle, also called the Eighty/Twenty Rule. This principle holds that twenty percent of your actions is responsible for eighty percent of your productive results. The key in life, therefore, is to identify and then target that twenty percent, to assure that you obtain the greatest possible results. This again will offer you the freedom to fulfill what inspires you most.

BEING OF SERVICE

Each of us has our own unique hierarchy of values, but we all share one key value: it is our nature to be of service. If you are of service, you are likely to feel more fulfilled, while if you are not of service, you are likely to remain unfulfilled. Even if you are well-rewarded for a job—even if you receive a high salary, prestige, and other benefits— you will likely not find those rewards as meaningful or as fulfilling if you do not also feel the fulfillment of providing a continuous and truly valuable service to others.

When you delegate everything that you aren't perfectly designed and inspired to do and then focus your efforts at working on that which is most meaningful and important to you, you harness your greatest resource of energy for providing service to others.

For example, I research, write, travel, and teach. Sometimes my teaching involves just a single student, which I call a "consult." Sometimes my teaching involves millions of people, perhaps on a television broadcast. Obviously, TV broadcasts are more efficient than teaching one person at a time, but there is a meaningful satisfaction I can find in teaching one-on-one that I choose not to give up. In that kind of teaching, I get instant feedback, which deepens my knowledge and skill and which also offers me an actual case study that I can use in reaching and serving a wider audience. So though my consults may not be as efficient as my television work per unit of time, they are meaningful because then I have fresh live information that I can use to inspire and serve even greater numbers of people. When you create your prioritized agenda, you want to include the most productive, profitable, and meaningful work among your priorities, as all of these types of work are important and inspiring.

RICARDO'S LAW

Ricardo's Law was the creation of eighteenth-century economist David Ricardo. It states that every country in the world has a resource or commodity that makes up its specialty niche: something that it is the greatest at or that gives it a competitive advantage. Whenever a country targets exporting that specialty, the economies in that country grow. This law also applies to your life. When you focus on your highest values, you are tapping into your greatest resources and sharing those resources with the world. When you "export" these resources, not only are you most profitable, but the world benefits.

THE "WRONG" JOB OR THE NEXT JOB?

I have suggested that you complete Exercise 1 to see how you can link the job description you are currently doing to your own highest values. In most cases, you are likely to discover connections that you previously had not suspected, which will enable you to find inspiration and fulfillment in a job that you previously may have minimized or found frustrating.

In some cases, however, you may discover that your current work situation is not the only or the most effective way for you to fulfill your highest values. When you took the job or started the business, you might have been trying to live by someone else's highest values. In that case, the frustration you might feel is there to get you to decide what you actually *do* love to do. The work you are currently doing is still playing an important role in your life: it is the step you had to do until you were finally ready to be true to yourself.

I have often had people say to me after hearing me speak, "I must be in the wrong job."

"No," I tell them, "there's no such thing as the 'wrong' job. You were simply in the *next* job—the job that was exactly what you needed as your *next step*. Now you're ready to stop subordinating or sacrificing your highest values to someone else's and to find a type of work that truly fulfills what is most meaningful and important to you."

A few months ago, I was presenting my Breakthrough Experience seminar in London. A woman came up to me and said, "Dr. Demartini, you are telling us to find a type of work that helps us fulfill our highest values. But what happens if you don't know what you want to do?"

"That doesn't exist," I told her. "You certainly do know inside what you would truly love to do."

"I don't know," she insisted.

"That's not true," I replied. "You simply have fears inside you clouding your mind and stopping you from declaring what you really would love to dedicate your energies or life to."

"I don't," she persisted.

"Yes, you do," I insisted. "You are afraid you might not be savvy enough, that you might fail, that you won't be making enough money in that other type of work, that you'll lose money trying to get into it, that your loved ones won't approve, or that you don't have the looks or the vitality to succeed . . . You're afraid of *something*, but you *do* know."

The woman shook her head, half smiling. "Okay," she said. "You got me. I suppose I *do* know what I want to do. But I *am* afraid . . ."

"So, what is it you know that you would you love to do?" I asked her.

"I want to do something to help educate children," she said. "But I don't know how to make enough money to do it, and I'm not qualified—"

"Wait a minute," I said. "The truth is that you *do* know, so can you first acknowledge that?"

"Yeah, I suppose I do," she admitted.

"So, if you don't have the degree that you think you need, do you have any reason not to go and gradually work toward acquiring such a degree at the same time that you are starting your desired career?" I said. "Or as an alternative approach, could you ask yourself how *not* having such a degree could actually be to your advantage? If you kept asking that second question, you could possibly turn your lack of a degree from something you perceive as a drawback to something you present as part of your unique perspective and contribution. I myself don't have degrees in all sorts of fields, but I have studied and learned and educated myself, and I go and work in different fields all the time. You don't have to let anything stop you."

This woman and I spoke for quite a while. Her immediate concern was that her job as an adviser in a financial planning firm had nothing to do with childhood education and that she herself had no credentials in that field. I wanted her to see that she was in exactly the right job for getting herself to the next step. So I simply began asking: "How is the job you're in now going to help you get to the next step and help you fulfill your dream of working with childhood education?"

It turned out that she had quite a bit to say in response to that question! She told me that she was making enough money in her current job to afford to take time off and get a degree in early childhood education. She was learning skills at her current job that actually would help her work with children. She was learning the necessary business skills and people management skills needed to run the educational programs she desired to found. She was making some important contacts that would assist her along the way. These were only some of the connections she identified between her current job position and the one she desired to pursue.

I encouraged her to identify more and more connections. I simply kept asking: "How is the job you're in now going to help you get to the next step and help you fulfill your dream of working with childhood education?"

Finally, the lightbulb went off. She realized that her current job was actually the perfect stepping stone for undertaking an ambitious plan of starting an educational foundation dedicated to early childhood education. The skills, social connections, and media contacts that she had developed at her current job turned out to be the perfect training for this new work. All along, the job that she thought was so frustrating and uninspiring was her ideal "school" for the fulfilling and inspiring service that she now intended to move into.

"I just wish I had understood this sooner," she told me when we finished talking. "All that frustration! All that complaining! I could have saved myself a lot of headaches if I had only seen that all along, I *was* pursuing my highest values. This wasn't the 'wrong' job. It was only the *next* job."

It had taken this woman a while to see how her current situation was linked to her highest values after all. But once she saw the connection, her frustration and resentment turned into gratitude and appreciation. She realized there was no mistake in her current positioning. That is the power of the Values Factor.

LOOK AT WHAT YOU LOVE

I had a similar experience with a man in Houston who attended my Breakthrough Experience seminar program a few years ago. This man was a nonstop talker. I've never seen anyone who could talk nonstop so smoothly and so fluently for such a long time! He spent most of his time studying personal development, reading books about human behavior, and attending "human potential" seminars. In fact, he was practically a seminar junkie! So when I asked him what he did for a living, I was a bit surprised to hear him say, "Oh, I'm in real estate."

"How are you doing in that field?" I asked.

"I'm doing okay," he answered. "Not great, but okay."

Well, given what I had observed, *that* didn't surprise me. A man who loves to speak and who spends every free minute studying human behavior and human potential is less likely to be doing as well in the real estate field than someone who spends every free minute studying real estate. So I said, "Would you like to hear my observation about you?"

"Sure," the man said. "What is it?"

"Well," I said, "you love talking! And you love learning. So it's almost insane for you not to learn and talk and get handsomely paid for it. Would you love that?"

"Absolutely!" he replied immediately. "That would be *great*! But how do I do it?"

"Well," I said, "why don't you develop a company around that?"

The man just stared—not even at me, but off into space. I could see him scanning his entire life. *"Wow,"* he said finally. "That would be really cool. But I don't think I can do it . . ."

"Really?" I said. "What remotely would make you think you can't do that?"

"Well, I just assumed I had to go out and get a job—a job that paid great money," he said.

"I can tell you right now, you're probably not going to find too many jobs that pay well enough to cover all that money you've spent on personal-development seminars," I said jokingly, but also seriously. "You talk most of the time, you're studying most of the time— why don't you take everything you've learned and *talk* about it?!? I've known you long enough to know that if you did that, you'll excel."

Now that he saw what was possible for him, this man was on fire to get started. "Would you be willing to consult with me and to show me exactly which steps to take to speed the process up?" he asked me.

"Certainly!" I said. "Instead of going to the next seminar next week, let's take the seminar fee and use it instead for a consulting session and sit down and map out the entire structure and all the priority action steps required to help you profitably fulfill what you know you would truly love to do. I'll spend the necessary time alone with you. So let's get you on track!"

We organized a step-by-step system to get this man on track with his new career of being a professional speaker. Before I met him, this man had been working at a job he wasn't quite fulfilled in and was unconsciously, spontaneously, voraciously reading, taking seminars, and talking to people while freely helping them. Then, after our consult, he saw his real estate work as a stepping stone because I also had him list all the ways his current job was essential to his mission and was going to help him along the way as a transition into his next, dream career as a speaker.

Now, after a few initially challenging months, he's on his path and he's making *way* more money than he did before, doing exactly what he loves to do, because he loves to talk and he loves to learn! He has tapped into the power of the Values Factor, and his heart is in his mission.

OWN YOUR OWN TRAITS

After this man I just spoke about consulted with me, he initially faced an interesting challenge. Once he had started creating a career as a speaker about human behavior and human potential, he began comparing himself with other, more established speakers. He occasionally felt discouraged, since comparing himself with someone else with more experience, whom he looked up to, often put him at a disadvantage. After all, some of these other speakers had been speaking about human behavior for several years or even several decades. This man was just beginning. But now he was wondering whether he would ever attain that higher level of achievement. Often, he beat himself up for not having started earlier, doubting his own ability to achieve what I and some of the other speakers had achieved.

So even though he had chosen to consult with me rather than to take my seminar, we had to engage a little bit in the Demartini Method anyway! As I do in the Breakthrough Experience, I had him identify all the traits he admired in the top professional speakers he was comparing himself with and I asked him to find out where he had those exact same traits in himself, to the exact same degree, in his own unique forms. I asked him to own within himself any traits he admired or felt intimidated by in any of these admired speakers, so that he could truly understand that he had everything he needed, wanted, or admired within himself to fulfill his dream. (And by the same token, he had every trait he disliked or looked down upon within himself also!)

Another challenge he encountered was that he felt a certain

amount of anxiety in charging people to hear him speak. So we had to go through my method of identifying more than one hundred benefits to the customer of him charging his desired fee, and one hundred drawbacks to the customer of him *not* charging his desired fee.

This is a common problem when people are beginning a business or a freelance career. They minimize themselves and exaggerate other people, thereby reducing the value of what they are offering and worrying about charging too high a price for it. Identifying the benefits to the customer of paying your desired price and the drawbacks to the customer of your *not* charging that price is an effective way of dissolving the tendency to self-minimize. This problem is primarily due to a lowered self-image and an uncertain mental attitude and can be solved by identifying your unique added values and your unique services to the customer or client.

For example, if you are a consultant who is charging too low a price, you will be forced to take on more clients to support yourself. Because your price is low, you will not have the time and energy to focus on each client to the extent that you might like. By raising your price, you free yourself to have a more selective or smaller client list— and then you can work in a more focused and effective way for each person on that list. So each client actually benefits from you charging them a higher price, which enables you to provide far greater service.

Likewise, if you are a freelance worker who is charging the bare minimum for the jobs you take on, you may feel resentful or frustrated when a job turns out to take up more time than you had initially planned. Charging a more realistic price for the job keeps you feeling grateful to be doing the job in the first place, even when things seem to go wrong, rather than feeling frustrated that your price allowed for no margin of error. It is of great benefit to your client to pay a higher price if that price means that you are well prepared for any difficulties or setbacks that arise and that you will remain grateful and inspired throughout.

So, step by step, this man went on to build a fruitful and financially rewarding career as a professional speaker about human development and human potential. Today he is doing what he loves and loving what he does—and getting handsomely paid for it!

BECOMING AN ENTREPRENEUR

In Chapter 9, you'll have the opportunity to look more closely at the leadership steps that are involved in actually being a leader, whether in business or in any other domain. Here, I'd like to offer a perspective for those of you who might like to become an entrepreneur.

Many people have inspiring business ideas, but then don't know how to take the next step in becoming an entrepreneur or a founder of such a business. Perhaps you have a potentially profitable idea, but you are hesitant to honor that idea because you don't believe you have the skills for initiating the founding of a business and then managing your idea in a profitable way.

However, what you may not realize is that here, too, you can delegate: you can have the idea and then assign to someone else the task of turning it into a business by selling your idea and making a profit. I have a friend in Houston who is one of the most amazing idea generators in the world. He comes up with ingenious business ideas, brainstorms them, and then works with a business planning expert and another savvy specialist involved in finance. None of them have ever actually led or managed their own companies long-term. They just put their highly talented brains together, create business plans, and then sell their concepts and plans to people who are skilled at viably implementing those ideas and plans. My friend and his team have made millions that way.

If you have an incredible idea but are not inspired about actually founding and running a company, you might want to partner with people who have other specialties and can do what you would prefer not to. Working with a team, you might be able to get your ideas off the ground and to do extraordinary things collectively. An incredible idea plus an incredible team might equal an incredible fortune!

In fact, one of my clients did make a fortune—from fortune cookies! He fiddled with a formula by a woman who knew how to bake that type of cookie, and then he had to figure out how to wrap it and package it. After three years, he sold the idea for a net of $8 million. As an idea guy, this man preferred to delegate the details to other people. But because he knew how to delegate those details, and because he was skilled at establishing teams, he was able to fulfill his vision by fulfilling what his highest values dictated to be his specialty—and his competitive advantage.

Any of your entrepreneurial adventures will probably start out with some form of inspired vision—one that fulfills and serves the highest values of others. Once the right hemisphere of your brain—the visionary, creative side—envisions this inspiring idea, it will cross-talk over to your left hemisphere—the practical, analytic side—sharing the initial vision. Your left hemisphere will then provide some additional structure to your visionary idea, putting it into a form that other people can understand through logic and reason. Then you might have to hire someone to put the details of your plan into action. Visionaries often require managers and technical workers along the way.

That's how some companies begin. And as your company grows, you go on to hire even more specialized people who can implement each of the specific detailed tasks that your company requires. You might even hire people to assist you in the development of your vision, and/or hire others who can help you with management and implementation.

Interestingly, many visionaries and entrepreneurs are those who perceived that they had received more challenge to than support of their highest values in their earlier life. By contrast, those people who perceive that they had received more support than challenge often remain more dependent and keep looking for security. They usually don't become entrepreneurs; instead, they work for other people, assuming that in this way they will receive some sense of security. But the people who felt they got challenged and maybe ridiculed and were perhaps given a lot of responsibilities often become entrepreneurs because they are accustomed to being independent and they like to think for themselves and do things on their own. Then they join with the person who likes security and who likes to build teams and put structures together and enjoys doing the smaller detail work.

Of course, being a visionary is not in any way better than being detail-focused, although it is more financially rewarding. But being a visionary and being detail-focused can be equally fulfilling—it is simply a matter of which path reflects your highest values.

You might say that the entrepreneur represents the right side of the brain, the visionary side, while the detail people represent the left side of the brain, the practical side. You might also say that the entrepreneur represents the heaven force that expands radiantly outward, while the detail person is the earth force or the gravity force that grounds the idea back to earth and asks, "How exactly are we going to do this?" Neither heaven nor earth is more valuable—both have their place. Although visionaries are more likely to be remembered, they would not be able to achieve their great goals without the earth force of the detail person providing a solid foundation beneath.

As you can see, most successful companies are usually started with an integration of the right and the left hemispheres of the brain. If you have individuals who have heavenly visions but are not associated with earthly detail people, they are probably not going to get off the ground. If you have a detail person without a visionary, the detail person probably won't take action, because they are afraid to act. So we require a whole brain, including both the heaven and earth forces, to make a viable company.

Another way to think about what a company requires is to look at the world of plants. When you take a seed and put it in the ground and it gets water and sunlight, the plant grows in two directions. The root grows deep into the ground, while the stalk shoots high into the sky. The stalk that grows up is phototrophic: it grows toward the light. It is radiant and grows outward. The root that grows down is gravitropic: it grows toward the source of gravity. It is "gravitant" and grows inward. The deeper the roots, the higher the stalk can rise. So you need both.

Now, you have the entire package inside you, and so does everyone else. But if you grew up with more perceived challenge than support, you tend to awaken the phototropic side of yourself, the part that has the expanded vision and wants to see. If you grew up with more perceived support than challenge, you tend to awaken the gravitropic part of yourself, the part that wants to take care of smaller details and ground things so they can be managed efficiently. These forces might also be seen as the masculine and feminine forces of the whole of nature.

The phototropic person is often what used to be called a type A personality. If you're this type, you like to "go for it," to compete, and to tackle challenges. You are oxidative—you can handle the rust!

If you're gravitropic, you are likely more of what used to be called a type C personality. In that case, you like security and protection. You are grounded, but you also like to hide in the earth, you might say. You won't rust or oxidize, because you are hidden safely in the moist, protective, reducing earth. You prefer not to be in the forefront and or to be held publicly accountable.

Now, again, you have both qualities, both personalities, and all traits inside you. But if you are like most people, in your public persona, you tend to activate one side more than the other. Then you require your opposite to create a whole, and so you attract that opposite. So if you are thinking of becoming an entrepreneur, you want to make sure that you are looking at the whole picture. You want to make sure that you are including both visionaries and detail people in your enterprise, so that everyone can do what is most inspiring to them according to their highest values, where they can embrace both support and challenge equally. This will allow you to take advantage of the Values Factor.

THE VALUE OF YOUR CAREER

Imagine for a moment what your life would be like if your vocation were truly your vacation; if you loved what you did and were paid handsomely for it; if your work appeared to you as the fullest possible expression of your highest values. Imagine if you lived a life serving others while fulfilling yourself and your mission. Imagine if you were able to link your current work to your highest values so that you found enormous meaning and purpose in what you spent the majority of your time doing. Imagine feeling inspired and clear about what your next career decision might be, whether it's staying with your current work, considering a new career path, or deciding to become an entrepreneur.

Now, don't misunderstand me. I'm not suggesting you indulge in some kind of juvenile fantasy of not having to work at all or of having wealth and success magically appear in your life without you making significant efforts to serve the world. Instead, I'm suggesting that you actively seek out the world challenges or services you find inspiring and then throw yourself into meeting them. After all, it is the challenges in life that make us grow. In fact, your mastery in life consists precisely in how many challenges you can conquer. Whoever tackles the greatest challenges, solves the greatest mysteries, resolves the greatest problems, fills the greatest voids, or serves the greatest needs becomes the greatest being. Your goal, therefore, is to choose the challenges that you find inspiring—the challenges that help you pursue your mission and fulfill your highest values and at the same time serve the greatest numbers of people. This is a great service to the world—and that is what produces great wealth.

You can find ways to make your vision become your reality when you structure your life according to the Values Factor. And in the next chapter, you'll discover how to use the Values Factor to build wealth and create financial freedom so that instead of you working for money, you can have your money working for you.

8

Growing Your Financial Freedom

No man can tell whether he is rich or poor by
turning to his ledger. It is the heart that makes a
man rich. He is rich according to what he is, not
according to what he has.

—HENRY WARD BEECHER

As I travel around the world and address thousands of people, I ask them, "How many of you would love to be financially free or independent?"

Immediately nearly one hundred percent of the people in the audience put their hands up and shout, "Yeah!"

Then I ask the same audience, "How many of you are already financially free or independent?"

Immediately ninety-eight to ninety-nine percent of the people in the audience put their hands down and become quiet. The only exception occurs when I am addressing a more specialized, executive-level audience that already has a higher value on leading companies, wealth-building, and financial independence.

But if it's a general audience, I go on to ask, "What is the average percentage of people who actually achieve financial freedom and independence?"

People usually shout out, "Only about one percent of the world, the one percenters."

Next, I ask them, "If only one percent of the people are going to obtain financial freedom, then who in this room is going to be among the one percent who achieve it?"

Everyone puts their hands up, assuming it is somehow miraculously going to be them. But then I say to them, "If that were true, you would probably already be demonstrating that you are on your way to economic freedom. You would already have evidence that your financial freedom is gradually becoming a reality in your life."

Now the room goes quiet. People are beginning to realize that in order to build great wealth, they will need a greater understanding of some additional principles and methods.

Many of my students and clients tell me that they want to grow their financial freedom. They want to build a business or a portfolio of investments that will create passive income for them—money that comes in "by itself" that they don't have to work for.

Then, almost invariably, they tell me that, for some reason, they're having trouble saving or investing money at the level they'd like. They say things like, "I want to save, but by the end of the month, I just run out of money," "I wanted to invest, but we had some unexpected expenses this year," or "I'd like to start a business, but I can never quite seem to get enough capital together."

When I come across statements like this, what I see is incongruency between these people's statements, goals, and highest values. People have fantasies about their financial goals, but their assumed financial goals are not aligned with their highest values.

Most often, the problem is that people don't understand the difference between "financial freedom" and "spending money." Many people tell me that they place a high value on money, but what they really mean is that they value *spending* money. They imagine financial freedom as being able to spend money on anything they want, and so it's very difficult for them not to just start spending now!

In fact, the way to grow your financial freedom is not to value *spending* money, but to value *saving* and *investing* it. If your highest values go toward spending—whether you are paying for new clothes, more education, or treats for your children—you are going to spend everything you have before you have the chance to save or invest any of it. If your highest values go toward saving and investing, you will stop before you make any purchase—whatever it is—because you will naturally be more interested in putting that money somewhere it can grow and pay dividends or interest back to you, giving you a return on investment (ROI).

Now at this point, you're probably wondering how you can ever grow your financial freedom—whether to build a business or simply to put away money for so-called retirement—if your highest values lie elsewhere.

The answer is simple: you can still build wealth if you *link your new financial goals to your present highest values*. In other words, link your goal of serving people and of saving or investing money to your current highest values—whatever they may be. After all, without serving others, you will have no money to save! *Deserving* is derived from *serving*. Service comes first, and then comes savings, as a result of services rendered. So if you link your goal of serving people, it will become easier to put money away—just as easy as it now is to spend it. The Values Factor makes it clear: whatever is truly highest on your values list, or at least linked to your highest values, is a goal you will spontaneously seek to fulfill.

Exercise 1, which is below, will help you link your new financial goals to your present highest values. Once you complete Exercise 1, you will have at least twelve hundred reasons for growing a business and building wealth that will serve yourself and others. By completing this exercise, you will almost certainly raise the value of business and wealth-building on your hierarchy of values until it is near your highest value and your most powerful sense of purpose. As a result, you will discover that you are now experiencing an Attention Surplus Order, Retention Surplus Order, and Intention Surplus Order for the goals of saving, investing, and growing your wealth:

- **Attention:** You will begin to *notice* more wealth-building opportunities that you'll then be able to act on.
- **Retention:** You will *retain* more helpful information that will assist you in building wealth.
- **Intention:** Your *intention* to build your wealth will grow in power.

Remember: The higher the value you place on serving people, becoming fairly rewarded, and building wealth, the more likely you will save and invest money and build the fortune that you say you want. The further away wealth-building is from your highest values, the more wealth-building and your highest values will conflict with each other. So if you truly want to build wealth, connect wealth-building to your highest values. Automatically, you will start seeing more opportunities and acting on them differently.

Exercise 1: Learning to Value Financial Freedom

Like every human being, you act according to your highest values, doing what you believe will provide you with the greatest advantage and reward, and avoiding what you believe will leave you with the greatest disadvantage and risk. So when I hear people say they want to build wealth in their life, I ask them the six questions that make up this exercise. Answer these questions, complete this exercise and you will raise the value of building wealth on your list of values and at least link your goal of financial freedom to your present highest values:

Instructions:

STEP 1: On a separate page or on your computer, answer each of the following questions. Make sure you answer each question thoughtfully, and make sure you provide each of the two hundred answers per question that I have specified. You will get the greatest results from this exercise by completing it thoroughly. You need two hundred answers for each question to truly shift wealth-building to a higher spot on your list of values. You also need to expend this amount of mental effort to remyelinate new pathways in your brain in order to neuroplastically transform your brain. If these two hundred answers were easily obtained quickly off the top of your head, you would have already been well into your journey of wealth building and your life would have already demonstrated that you had made those connections. Just as in fitness training, it takes more and more reps to get results beyond your present comfort zone and ability level, so in this mental work, you do need to expend some extra effort to transform your thinking and your brain. So dig for legitimate and powerfully meaningful answers. Persevere until you can genuinely see that your perceptions, decisions, and actions have truly transformed with regard to your financial management.

1. How can building a business that serves ever-greater numbers of people be of great service, value, and benefit to you? Answer that question at least two hundred times. Do not list the benefits of spending any of the money that you will make. Write only the benefits of actually building the business.

For example:

1. To be able to lead and influence the lives of those I employ

2. To be able to employ people and add to the number of economic exchanges

3. To be able to serve and make a difference in the lives of millions of people

4. To be able to master the skills of business management

5. To be able to create a business that I can leave to my offspring

2. How can managing your business more effectively and efficiently to maximize your profits be of great service, value, and benefit to you? Answer that question at least two hundred times.
For example:

1. To be able to master the skills of governing and leading people

2. To be able to hire and inspire teams to fulfill their lives

3. To be able to prioritize my and my employees' actions to reduce stress

4. To be able to maximize profits, keep costs down for customers, and sell more

5. To be able to determine what is working and not working

3. How can saving an ever-greater portion of profit from your business be of great service, value, and benefit to you? Again, answer that question at least two hundred times.
For example:

1. To be able to stabilize my primary business

2. To be able to attract more qualified clients

3. To be able to associate with wealthier clients and receive more ideas and expanded options

4. To be able to capitalize on the beauty of compound interest

5. To be able to calm my volatile emotions and economic stress levels

4. How is investing and learning the art of *progressive investing* with greater degrees of leverage and return going to be of great service, value, and benefit to you? ("Progressive investing" means that as your wealth grows, you are able to take ever-greater risks. For example, you might begin by putting $100 each month into an interest-bearing account. When you have accumulated a few thousand dollars, you might put half of your wealth into a collection of blue-chip stocks. When that wealth has grown larger, you might put a portion of it into a collection of smaller and newer stocks that is riskier but that offers a potentially greater rate of return. As your wealth grows, you are able to take greater risks—and achieve greater rewards.) Once again, answer that question at least two hundred times.

For example:

1. To be able to take advantage of more progressive and elevated returns

2. To learn about companies and their financial strategies

3. To build a stable stack of cushioned investments

4. To diversify my portfolio to take advantage of different classes and sectors

5. To pool my money with other sophisticated investors

5. How is building and amassing a vast financial fortune going to be a great service, value, and benefit to you? Yet again, answer that question at least two hundred times.

For example:

1. To be able to build a stable nest egg

2. To be able to draw in even more wealth-building opportunities

3. To be able to endure any form of socioeconomic volatility

4. To be able to build an enduring brand

5. To be able to select the individuals or companies I associate with

6. How is identifying or creating a financial cause—something you can dedicate your life and your wealth to—that leaves a legacy that lasts more than one hundred years and serves vast numbers of people going to be of great service, value, and benefit to you? Answer that question at least two hundred times.

For example:

1. To be able to create a lasting foundation that serves the world beyond my life

2. To be able to have a multigenerational family structure that serves the world

3. To be able to master more sophisticated estate and trust planning

4. To be able to participate in philanthropy

5. To be able to leave a lasting family or corporate legacy

As you answer these six questions thoroughly, you will notice creative new ideas and resources within and around you that you have not been aware of before, and you will see how you can more efficiently begin building your desired wealth through fulfilling people's highest values and providing greater service to the world, as well as through valuing yourself more fully.

STEP 2: Next, cross-link each of the previous six questions or actions to your present three highest values by asking the following two questions:

1. How specifically does each of the previous six questions, their answers, and any actions you might take as a result help you fulfill what you would love to fulfill based on your present three highest values? Answer that question at least fifty times.

For example: If your present three highest values revolve around your family, you might ask: How can building a business that serves ever greater numbers of people be of great service, value, and benefit to your family?

2. How does fulfilling your three highest values help you fulfill the previous six questions or actions? Answer that question at least fifty times.

For example: How can spending time with your family help you build a business that serves ever-greater numbers of people?

ALIGNING YOUR HIGHEST VALUES WITH YOUR FINANCIAL FREEDOM

When your goal of financial freedom and your highest values are *not* aligned:

- You will probably live in a financial fantasy with unrealistic expectations.
- You will probably devalue yourself or feel less worthy due to your unrealistic expectations.
- You will probably be less likely to pay yourself first and less likely to save and invest. ("Paying yourself first" means that as soon as you receive income, your first step is to put a portion of it into your savings or investments; then you pay your bills with the remainder.)

- You will probably be less financially ambitious.
- You will probably be less likely to manage your time and money wisely.
- You will probably be more likely to pass up or give away your financial opportunities.
- You will probably feel less worthy of receiving financial rewards.
- You will probably be less likely to recognize your *true hidden higher financial worth*. (I explain what I mean by this phrase in the section that follows entitled "You Are Already a Billionaire" on page 268.)
- You will probably be more vulnerable to immediately gratifying get-rich-quick schemes.
- You will probably be less emotionally stable with money and less able to manage your money.

When your goal of financial freedom and your highest values *are* aligned:

- You will more likely feel worthy of wealth and affluence.
- You will more quickly dissolve past baggage and belief systems that hinder wealth reception.
- You will generate stronger reasons to build businesses that generate wealth.
- You will more likely desire to learn more about financial matters and investments.
- You will more likely pay yourself first so that you can save and invest your well-earned money.
- You will more effectively manage your emotions, regarding both wealth and finances.
- You will more likely stick long-term to the financial strategies that you have chosen.
- You will more likely expand your purpose, vision, and cause of wealth-building and social contribution.

THE PRINCIPLES BEHIND GREAT
WEALTH-BUILDING

Now that you know how to increase or raise wealth-building on your scale of values, you are ready to learn some secrets of creating greater wealth:

- **Create a clear business mission statement.** Your rewards of vast wealth will come as a result of your creativity and dedicated hours of service. You serve most when you are clear on what your mission for service is. A business mission statement will help clarify your service. Your ultimate business service will be to fulfill the highest values of others.
- **Take on a global problem.** Leaders tackle globally challenging problems that serve or fulfill millions of people's highest values.
- **Create, locate, or affiliate** with someone who has innovative solutions to those global problems. If you do not have the answers, then find someone who does and someone who is most inspired by, creative toward, and congruent with providing such global solutions.
- **Tap into the highest values or inspiration of the people you desire to market to.** If you do, they will desire to consume your product, refer other people to you, and somehow become part of your growing social or entrepreneurial cause. People will do whatever it takes to fulfill their highest values.
- **Create a compensation for all participants.** Everyone involved in your wealth-building project desires and deserves to have their highest values fulfilled and to be fairly compensated.

OWN THE TRAITS OF
THE FINANCIAL MASTERS

Once you have elevated wealth-building on your scale of values and understood the secrets behind creating a wealthy mind-set, your next step is to own the traits of the great financial masters. You may believe that the people whose financial achievements you most admire have qualities that you do not have—either supportive qualities that you admire as positive or challenging qualities that you dislike as negative.

In fact, every quality or trait that you see in anyone else—whether admired, despised, or anywhere in between—is present within you, to exactly the same degree that you have observed it in anyone else. Over the last quarter of a century, I have taught the Breakthrough Experience seminar program around the world. In so doing, I have facilitated the Demartini Method and have proven time and time again to tens of thousands of people that whatever they perceive in others they have in some form or another to the same degree. Although many attendees question this principle when they begin the seminar program, no one does by the time they finish.

This is significant since you may have believed that building great wealth was out of your reach because you didn't have the qualities needed to do so. You may also have wanted to avoid building great wealth out of an unwillingness to take on the supposedly negative qualities that you may have previously associated with it. Knowing that you demonstrate both the admirable and the so-called despicable qualities—regardless of whether you build wealth or not!—will help free you to build wealth once you decide that it will truly serve your highest values.

Exercise 2: Owning the Traits of the Financial Masters

To become a financial master, you will likely find it empowering to discover that you already have within yourself the traits of every great or even legendary financier, entrepreneur, and wealth builder you may ever admire. This exercise will help you identify and own those traits so you may play in a new field of financial possibility.

Instructions:

STEP 1: List the three most powerful financial masters that you know of, admire, or would love to play in the same field of financial possibility with:

1. _____

2. _____

3. _____

STEP 2: Research everything you can discover about these three individuals. Then list the five traits you admire most and the five traits you dislike most about each.

Five Traits of Financial Masters That I Admire Most:

1. _____

2. _____

3. _____

4. _____

5. _____

Five Traits of Financial Masters That I Dislike Most:

1. _____

2. _____

3. _____

4. _____

5. _____

STEP 3: Complete this special modified and selected portion of the Demartini Method on each of these three financial masters until you have completely owned all of the five most admired and five most disliked traits of each of these leaders to the same degree and neutralized any admirations and dislikes you presently have about them. By one hundred percent owning and neutralizing their traits, you will be able to begin to play in a new and greater field of financial possibility and opportunity. Be sure to look in all seven (spiritual, mental, vocational, financial, familial, social, and physical) areas of your life for your hidden character traits. The seer, the seeing, and the seen are the same; that is, what you perceive is in you, and by the process of being able to see it, you reveal that it is in you. If you see a trait in anyone else, the fact that you perceive that trait is a sign that the very same trait is within you. So whatever traits you perceive in the financial masters you have identified, you have in yourself as well.

For each of the three powerful financial masters, you are to answer the following specific question: where, when and how are you demonstrating or have you demonstrated this admired or disliked trait one hundred percent to the same degree? You will need to answer these questions over and over again for each of the five admired and despised traits and for each of the three financial masters until you can truly see that you own all of the ten traits for each of the masters one hundred percent. It may take as many as twenty answers or even more to fully own some of the traits. Keep searching for the answers until you own every trait one hundred percent.

Admired Trait 1		
Where?	When?	How?
Where?	When?	How?
Where?	When?	How?
Where?	When?	How?
Where?	When?	How?
Where?	When?	How?
Where?	When?	How?
Where?	When?	How?
Where?	When?	How?
Where?	When?	How?
Where?	When?	How?
Where?	When?	How?
Where?	When?	How?
Where?	When?	How?
Where?	When?	How?
Where?	When?	How?
Where?	When?	How?
Where?	When?	How?
Where?	When?	How?
Where?	When?	How?

Admired Trait 2		
Where?	When?	How?
Where?	When?	How?
Where?	When?	How?
Where?	When?	How?
Where?	When?	How?
Where?	When?	How?
Where?	When?	How?
Where?	When?	How?
Where?	When?	How?
Where?	When?	How?
Where?	When?	How?
Where?	When?	How?
Where?	When?	How?
Where?	When?	How?
Where?	When?	How?
Where?	When?	How?
Where?	When?	How?
Where?	When?	How?
Where?	When?	How?
Where?	When?	How?

Admired Trait 3		
Where?	When?	How?
Where?	When?	How?
Where?	When?	How?

Admired Trait 3		
Where?	When?	How?
Where?	When?	How?
Where?	When?	How?
Where?	When?	How?
Where?	When?	How?
Where?	When?	How?
Where?	When?	How?
Where?	When?	How?
Where?	When?	How?
Where?	When?	How?
Where?	When?	How?
Where?	When?	How?
Where?	When?	How?
Where?	When?	How?
Where?	When?	How?
Where?	When?	How?
Where?	When?	How?

Admired Trait 4		
Where?	When?	How?
Where?	When?	How?
Where?	When?	How?
Where?	When?	How?
Where?	When?	How?
Where?	When?	How?
Where?	When?	How?

Admired Trait 4		
Where?	When?	How?
Where?	When?	How?
Where?	When?	How?
Where?	When?	How?
Where?	When?	How?
Where?	When?	How?
Where?	When?	How?
Where?	When?	How?
Where?	When?	How?
Where?	When?	How?
Where?	When?	How?
Where?	When?	How?
Where?	When?	How?

Admired Trait 5		
Where?	When?	How?
Where?	When?	How?
Where?	When?	How?
Where?	When?	How?
Where?	When?	How?
Where?	When?	How?
Where?	When?	How?
Where?	When?	How?
Where?	When?	How?
Where?	When?	How?
Where?	When?	How?

Admired Trait 5		
Where?	When?	How?
Where?	When?	How?
Where?	When?	How?
Where?	When?	How?
Where?	When?	How?
Where?	When?	How?
Where?	When?	How?
Where?	When?	How?
Where?	When?	How?

Disliked Trait 1		
Where?	When?	How?
Where?	When?	How?
Where?	When?	How?
Where?	When?	How?
Where?	When?	How?
Where?	When?	How?
Where?	When?	How?
Where?	When?	How?
Where?	When?	How?
Where?	When?	How?
Where?	When?	How?
Where?	When?	How?
Where?	When?	How?
Where?	When?	How?

Disliked Trait 1		
Where?	When?	How?
Where?	When?	How?
Where?	When?	How?
Where?	When?	How?
Where?	When?	How?
Where?	When?	How?

Disliked Trait 2		
Where?	When?	How?
Where?	When?	How?
Where?	When?	How?
Where?	When?	How?
Where?	When?	How?
Where?	When?	How?
Where?	When?	How?
Where?	When?	How?
Where?	When?	How?
Where?	When?	How?
Where?	When?	How?
Where?	When?	How?
Where?	When?	How?
Where?	When?	How?
Where?	When?	How?
Where?	When?	How?
Where?	When?	How?

Disliked Trait 2		
Where?	When?	How?
Where?	When?	How?
Where?	When?	How?

Disliked Trait 3		
Where?	When?	How?
Where?	When?	How?
Where?	When?	How?
Where?	When?	How?
Where?	When?	How?
Where?	When?	How?
Where?	When?	How?
Where?	When?	How?
Where?	When?	How?
Where?	When?	How?
Where?	When?	How?
Where?	When?	How?
Where?	When?	How?
Where?	When?	How?
Where?	When?	How?
Where?	When?	How?
Where?	When?	How?
Where?	When?	How?
Where?	When?	How?
Where?	When?	How?

Disliked Trait 4		
Where?	When?	How?
Where?	When?	How?
Where?	When?	How?
Where?	When?	How?
Where?	When?	How?
Where?	When?	How?
Where?	When?	How?
Where?	When?	How?
Where?	When?	How?
Where?	When?	How?
Where?	When?	How?
Where?	When?	How?
Where?	When?	How?
Where?	When?	How?
Where?	When?	How?
Where?	When?	How?
Where?	When?	How?
Where?	When?	How?
Where?	When?	How?
Where?	When?	How?

Disliked Trait 5		
Where?	When?	How?
Where?	When?	How?
Where?	When?	How?

Disliked Trait 5		
Where?	When?	How?
Where?	When?	How?
Where?	When?	How?
Where?	When?	How?
Where?	When?	How?
Where?	When?	How?
Where?	When?	How?
Where?	When?	How?
Where?	When?	How?
Where?	When?	How?
Where?	When?	How?
Where?	When?	How?
Where?	When?	How?
Where?	When?	How?
Where?	When?	How?
Where?	When?	How?
Where?	When?	How?

BILLIONAIRES' TRAITS

Following are some key traits that billionaires tend to share. However you feel about these qualities, whether positive, negative, or neutral, find them within yourself to know that you also share these traits. You actually already have more in common with billionaires than you think!

1. Billionaires just know they are destined to be wealthy: that being wealthy is aligned with their highest values.

2. Billionaires start simple, humble, small, and from scratch and then patiently and methodically keep serving others and continue working toward building their wealth: they build financial momentum through living congruently with their highest values.

3. Billionaires think big, are hungry for service-driven wealth, and desire to be exceptional and not hinder themselves by others' outer limitations: they do not subordinate to another's highest values.

4. Billionaires take ever larger calculated risks and have risk management strategies that they apply to both their own and other people's money: they have Attention Surplus Order when it comes to financial risks and rewards.

5. Billionaires seek, love, and thrive on challenges, are competitive, and have thick skins: living according to their highest values, they thrive on the balance of support and challenge.

6. Billionaires keep making their businesses more effective and efficient: they live congruently with their highest values and become most efficient in their actions.

7. Billionaires are focused on their primary specialties without becoming distracted by too many secondary ventures: they do not subordinate to another's highest values or to lower-priority distractions.

8. Billionaires are vigorously driven by their purpose, vision, inspiration, calling, and desired legacy, and are willing to consistently put in the long hours and work required by their continually re-

continued . . .

fined strategies: they are focused upon fulfilling their highest values.

9. Billionaires set high and challenging goals that are nevertheless realistic and attainable; they intend to be the richest people in the world, or at least, some of the richest: that is one of their highest values.

10. Billionaires are innovative visionaries who thrive on criticism and are even inspired by it: they live congruently with their highest values and become independent visionaries able to handle great challenges.

11. Billionaires use both supportive and challenging news as simply feedback: by living according to their highest values, they embrace the balance of support and challenge equally.

12. Billionaires are strong-willed and have strong self-imposed uncompromised standards while keeping a close eye on both their wealth and their wise, frugal expenditures: their congruence allows them to continually raise their already high standards.

13. Billionaires are true to themselves and their philosophies: they know and live by their highest values.

14. Billionaires believe in themselves, are self-confident, take charge of their financial destiny, and stick to what they believe; their alignment with their highest values allows them to be more certain.

15. Billionaires press on and are persistent, determined, tough, and unyielding: they spontaneously love to do what they feel called to do and thereby bring great service to the world.

16. Billionaires transform obstacles and challenges into opportunities and refuse to throw in the towel: they see their challenges as *on* the way, not *in* the way.

17. Billionaires are unyielding and committed long-term—perhaps even until death—as they are too busy to have time for dying or resting: their higher level of congruence with their own values expands their time horizons.

18. Billionaires learn quickly from their so-called mistakes, innovate, and then keep growing: they embrace feedback so as to refine their vision and their decisions.

19. Billionaires thrive on pressures and uncertainties while seeking out and even thriving on stresses: their values give them Intention Surplus Order to help them fulfill their intentions even under pressure.

20. Billionaires, once wealthy, are less interested in just making money than they are in using their earned money to keep score of their services: their highest values involve service as much as reward.

21. Billionaires love to play the business game and make deals: they do what they love and love what they do.

22. Billionaires are opportunistic solution providers and are on the lookout for ways to solve people's problems. They move into markets and buy when others move out and sell: their values give them Attention Surplus Order to spot opportunities and Intention Surplus Order to act upon what they see.

23. Billionaires manage leveraged debt to their advantage to get richer while ensuring that others take some of the risk and pay for it: their highest values involve the inclusion of others.

GETTING REAL

A lot of people live in a fantasy world when it comes to wealth-building. But I prefer that you have the option of breaking free of that. I would love for you to become grounded enough to realize that if you don't raise the six steps to wealth-building[1] up to become some of your highest values; if you don't study financial or wealth management; if you don't bring order to your financial structure and habits; and if you don't own the traits of the wealthy, you are probably going to live in a delusion about your financial future. You are going to be like a woman I met once, who told me that she had seen *The Secret* and then said to me, "Dr. Demartini, every day, I go out to the mailbox with a clear intention that a million-dollar check will be there for me—but somehow it never is. What am I doing wrong?"

Well, of course, that is a total misunderstanding of what was stated in *The Secret* and what I am saying in this book. No one manifests great wealth solely by thinking about it. You will require a clear and inspiring goal of creating and building wealth that aligns with your highest values and that serves a vast number of other people's highest values. Then you will need to implement clear, sound savings and investment strategies and make effective business and financial

---

[1] The Six Steps to Wealth Building: Dr. John Demartini's six primary steps to building a financial fortune as presented in his *"Where's My Billion"* seminar program: 1. Building a business that serves ever greater numbers of people. 2. Managing the priorities and performances within the business to maximize profits. 3. Saving an ever-progressive portion of the profits. 4. Investing in investments that provide ever-progressive levels of risk and reward. 5. Accumulating a vast fortune. 6. Creating a financial cause that leaves a philanthropic legacy. Go to drdemartini.com and click "Programs" on the left-side menu.

decisions that are actually going to help you make a difference in the world so that you can build your fortune.

So let me ask you what I ask in some of my seminars: what would you do if you had $10 million unexpectedly handed to you right now? Take a moment right now and list the first ten things you would do.

Now, look at your list and answer this question for me: After you've taken those first ten actions, how much of that $10 million is left?

So, what did you write down? Did you plan to buy a house? Send your children through college? Take a great vacation? Give fabulous presents to yourself and your loved ones? Buy a new car or take a long-awaited luxury vacation?

If you're like most of my general audience attendees, you will realize that what you did with that $10 million is *spend* that money. Even if you bought a house, you haven't really made an investment because, generally, real estate depreciates and costs as much as it appreciates unless it is used as a rental property or bought with the explicit intention of being improved and/or flipped for resale. If you plan on living in a house, buying it is usually a break-even deal at best. And if you spent the money on college tuition, travel, or gifts, from the point of view of wealth-building, you have basically just potentially diminished your net worth, unless you explicitly intended those expenditures as investments in a particular career or business that you plan to build. Otherwise, you are behaving as a consumer, not an investor. You are spending wealth, not building wealth!

This is the exact opposite of what a financial master would do. A financial master's first thought would be to invest that $10 million to produce passive income—income that he or she doesn't have to work for. Financial masters would invest in "appreciables"—items whose value can reasonably be expected to increase—not disperse their money into "depreciables" or consumables—items whose value can be expected to decline or even evaporate. Investing in appreciables is how you would build true financial freedom for yourself and your family, and how you eventually go on to leave a financial legacy that outlives you.

This is why I suggest that if you want to build wealth and create financial freedom, you link that goal to your highest values—but in a real way. Financial freedom is not about spending money; it's about building wealth. Only people who are clear about that distinction are likely to create financial freedom.

SAVING AND INVESTING

I very much want you to understand the reality of what it takes to build wealth. The first step is saving, followed closely by investing, and then, when your portfolio of investments is in great shape, by possibly speculating.

Most people put off saving "until"—until their bills are paid, until their debts are paid, until a more comfortable time. Well, I have news for you: it's almost never a more comfortable time, and yet, it's always possible to start saving. Parkinson's Law makes it clear that if you don't save your money or invest it into high-priority wealth-building vehicles, it will automatically become consumed by low-priority distractions and unexpected bills or wealth destroyers.

I started saving in my twenties when I realized, "I can't sit here and fantasize about being wealthy; it's time to be strategic and tactical. I need to ask myself, 'What's it going to take? If I'm going to build financial stability and then financial independence, how much do I need to save and how much do I then need to invest? If I want to earn enough money to both save and invest, how many people do I need to serve?'"

I started calculating how much service I needed to do to get a net return of an amount that would allow me to get real about serving, saving, and investing. And that was the beginning of my business and wealth-building. But I had to have a big enough reason for doing it or I wouldn't have even bothered taking action. I had to put wealth-building and achieving financial freedom high enough on my list of values to really be inspired to do it. When your *why* is big enough, your *hows* take care of themselves.

At the time, I was scared because I was behind on my bills. I was in my twenties and just getting started. I was a doctor, I had recently expanded my office, I was paying for a house, for a car, and for loans I'd taken out to go to school and to develop my office. Plus, I was facing a bunch of stresses in my life, and I didn't think I could afford to save at that moment. Like many people, I thought, "When I get out of all my debt, then I will start saving and maybe someday begin investing."

Don't live in that illusion! Impoverished people think that way. The wealthy pay themselves first. But the impoverished pay themselves last. The poor devalue themselves. When you live congruently according to your highest values, you achieve more, you value yourself more, and when you value yourself, so do others. One of the ways that you know you are valuing yourself is that you are paying yourself first.

Finally, I realized that there were no real risks involved in beginning to save. Yes, there was a possibility of inflation or some lost investment opportunity, but the worst thing that I could imagine happening if I saved was that I might think I would have to pay my bills and debts during a low-income period or some other worst-case financial scenario or emergency. So I said, "I'll just do it."

I started with $10 a day, $50 dollars a week, and $200 a month. That wasn't a lot, but I was still a bit anxious. I was overwhelmed by debt and I was thinking, "Wow, it's going to take me ten years to pay this off—I won't be able to start saving for ten years." I felt burned out and trapped in the dream of trying to get ahead in life. But somehow I managed to start saving. And at the end of the first month, I had made it. So I did another month. That worked out, too. Three months went by and I didn't even miss the money I had saved.

Even better, amazing things began to happen. An extra patient would come in. Someone would take me out to dinner. Somehow, I always had the extra money. So I said, "You know what? I am getting comfortable with this. I think I can do more than $200. I think I can raise it to $300." So I did that for three months. Then I said, "You know what? I am not missing this saved money. I attracted some more new patients and some other business opportunities are starting to appear." So I raised my savings amount to $500, then to $750, and then to $1,000.

Now I was starting to see light at the end of the tunnel. And now some interesting opportunities started emerging. I noticed that my business was growing stronger and more stable. I calmed some of my anxiety because I started accumulating a little cash, also known as *liquidity*. The quality of my clients went up. The people that I associated with changed; now I was dealing with a higher echelon.

So I started having more confidence. I started being able to say to patients that I really didn't resonate with, "No, you would be more effectively served by another service provider." At the same time, I started giving my patients an even greater quality of care. I was giving more and more service—and I was saving more and more. In fact, I had saved enough that I was able to begin investing.

I kept increasing the amounts I saved and invested, doubling those amounts again and again, and I started watching things happen. When you manage your money wisely, you start attracting more money to manage. Then I started studying money and finances even more thoroughly: the value of money; how to manage it; how to invest it.

First, though, I started with savings. And that is why I advise, start with savings. After you have built up a stable cushion of savings, then you can invest additional income on top of that, and then you can speculate, if you ever chose to, again on top of that. But you want to begin with some liquidity, a cushion to stabilize your primary business before you go investing and possibly gambling, which is what so many people unwisely do. They rise and crash. But I didn't handle my money that way, and I don't want you to handle yours that way, either.

Now, guess what else happens when you start saving and then investing the money you have generated by performing services? You create a whole new set of people you get to associate with. When you have $10 saved, you hang out with ten-naires. But when you have $100 saved, you hang out with hundred-aires. When you have $1,000 saved, you hang out with thousand-aires. And when you have $1 million saved, you get to hang out with millionaires.

And so your wealth keeps building and your life circumstances keep transforming. When you have $10 million saved, you get to hang out with decamillionaires, and when you acknowledge that you have a billion, you hang out with other billionaires. Yes, compound interest grows as you save and wisely invest your money, but that is not the greatest thing. Building wealth also increases the associations, opportunities, and ideas that you have, the quality of clients that you start to attract, the brand that you get to stand behind, and the greater circles of people you have the opportunity to serve.

Now most people's tendency is to start spending money as soon as they make it. They desire immediate gratification. But if all you do with your money is spend it, you make it harder and harder to ever achieve financial independence. So I consistently say to my attendees and clients, don't raise your lifestyle unless you are willing to raise your savings or investments and taxes by equal amounts. Otherwise, you will just put yourself further into financial burden or debt, and you are going to spend more of your life working for money instead of having it work for you.

You will be a slave to money if you have to work for it all your life. But you will be its master if you have it starting to work for you. And your money won't ever start working for you until you begin to save and invest it. At first, the process will seem slow, but if you give it some time and let it build momentum, massive financial changes occur in your life. So just start. The key is not how much you save; it is the habit of saving and investing. When wealth-building rises higher on your list of values, your clarity of vision and patience for its accumulation expands. This is the power of the Values Factor.

KEY PRINCIPLES OF THE GREAT FINANCIAL MASTERS

- The financially wealthy pay themselves first, but the financially unwealthy pay themselves last. So whenever you receive any money, make sure you put either a minimum amount or some percentage of it—whichever is greater—into your savings and/or investment accounts, or into other investments.
- Pay your personal taxes. By the inch, it's a cinch; by the yard, it's hard. Chunk your tax payments down into smaller times and sizes so that you make sure to stay current.
- Pay all of your payables according to priority. Prioritize all payments and stick to that set of priorities no matter what. When you manage your money wisely, you receive more money to manage. Pay your budgeted personal lifestyle bills according to priority. Pay your business taxes by priority. Pay your budgeted business bills according to priority.
- Keep your money flowing if you would love to keep it growing. Keep investing it.
- Appreciate a challenging upbringing, when you may have undergone financial struggles. A challenging background

makes you hungrier to earn what you receive. As we have seen, challenges create voids that then create values. The greater the challenge, the greater the void . . . and the greater the value.

- Work in careers or jobs that you truly love or link whatever job duties you have to your highest values so that you can be inspired and, like Warren Buffett, "tap-dance to work."
- Work, work, work . . . Serve, serve, serve . . . Save, save, save . . . Invest, invest, invest . . .
- Become a global macro-visionary: bring service to the world. Link "being of service" to your highest values.
- Educate yourself on investing. Warren Buffett had read every book on investment in an Omaha public library by the time he was eleven. The earlier you begin your studies, the better. If you truly begin to value wealth-building, you will build it.
- Study probabilities, statistics, and money management principles. When you truly value investing, you will study its laws.
- Mentor others on investing so you will learn by teaching.
- Don't pretend you know everything about investing: remain humble and open to continued learning. Likewise, don't always think you are right—pride goes before a fall.
- Don't venture beyond your sphere of knowledge until your sphere of knowledge extends beyond your venture. Study investments class by class.
- Save before you invest and before you speculate. Build a stable foundation so that your building won't sway.
- Be a long-term investor more than a short-term speculator. Stay the course for twenty to fifty years. That keeps greed and fear out of investing. The time in the market is more important than the timing of the market. Be a patient investor, not a daily trader who seeks immediate gratification.

continued . . .

- Know the downside as well as the upside of each investment. When you live according to your highest values, you will embrace both sides equally.
- Maintain discipline; avoid chasing fads or following fashions. Be a principled and disciplined investor, not a gambling opportunistic one.
- Stick to the fundamentals; markets regress to a mean regardless of cycles.
- Make large, significant investment decisions only when you are certain that markets are at extremes—generally every five or ten years. The average market cycle lasts between five and ten years. At those points, be a contrarian: every manic has a panic. In other words, when the market is at its peak, during a so-called bubble, that is usually a wise time to sell, even while everyone else is buying. When the market is at its lowest, during a crash, that is usually a wise time to buy, even while everyone else is selling.
- Wait, wait, and wait until you can see a great bet: patience is wisdom. Buy and hold value with patience.
- Diversify to reduce volatility. Don't put all your eggs into one basket, even if it is your own company. Select a few investments and hedge your bets. Balanced portfolios become timeless.
- Unless you are an investment specialist, consider buying the whole haystack in an index rather than spending time and money searching for needles. (An index is a collection of stocks, bundled together by a financial firm. It is generally held for at least a year, enabling you to take advantage of long-term capital gains.)
- Seek low-cost index fund investments to keep the cost of investing and trading down. Performance isn't the only thing that counts—the expenses are often just as significant.

- Beware of overpriced, highly volatile, unregulated hedge funds.
- Work your way up the investment class spectrum, not down—earn the right to risk.
- Beware of unrealistically thinking that you will pick only winners or stocks that will only rise in value. You will pick at least some losers as you invest, and you must budget for that. This is why I advise progressive investment. When your wealth is small, invest conservatively, in an interest-bearing account or a CD. When your wealth is greater, invest in an index or mutual fund or some other form of stock accumulation that hedges against risk. When your wealth is greater still, you can take greater risks, because you will have a financial cushion to soften the blow of the inevitable losing stocks.
- Invest in companies that are managed well: people make the difference.
- Beware of forecasts and predictions of markets, they can be biased gambles; remember that the people who make the predictions have their own biases.
- Concentrate your efforts on what you can control, notably keeping costs and taxes to a minimum.
- Master the science of asset allocation: keep to the big picture and to your overall investment strategy. If you are continually buying and selling, you raise the cost of investment. If you are able to hold on to your assets longer, you benefit from capital gains. Sometimes you need to move your assets around to respond to a change in the market, but if you master the science of when and how to do this, you will save yourself money in the long run.
- Review and rebalance your investment portfolio after each year to maintain your asset allocation according to your strat-

continued...

egy. Work with an adviser to determine the strategy that makes sense for you, and then make sure that *you* decide rather than allowing the market to do so. Don't let your portfolio drift. Have your adviser explain the plan to you and make sure that conscious decisions are being made for every investment.

- Maintain some liquidity and be conservative. Don't ever lose sleep over trying to gain a few extra percentage points. It is better to take fewer risks and feel more confident, rather than taking big risks that will keep you up at night. Keep plenty of liquid cash on hand so you can respond to emergencies and opportunities as they arise.
- What the wise man does in the beginning, fools do in the end!
- Hedge against all extreme outcomes. Big biases can destroy portfolios. For example, if your bias is toward tech stocks and you have not balanced your portfolio, you are vulnerable and likely to lose a great deal and destroy your stock portfolio when any tech bubble bursts, as it did in the 1990s. Or if your bias is toward real estate and then the real estate market crashes, you could destroy your portfolio unless you balanced it with some investments in other areas.
- Know the risks and dangers of leverage. "Leverage" is a financial term for any technique used to multiply gains and losses. For example, if you wanted to start a business, you might *leverage* the value of your house by taking out a mortgage on it and using that money to start your business. Now your house is even more valuable than it was before—because it is both a valuable piece of real estate and the foundation of a profitable enterprise. However, as you can see from this example, leverage poses risks, as well. If your business fails, you might also lose your house. Leverage multiplies your potential gain, but it also multiplies your potential risks. Understand leverage

thoroughly in your business dealings, and take no unnecessary risks.

- Set realistic objectives and lower your unrealistic expectations. Beware of overzealous returns.
- Factor in inflation to determine real returns and real wealth.
- Over the long term, currency movements cancel each other
out, so keep an eye on foreign investments.
- Develop an investment team.
- Use debt sparingly, if at all, and only if with long-term, low,
fixed rates and if your debt produces more than it costs. For
example, suppose you borrow money at six percent a year to
start a business that, in three years, has a return on investment
of twenty-four percent. Because your business is bringing in
far more than the interest rate on your debt, your debt has
produced more than it costs. However, if you borrow money
to buy a car or put some new clothes on your credit card, your
debt is costing you money—and it is not producing any
money—unless your new car can truly be demonstrated to
assist you in making you more return on your investment than
the car loan cost. Consumer debt is one of the reasons that
many people find it difficult to get ahead financially. They are
spending money on debt that does not produce any income.
- Be reasonably calm and prepared for ups and downs: that is
just the feedback that the market is giving you.
- Develop a creative capitalistic mind-set that includes accountable philanthropy. Philanthropy can be a very meaningful use
of your money, but it must be *accountable* philanthropy,
whereby the money that is distributed makes recipients accountable, responsible, productive, and dignified, rather than
fostering dependency, irresponsibility, and shame.

YOU ARE ALREADY A BILLIONAIRE

Now here is something else I consistently share in my financial wealth-building seminars, which often surprises my attendees and which might surprise you: everyone already has a billion dollars' worth of wealth—but not always in the form of classical assets or money. So now you have the opportunity to transform your present form of a billion dollars into the exchangeable and financial forms of money.

Let's begin with a definition of what true wealth is. The word "wealth" comes from the Old English words "weal" ("well-being") and "th" ("condition") which taken together means "the condition of well-being." (By the way, the word "economic" comes from the Greek "oikonomia," meaning "the management of the household." And the word "mortgage" means in French "a pledge unto death" or "a grip of death"!)

As the name suggests, genuine wealth represents the things that make life worthwhile or valuable. It is the experience of a life worth living, a life that is aligned with our highest and most meaningful values, not only as individuals, but also collectively as families, communities, cities, states, nations, and the world. Put another way, wealth is the condition of our collective well-being in all seven domains of life: spiritual, mental, vocational, financial, familial, social, and physical.

Genuine wealth is measured by the condition of anything that makes life worthwhile. That's why genuine wealth implies total life wealth. Many people are accustomed to looking at wealth strictly in financial terms or as property and possessions. But genuine wealth is much more than that—and we know it intuitively.

Conventional economics and business indicators of prosperity such as GDP (gross domestic product), stock market indices, and other economic indicators that we hear reported daily are only part of what we would define as genuine wealth. Indeed, many of these indicators, such as GDP growth, do not distinguish between expenditures in the economy that actually contribute to genuine wealth development versus those that depreciate or erode our social fabric or the strength of our relationship with nature.

Genuine wealth represents all the things that make life worthwhile, all the things that resonate with and fulfill our highest values and hearts. Genuine wealth is an accounting of life: a window into our innermost being, a mirror image of our genuine selves. Recognizing our wealth involves being in touch with our highest core values, our complete life assets, and our full awareness and potential. Our wealth includes all the assets that contribute to our complete and balanced state of being. And it accounts for what we value most. Genuine wealth allows us to objectively assess our real assets—our strengths—and to understand our true opportunities for developing our real wealth potential.

Whether your wealth comes in the form of your savings, your investments, your children, your friendships, your vocation, or some other form, it represents an expression of your highest values. In fact, everybody has great wealth—as I stated earlier, a billion dollars' worth—they just have it hidden in the form of their highest values. Some people have intellectual property wealth: great ideas that they have never packaged and turned it into sellable products and cash. Some people have wealth in the form of social interactions and networking contacts, leverage of people that they have never converted into cash. Some people have physical bodies that are so hot that people will pay millions to go out with them. I know a lady in Houston who, because of her beauty and confidence, will not even go out on a date unless the guy is wealthy and of high standing. She doesn't want to date anybody who is worth less than half a billion. Her genuine wealth—*her* "billion"—is in the form of her confidence, social skills, poise, and attractive appearance.

I know people who spend a vast fortune on education that they never turn into cash. I know people who spend a vast amount of money on their fitness and then never turn that into cash. Some people have spiritual awareness that is worth a fortune, but they don't charge for it. And then there are the people who have transformed their wealth—in any area of life—into a massive financial fortune because whatever else they valued highly, they also highly valued financial wealth.

So as you can see, everybody has wealth potential. The hierarchy of your values dictates your financial destiny and the form that your genuine wealth can take. But if you place a higher value on creating wealth—as was the goal of Exercise 1 in this chapter—then you will soon be able to begin converting your current form of wealth into a savings and investment form of wealth.

There is really no form of wealth that cannot be converted into cash: intellectual property, spiritual abilities, beauty, family relationships. Whatever area you are currently inspired by and presently store your hidden wealth or assets in, you can turn into money. But if you don't restructure your value hierarchy to place a higher value on building wealth in the form of savings or investments, your wealth will likely remain in a form that will never be capitalized on.

I know a gentleman who had a radio station in a network that reached millions of people across the world. More than 55 million people listened to him daily. But he had to get donations on a daily basis to keep his station alive because he didn't have a high value on saving or investing money.

He did have a value on intellectual property, and he had easily a billion dollars' worth of assets sitting in his storage in archives featuring the most famous people across the planet whom he had interviewed in the last forty-eight years. Because he and I have worked together, he is finally converting those archives into packages to sell.

Now, there is nothing right or wrong with keeping your wealth in any form you choose. You just don't want to have a fantasy that your wealth will suddenly appear in the form of cash, liquid savings, or investments and then beat yourself up when you don't have the highest values that will lead it there. The following exercise can help you find assets you never before suspected—aspects that you might well be able to turn into cash savings and financial investments.

Exercise 3: Discover Your Hidden Assets

According to economist Alfred Marshall, every muscle movement you make can be initiated or inhibited by someone who offers a specific amount of money. In other words, any action that you take can be translated into wealth, even though this potential wealth may be hidden from you until you understand how to see it.

For example, say that you have some intellectual property that you have not yet translated into a product that can be sold for cash. Maybe you know all the best places to eat in your neighborhood; you could produce a restaurant guide and sell it to local tourists, or start a website and sell ads to local restaurants. Your knowledge of the best places to eat in your neighborhood was a *hidden asset* until you realized its value and decided to use it.

Or perhaps you have some social contacts that have not yet been leveraged and converted into money. For example, maybe you know someone who has access to a famous writer or a major political figure. Suppose you decided to start a magazine or a foundation, and, through your friend, you were able to reach out to the writer or politician and convince them to be on your board of directors. Now your new magazine or foundation has credibility and can raise money from other sources. Knowing someone who had important social contacts just turned into a financial asset for you.

Your hidden assets might well add up to more than a billion dollars once they are converted into cash.

To discover all of your hidden assets, look carefully through all seven areas of your life: spiritual, mental, vocational, financial, familial, social, and physical. For example, if I were considering my own spiritual assets, I would consider my mystical or philosophical understanding of the nature of reality and the essence of my being or my present state of gratitude for the many experiences I have had throughout my life. For mental assets, I would consider my intellectual property in my Demartini Method for dissolving grief or conflict or my understanding of how to build wealth. For vocational assets, I would list my business management skills, my business contacts, and my business brand leverage. All of these assets are worth millions to me.

As you complete this exercise, consider which assets are worth millions or possibly billions to you—whether or not you can convert them into cash savings or investments.

Instructions: For each of the following areas of life, identify your greatest hidden assets. Your assets will be stored most in the areas of your highest values.

1. Spiritual	1.
	2.
	3.
	4.
2. Mental	1.
	2.
	3.
	4.
3. Vocational	1.
	2.
	3.
	4.

4. Financial	1.
	2.
	3.
	4.
5. Familial	1.
	2.
	3.
	4.
6. Social	1.
	2.
	3.
	4.
7. Physical	1.
	2.
	3.
	4.

SPIRITUAL VALUES AND BUILDING WEALTH

Too many people consider wealth-building as somehow opposed to spiritual values. I couldn't disagree more. There is no contradiction between an interest in spiritual issues and a commitment to building wealth and well-being. In fact, the two are inseparable and can definitely reinforce each other.

One of my most inspiring experiences linking the notion of

wealth-building with higher values took place at a seminar I once did in Seattle. A man came to my evening program and then afterward came up to me and asked for a consult. I agreed to see him the next morning at my hotel.

When the man showed up, he was agitated and distressed. He was a tall, thin man in his late thirties who had his own clinic, where he did natural and spiritual healing. He had been in business for himself for about ten years, and at this point he was $60,000 in debt; he and his wife were basically just scraping by from month to month. His wife had become deeply frustrated with the situation. She felt that at their current income, they couldn't afford to take care of their family, and she was unwilling to raise her children in a financially unstable environment. She had grown up with an absent father and a struggling single mother, and she was adamant about not imposing a similar set of stresses upon her own children.

So they were at an impasse. In fact, his wife was about to leave him, which is why he had been inspired to come to me in order to reconcile what he saw as these two warring goals: spiritual development and growing his healing business.

The first thing we did was look at his hierarchy of values. Of course, they were all about metaphysics and spiritual healing, which made sense, because he was certainly a metaphysically oriented guy. He was living in a fantasy that he was going to somehow get ahead financially doing what he was doing. But every time he would get extra money, instead of using it to build his business or wealth, he would buy metaphysical books or he would go off to seminars on yoga, meditation, healing, and other topics of that nature.

Of course, since we also attract people who challenge our highest values, he had married a woman who had become more and more practical and materialistic. This was the balance he needed to ground his idealistic and metaphysical outlook.

When this became clear to me, I said, "Look. With your set of values, you are not going to get ahead businesswise or financially, because your highest values are going to dictate your business and financial destiny, and you are going to keep spending money on the metaphysical and spiritual healing studies that you currently truly value. So you can do one of two things here: decide that you are willing to let go of your relationship, because clearly your wife is not going to stay in this situation any longer. Or else adjust your highest values so that you can begin to finally build your business and wealth. Which would you love to do?"

The man said, "I don't want to say good-bye to my wife. She means the world to me, and she's stuck by me all these years, and I think we can still have a beautiful family together. But I see that she's unfulfilled now, and I don't know how to fix things."

"Well," I told him, "You are floundering businesswise. So we are going to sit down and identify all the potential benefits you might get from serving people, growing your business, and building wealth. And we are going to find out how creating financial freedom for yourself and your wife will help you fulfill your metaphysical or spiritual and healing needs."

"Oh, no," he said. "I've tried that. I have read books on business, and I know what they all say, and I don't disagree—but I just can't seem to follow them or stay focused on them."

"That's fine," I said. "You don't need to worry about that. Now let's simply begin to adjust your hierarchy of values." So we started with just that basic question: "What are the benefits of building a business that serves ever greater numbers of people?"

Well, at first, he was blank—just staring at me. "It bores me," he said. "I only have this business so I can do what I want to do."

I said, "Let's look at how building and refining your healing business can serve you. For example, could building your business bring you more patients that you could share your metaphysical and spiritual teachings with?"

"Oh," he said. "Well, that is a neat idea. Yes, I could do that."

"All right. Now, do you think you could build a social network out of all your patients with whom you could also share your inspirations and your insights from your metaphysical studies? Would building a business help you build a network of that type?"

"Why, yes. Yes, it would."

So I continued asking him this question until we had seventy-five answers for the question. And along the way, you could see an inner transformation taking place. His eyes started lighting up and he began to get enthused, and he even started jotting down one or two ideas that were coming to him about ways that he could attract some new patients and deepen his ties with his current patients.

"Now I see what I can do!" he exclaimed at one point. "I never thought of it this way before!"

So then I asked him, "How about saving and investing money?"

He said, "I have always had an issue with saving money, I have to admit."

"Then let us break through that," I said. I could see that he had bought into a kind of Eastern mysticism that celebrated austerity as the only true spirituality. But spirit without matter is expressionless, just as matter without spirit is motionless, so I helped him revamp his thinking by linking the process of making, saving, and investing money to his spiritual quests. I wanted him to see the benefits of helping people spiritually by saving, investing money, and building wealth. For example, the more money he made, saved, and invested, the more money he would also have to invest in his spiritual studies and philanthropic activities.

Once again, as he began to get the idea, his eyes lit up and he began coming up with his own ideas. So we moved on to the next question: I asked him how studying business could be of value to him, and how it could be of value to invest and build his wealth. I wanted to link wealth-building and investment with his metaphysical values, so I started correlating investments with ecosystems and his metaphysical interests. I suggested that every time we build wealth, we go up into higher echelons of social contribution and spiritual awareness, so that when we've reached the highest echelon of socio-spiritual development—where nothing within us is missing—when we have the highest abundance—then we are actually mastering our highest metaphysical or spiritual expression. I kept linking every-thing we were saying about money and wealth back to what he per-ceived his metaphysical mission to be.

Next I said, "Look. You say that you don't want to be a slave to money, but you actually *are* a slave to money because you are working for it and worrying about it most of the time. If you are saving and investing money, you'll get to the point where your money starts working for you and you will be its master. Then you won't have to worry about money so much and you'll no longer be a slave to it." I asked him to write down how having a vast fortune and true financial independence could actually serve his spiritual quest. We kept stack-ing up these links between growing his wealth and his highest values until he was really on fire with these new ideas.

Finally, I asked him what would happen if he built his business and accumulated wealth with the goal of contributing it to a cause—a spiritual cause of some kind, such as starting a metaphysical school or helping other spiritual teachers become viable or sustainable with their writing and their spiritual practice.

That is when his eyes really lit up.

"Okay," he said. "I got it."

So by the end of the process, he had more than a hundred reasons why various aspects of business and wealth-building and investing would support his highest value of spiritual growth. I asked him to continue working on the linking exercise on his own, and he enthu-siastically agreed.

His wife came in toward the end of the exercise. She was tentative at first, but when she saw what he had done, she started weeping with appreciation and hugging him, and said, "I wish we had done this a decade ago. Because now I see there are possibilities for you."

Ironically, his wife was all ready to spend this new money she saw coming in on a better house and on other things for her family, but I told her that if she was primarily focused on spending money, she was going to defeat the whole approach. I told her that before she could change her lifestyle, she had to make sure that the two of them were saving and investing and remaining current with their taxes, because otherwise, they were right back in the same cycle, only instead of spending money on his spiritual books, they were spending it on a house and nursery-school fees. Either way, though, they weren't going to build true or lasting wealth. To build true and lasting wealth, they had to focus on saving, not spending, investing, not "lifestyling." It is wise to raise your lifestyle only when you can raise your savings and taxes at equal times and in equal amounts.

They both understood what I was saying, and they left the hotel ready to make a fresh start. I heard from them a few months later. He had gotten out of debt pretty quickly, and a few months after that, he had grown his business by fifty percent. I heard from him about a year after that, when he felt that he was well on his way to having a thriving business and true financial freedom. And he is still pursuing his metaphysical quest because now he has linked his financial freedom to it. In fact, now he sees them as one and the same.

MISTAKEN NOTIONS OF ALTRUISM

If spiritual pursuits and wealth-building can go hand in hand, what about altruism? Although I do believe in service, I am generally suspicious of the actions that many have unwisely called altruism. I consider that what is usually called "altruism" is most often a compensation for feelings of shame and guilt that frequently prevent us from receiving the wealth that we might otherwise build or attract.

Recently, I was working with a gentleman who was attempting to break through his block against receiving and holding on to money.

No matter what he'd tried to do, he didn't seem to be able to get ahead—in fact, he could barely even get by.

This man was very bright, very intelligent, and very involved with charitable giving. He asked me if there was anything he could do to transform his relationship to money.

"Absolutely!" I replied. "I want you to write down a list in which you identify every single thing right up until today that you feel shame or guilt about. I want you to write down every time you feel you messed up, did something wrong, hurt somebody, or deserve blame of any kind."

I knew that often when we minimize ourselves, it's because we feel shame and guilt for doing or not doing something that we misperceive to be more of a drawback than benefit to other people. Although we actually have also simultaneously been of service to these same people, and perhaps frequently have been of a great hidden service, we don't always remember or realize that. Instead, we hold on to our unconscious shame and guilt, which we keep buried deep inside.

Any action or inaction that we haven't cleared or balanced out by finding how it served people can end up diminishing our image of ourselves deeply and unconsciously. So as compensation, we sometimes create the belief that altruism will make us feel "better" about ourselves. Instead of asking for fair and appropriate compensation for our services, which sets up a fair exchange within the socioeconomic world that keeps products and services sustainably flowing, we give away our services because we are afraid to ask for money. Whenever we feel "good" making a difference but don't want to be compensated, it's likely that we are compensating for the shame and guilt of the past—or else that we have a hidden agenda for the future.

So I asked the man who approached me to write down every instance that was provoking his shame and guilt. I asked him to identify how the incidents he felt ashamed of and guilty about served him and the people involved.

"Don't stop until you're truly grateful for whatever you did!" I told him. "Otherwise you will be thinking you are giving away money for charitable purposes—but it will partly be compensation for those buried feelings."

In fact, the number one cause that keeps people from building wealth is guilt and shame. They don't feel worthy of receiving. They don't value themselves. And yet, 99.9 percent of everything that you have been beating yourself up about is because you haven't looked deep enough to see that whatever you did, it was *not* a mistake. There were benefits to you and to the other people involved, which your guilt and your shame are keeping you from seeing.

Meanwhile, your guilt and your shame are causing you to minimize yourself, and as you do, you automatically put wealth-building lower and lower on the hierarchy of your values because you feel unworthy. You are unwilling to receive. And so you are simply spending your money on immediately gratifying consumables and giving other people your money instead of producing, saving, and investing.

At the root of the problem is your effort to live by another person's values rather than your own, which means that even your altruistic service will not be fulfilling for you because your guilt and shame keep you from feeling fulfilled. It's a vicious cycle, because if you're not fulfilling your own highest values, you'll be compensating for that by immediate gratification and consumerism on the one hand . . . and by charitable works and altruism on the other. True service to the world is not giving to others out of guilt or shame or rescuing them from their presumed desperation. It is initiating fair exchange with others and not robbing them of dignity, responsibility, accountability, or productivity. It is seeding in them opportunities to grow their own lives and making them sustainable.

The solution is to clear up your shame and guilt so that you can truly and more fully value yourself. Because when you value yourself, so will the world. Until you live by your highest values, you will likely not value yourself and feel your greatest self-worth. And until you value yourself and money, you will have a hard time holding on to it.

Remember: money circulates through society from whoever values it least to whoever values it most. People who don't value it will have a very hard time staying in business. They are the kind of people who lower their value to get a deal instead of adding their value to receive a fair and sustainable price.

For example, when I first began my professional teaching career, I had difficulty asking for and receiving money for my services as well as difficulty saving or investing anything that I received. But I soon realized that unless I valued my teaching, no one else would. I learned how important it was to value the ideas I was presenting and to value my service as a skilled teacher; otherwise, my contribution to the world through my teaching would be lost.

I also learned how important it was to value money in general. Otherwise I would not be able to first survive and then thrive in the business world of inspired teaching. Every time I valued my ideas, my teaching, and money, my business grew. Now I teach all over the world and I have money working for me instead of me having to desperately work for money.

This sheds an important light on the issue of so-called altruism. When I started teaching professionally, my lowered self-worth made me appear to be altruistic. In reality, though, I simply did not value myself as much, and as a result, I led my students and potential students to value me less as well. When I valued myself and my contribution correctly, I was able to bring my career into balance and to base my work on creating and maintaining true fair exchange.

The irony is that some of the more common forms of altruism are false forms of service. If you really value humanity, you will care enough to figure out the needs and highest values of other people and find a way to fairly serve them, directly or indirectly. In turn, you will help them maintain fair exchange, because otherwise you can rob them of their dignity, fulfillment, and service. So it is wise to build a business that serves ever greater numbers of people by focusing on sustainable fair exchange. Then it is also wise to refine and polish your business, making it as effective and efficient as possible so as to guarantee quality service for your customers or clients and maximizing your company's profits. As you produce those profits, your effort and work will begin to pay off and ultimately serve everyone involved: yourself, your employees, your customers, and your local and global economy.

What some so-called altruists may not realize is that fairly exchanged business is one of the highest forms of service. Running a successful business means that you value people enough to make your company as effective as possible so that you can keep your costs down to compete in the marketplace—which means that you are providing a service at fair cost. You care enough about your employees to make sure their job duties are effective and competitive in the global market, ensuring that they work in an honored and respected business with cutting-edge methods, all of which will make their professional lives more fulfilling in both the short and the long run. And you care enough about yourself to extract enough surplus value out of your labor force so that you receive a profit that gives you enough of a cushion to stabilize the volatilities of your company so you can continue to grow, serve, and awaken your own and others' financial freedom.

YOUR HIGHEST VALUES ARE THE KEY

When I was conducting the Breakthrough Experience in Los Angeles a couple of years ago, a woman came up to me at the end of it and said, "Dr. Demartini, I have one more question that I was afraid to ask during the program. I have been in business for many years and I am just afraid that my business has plateaued. I can't seem to get over this hump, and my overhead is going up while my profit margins are going down. Is there anything you can do to help me with that?"

I said, "Sure. What is the most valuable thing in your life?"

She said, "My daughter."

I walked up to her nineteen-year-old daughter, who had just come to pick up her mom, and said, "Would you please follow me?" I walked her about sixty feet away from her mother, who said, "Dr. Demartini, where are you going?"

I said, "I am taking your daughter. Didn't you say she is the most important thing in your life?"

"She is."

I said, "I am taking her and you will never see her again, until you have $500,000 and your business is double its present size and making greater profits." I looked her straight in the eyes, and I said, "If you don't do this in the next three months, your daughter will die."

Even though at first she could hardly imagine that I was serious, somehow, for just a moment, my Al Pacino act got through to her and she believed me. So I kept going. I said, "The only way to save your daughter's life and get your daughter back is to get $500,000. And you can't borrow it, you can't steal it, and you can't have it given to you. You have to go and double the size of your business and make $500,000 in profits for savings, and you've got three months to do it. If you knew your daughter was going to die and was never going to be seen again, could you do that?"

"Absolutely," she said. "Nothing would stop me."

So I asked her, "What went through your mind as I did that?"

She said, "Dr. Demartini, this has been amazing. As you were saying that my daughter would die, my mind thought of a series of different actions I could do immediately to generate more clients and money in my business."

So there is your proof. As Napoleon Hill, author of groundbreaking book *Think and Grow Rich*, has told us, if you have a burning desire to do something, and it is the highest value in your life, nobody will have to motivate you. You will just automatically come up with creative ways of doing it. When the *why* is big enough, the *hows* take care of themselves.

So to amass wealth, you have to truly value building wealth. In addition to clearing out the guilt and the shame, you need to write down twelve hundred reasons why you want to build a business that fairly serves the public and why you want to build your wealth, until your brain has so many reasons that, like that lady, you can't imagine doing anything but getting your desired outcome. And then you will build wealth, grow your financial freedom, and lay down another foundation stone for a fulfilling and inspired life. That again is the power of applying the Values Factor.

9

Expanding Your Influence

We're here for a reason. I believe a bit of
the reason is to throw little torches out
to lead people through the dark.

—WHOOPI GOLDBERG

Every one of us has an inspired leader within. The question is not
whether we have the capacity to become a leader—each of us
does, from the poorest resident of a Calcutta slum to the most glam-
orous member of a royal family. The question is whether we choose
to awaken and embrace our inherent capacity for leadership or to
overlook and be oblivious to it.

Most of us want to truly make a difference, to be valued enough
to be remembered, and to leave a legacy behind us. Can anyone really
say they want to be forgotten or insignificant? The greater our service
to the world and the more powerful our influence, the more likely we
are to leave our mark in history—not for the sake of grandeur, but for
the sake of higher fulfillment and contribution.

When you think about your own desired level of influence and
leadership, you might aspire to be an entrepreneur, a political leader
or social visionary, the founder of a philanthropic charity or founda-

tion, a leader in the arts or entertainment world, a cutting-edge scientist or inventor, a pioneer in education or medicine, a style-conscious trendsetter or designer, or some type of spiritual leader. Or perhaps you see yourself as a leader on a smaller, more personal scale: in your relationship, family, community, or workplace.

Whether you envision the scope of your leadership as large or small, global or personal, you become an authentic leader by getting in tune with your highest value, which is your purpose, or what you might call your mission.

Do you already see yourself as a leader and wonder how you can expand the scope and effectiveness of your leadership? Or do you yearn to further develop your leadership and wonder why you haven't yet attained the influence you seek? Perhaps you haven't yet dared even to aspire to leadership, believing that true leaders have qualities that you believe you lack?

One of the more powerful moments of my seminar the Breakthrough Experience is when my participants are working with one of the sets of questions contained within the Demartini Method. Upon deep introspection, they discover that they already possess every quality they admire, as well as every quality they dislike, to precisely the same degree as those whom they admire or dislike the most. The Breakthrough Experience also reveals to my participants that their social world is assisting them in awakening their most authentic nature so that they can become the leaders they have the potential to be. To paraphrase Marianne Williamson, we serve the world by shining, not shrinking.

To help you achieve *your* potential, I'll share with you the secrets to becoming an authentic leader, including the insights I provide to the business leaders for whom I regularly do training and consultations. Whether you are a leader in a religious organization, an educational institution, a profit-making enterprise, a company, a department, an area of expertise, or a family, you can benefit from understanding how your highest values guide and shape every aspect of the group you lead. The Values Factor can help you realize your leadership potential and become the great leader that you have it in you to be.

THE SEVEN FEARS THAT BLOCK YOUR PATH

Like everyone else in the world, you have a unique mission of service. And though you may assume or claim that your mission is unknown or at least unclear, it still remains silently within, yearning to express itself. If you feel you are unclear about your own mission or if you do not see yourself as a leader inspired by that hidden inner mission, you may be allowing the following fears to block your vast potential:

1. Fear of Breaking the Morals and Ethics of Some Spiritual Authority

Have you ever wanted to do something that you felt was deeply meaningful but stopped in your tracks for fear of what some spiritual authority might think about you? Perhaps you feared acting in a manner that someone or some group might not perceive as being "spiritual" or moral enough. Or perhaps you feared being rejected by some spiritual authority, or being shunned by some religious or spiritual leader or movement. You might have denied the truth of your own highest values and subordinated them to a so-called spiritual authority, or you might have avoided actions that seemed to be called for by your highest values. You might even have been immobilized by fear of disapproval, rejection, or shunning.

Perhaps you were simply following the spiritual rules taught to you by your parents, whether or not those rules have any relevance—to you *or* your parents! I'm thinking of the story about the lady who cut the leg off the turkey because that's what her mother, grandmother, and great-grandmother did. When the family finally asked the great-grandmother why she had always prepared turkey in that way, she said, "Because I had a short oven and I couldn't fit the whole turkey in there." Yet three generations later and with a huge oven, her family was still cutting the leg off the turkey—simply because they had never questioned *why*.

You might want to ask yourself whether, like that family, you are subordinating yourself to some spiritual dogmas, values, or principles that you have been taught without stopping to question them or to ask whether they fit your own authentic highest values. I am not denying that many spiritual traditions do contain many valuable ideas, principles, and guidelines; I am just suggesting that before you blindly follow any dogmatic idea from any tradition, it is wise to make sure that the idea is sound or meaningful to you.

Ironically, many of the inspired people who initiated those spiritual teachings and their evolving traditions did not subordinate themselves to other previous spiritual teachers or leaders. They had their own authentic, inspired, and in some cases mystical visions and then passed their torches from their hearts to others. If you admire the founder of some spiritual tradition, give yourself permission to acknowledge and awaken within yourself whatever you see in them. Allow yourself to stand on their shoulders instead of living in their shadows, and be willing to question every precept before you blindly follow or subordinate yourself. If you find that something is true to you, incorporate it and live it. But don't blindly do anything simply because you have been told to do so. Like the spiritual leaders who inspired you, find the authentic leader that lives within you and manifest that leader into the world. By living congruently according to your highest values, your leadership will spontaneously emerge from within, along with your inspired mission. There is no reason that we cannot bring forth today just as great a spiritual leader as we have ever had in the past.

2. Fear of Not Being Smart Enough

Perhaps you are shrinking from manifesting your authentic leader because you're afraid of not being smart enough. Or perhaps you're afraid of not having the right degree, credential, or background. Not having a degree doesn't have to stop you—but *fear* of not having a degree might cause you to hold *yourself* back.

However, there is nearly always somebody out there with no degree who goes out and changes history. Did you know that people can get an entire PhD studying just one tiny portion of another person's life? And that the average PhD takes about four more years to acquire after someone has gotten their undergraduate degree? So if you are between the ages of thirty and seventy, you have in you anywhere from seven to seventeen PhD's worth of experiences! Someday, someone could make a PhD out of studying your life—if you honor yourself and give yourself permission to do something extraordinary. So I want you to go and look into the mirror and tell yourself, "I am amazingly intelligent, and my life has earned me multiple PhDs!"

I am not telling you not to get an advanced education. I myself had nearly ten years of college and professional training and then continued on with an extensive schedule of diverse forms of advanced education. I am all for education, whether it is self-taught or comes from somebody else, but I don't want you to let a lack of diplomas or the standards of any school stop you from your dreams, because many if not most schools are going to set lower standards than I hope you set for yourself. Even some Ivy League educational institutions demand from their students less than is truly required to excel in the real world of business and the professions. So don't go for the bare minimum—go for your most ingenious dreams.

I can make a list of so many people who never finished high school but who today are multimillionaires, billionaires, or world leaders in various fields. Even before I got my advanced degree, I wanted to be among those leaders, because I fully intended to make a contribution to planet Earth. I didn't want to make some vague contribution; I wanted to leave a mark and make a memorable contribution to history. I am very inspired to contribute enough service to the world to achieve that. And the most effective way to make that kind of mark is to be authentic—to stand up and break through the limitations of any stagnant belief systems that you might hold. The key is knowing that deep inside you, with or without your degree, you possess something really magnificent: the power to be an extraordinary individual and a unique leader.

I wonder what would happen if you allowed your inner leader to come out into the light of day. I wonder what would happen if you set yourself socially impacting goals that you knew you were willing to work toward. I wonder what would happen if you chunked those goals down into small enough bites so that you could overcome any resistance about taking each step and relentlessly pursued them. I wonder what would happen if you surrounded yourself with people who wanted you to achieve those goals, and if you delegated whatever you could to other people—friends, colleagues, employees—so that you personally could stay completely focused on your vision of leading. (For more about delegating, see Chapter 7 as well as further on in this chapter.) You might find that focusing on your mission—the reflection of your highest values—while owning the traits of anyone you imagine to be more intelligent, drives out any fears about intelligence, credentials, or degrees, allowing you to expand your influence and manifest your inner leader.

3. Fear of Failure

I don't believe in the idea of failure. I believe that what most people call failure is simply feedback. When you are truly inspired by something, and it is linked to your highest values, you cannot fail, because you don't give up. You just keep pursuing your objective. You might fall, maybe even several times, but you will just keep getting back up again.

So if you fall and do *not* get back up, what is that? That is a gift, because your unwillingness to get up again is letting you know that what you are going after isn't really all that important to you. You don't give up on the things that truly matter to you. You only give up on the things that don't.

This is why I say that there is no failure; there is only feedback. Failure is just a label that you impose on yourself when you were expecting yourself to achieve something that isn't truly aligned with your highest values. That expectation was a fantasy, because you were expecting yourself to live outside your highest values, which simply cannot be sustained. So what looks like failure is nothing more than feedback, pushing you to set more meaningful goals that truly are important to you.

Most super-achievers have a list of so-called failures greater than yours. But they don't view those experiences as failures; they, too, view them as feedback that allows them to further refine their goals, giving them information about what works and what doesn't, or helping them to see more clearly what matters to them most. Each time a super-achiever falls, they get back up on their feet again because they perceive that the world is working on their behalf.

That's what happens when you set a goal that is completely aligned with your highest values: You tend to walk your talk. You tend to awaken your leadership and your certainty. You tend to feel grateful. And you begin to believe that everything is working on your behalf. When you live by your highest values, you are not a victim of your history but rather a master of your destiny.

On the other hand, every time you set a goal that is not congruent with your highest values, you are likely to procrastinate, hesitate, and be frustrated in your attempt to fulfill your objective. You are likely to experience the ABCD's of negativity and to minimize yourself. Then you begin to doubt yourself and compare yourself with the people whose values you have injected into yourself . . . and then you might give up on your goal. Instead of living on the shoulders of giants as your true, authentic, and empowered self, you begin to live in other people's shadows and shrink.

So if fear of failure is stopping you, the solution is very simple: reconnect to your highest values and make sure that your mission, your highest values, and your goal are completely aligned. Make sure you have identified your highest values and then find at least two hundred ways that reaching your goal will help fulfill those values. When you are in pursuit of your highest values, you are willing to experience both pleasure and pain, and so-called failures look just like momentary feedback. Once again, the Values Factor is the key.

4. Fear of Losing Money or of Not Making Money

There is no lack of money on this planet. There are, however, some people who are not driven enough to go out and perform the services that many other people need in order to generate or earn it. And there is a lack of creativity about coming up with inspired ways to perform those services. People who vastly care about others find ways to serve them and in turn have access to nearly unlimited reservoirs of money.

There is nothing outside of you that is keeping abundant sources of money away from you. Being your true and empowered self certainly doesn't keep money away from you. Not providing a service, not appreciating the value and purpose of money, and not valuing yourself is what keeps money away from you. The greater the service you provide, the more money you can potentially generate. The more you value money, the more money you will wisely manage and keep. So if you are not saving, investing, and accumulating money, you might want to go back to Chapter 8 and link your goal of building wealth to your highest values. And if you are not generating or receiving money, you might want to figure out whom you are not serving.

Every time you set a goal that is congruent with your highest values, your self-worth goes up. When I teach the Breakthrough Experience, I work with people who have attempted for years to run their life according to social ideals and unrealistic fantasies, and they inevitably minimize themselves in the process. Then I help them recognize their true highest values and then to set goals that are congruent with those values, and suddenly, they see how to break through their issues and build momentum moving forward, because they finally understand what truly drives them. Then they become more consciously congruent with their highest values, and their self-worth suddenly grows. They can more freely ask for what they want because their "deserve level" begins to expand. This is why it is so important to master the Values Factor.

5. Fear of Losing Loved Ones or the Respect of Loved Ones

Perhaps, like many people, you fear that if you pursue fulfilling your highest values and become an inspired leader, your spouse will leave you, or your kids will think you failed them, or your parents will disown you. If these are your fears, I invite you to consider what your highest values truly are.

In some cases, people's highest values revolve around their loved ones. I worked with a woman in Florida who told me that she had long desired to start her own business but then became trapped when she became married and pregnant with a series of children. She kept fantasizing about her business and beating herself up over not ever starting it. In the back of her mind she assumed that when her children grew up, *then* maybe she would do the business she imagined she wanted to do.

Twenty years went by, her children all grew up and went off to college, and, she told me, "Now I keep concerning myself with my children's lives, and I can't seem to ever get around to starting up my business. I am beginning to think that maybe I am too old now."

I asked what it felt like inside to say she wanted to do something and then not do it.

"I feel like a failure," she told me.

I shook my head. "What this really means is that your highest value all this time was your children," I said to her. "Your business was not truly the most important value to you. If it was, you would have started it up a long time ago. So instead of torturing yourself with unrealistic expectations, why don't you just acknowledge that your children were the most important values in your life and that it is perfectly okay. There is nothing wrong with you. Your highest values dictated your destiny over the last twenty years, and they are dictating your destiny right now. They dictate what you see, what you decide, and what you act upon. Your whole life is an expression of your highest values. So if you are not fulfilled in life, it's not because you 'failed' to do things. You are simply not appreciating yourself and your life because you unrealistically expect yourself to do something that is not truly highest on your values."

As that woman questioned herself, I invite you to question yourself by considering what your life has truly demonstrated. Have your loved ones been your true highest values? Have you injected into yourself some social idealisms or the highest values of some authorities or loved ones? Do you think you "should" fulfill these values or social idealisms but yet are not actually pursuing them because something else is *truly* more important to you, such as your children or some other value?

You can get clarity on these issues and overcome your fears if you keep asking yourself, "What are my true highest values? What is my inspired mission? Am I consciously living congruently with my highest values and my mission, or am I subordinating my highest values to someone else's and attempting to be someone I am not?" Answering those questions can help put your fears into perspective. It could be wise to review once again the thirteen value determinants from Chapter 2.

When we admire, are infatuated with, or become subordinate to our loved ones, we often live in fear of what they might say or do if we don't attempt to live according to their values. Until we set ourselves free of this subordination, we will live with moral dilemmas and internal conflicts, and we will judge ourselves by their values with the superego that we have internalized from them or from other authority figures. Yet all the while, we are still unconsciously living according to our own true highest values.

Wouldn't it be more fulfilling to simply identify those values and structure our lives around them? Or, alternatively, wouldn't it be more fulfilling to change our highest values to match our intended goals? Otherwise, we are living a kind of divided life, which keeps us from finding the fulfillment and inspiration that we might otherwise attain.

6. Fear of Rejection

Have you kept yourself from becoming an authentic leader because you fear that someone would reject you for doing what you love or for pursuing your highest values? This powerful fear might be keeping you not only from acknowledging and awakening your inner leader but from even imagining that you could.

We only fear the rejection of those whom we have put above us and whom we have subordinated ourselves to or are dependent upon. The moment we own that the admired traits that we imagine in these other people are inside ourselves to the same degree, we liberate ourselves from the fear of their rejection, and we give ourselves permission to play in a greater arena of leadership opportunity.

Allowing your vision to grow and expand is one of the keys to reaching your full leadership potential. My earliest postgraduate profession was being a chiropractor. I worked with spinal conditions, and I did very well. I owned one of the largest facilities in Houston.

Eventually, I felt it was time for me to expand further. As I recommended in Chapter 7, I started delegating the lower-priority work that I found less inspiring so that I could focus only on what I found most inspiring. I hired another doctor and some staff; then I hired a second doctor and some more staff. I ended up employing thirteen doctors over the years, with five doctors working for me at any one time.

Then I realized that public speaking in the mornings, at lunch, or in the evenings could generate more patients than just sitting in my office treating patients all day. So I began speaking throughout the city of Houston, on radio, and on television, where I had my own show, *Dr. Demartini Health Hints*. I realized that what I did best was reaching out to people and inspiring them toward a wellness lifestyle and more fulfilled living.

Next I realized that I was still limiting my service to just my own office. If I wanted to expand my influence any further, I would either have to go out and build another set of offices, or else I would have to go out and teach other doctors how to do what I did while getting handsomely paid for it.

I chose the latter. Then, after speaking to and consulting for thousands of doctors, I realized that I was limiting myself to influencing primarily health professionals and that there was a whole world of additional industries that I could reach!

And so I gave myself permission to open that doorway and just keep going. Today, I actually influence more patients than I did in my office because now I sometimes speak to as many as nine thousand doctors at a time while reaching out to hundreds of additional industries.

My influence expanded, in other words, when I realized that I had to give myself permission to release the shackles of my limited thinking and allow myself to do what I was inspired to do. The more I delegated responsibilities and the more congruent with my highest values that I became, the greater my vision and sphere of influence. I wonder what *you* could do if you kept breaking through the limits of your own fears—particularly the fear of rejection. Fear is simply an unrealistic expectation based on an imbalanced perspective. It is the assumption that as we imagine the future, we will experience more challenge than support, more pain than pleasure, more negative than positive, or more loss than gain.

But the world does not ever truly provide such an imbalance. It does not have a negative without a positive. So as long as we live with the unrealistic fantasy of obtaining a positive without a negative, or as long as we live in fear of a negative without a positive, we will be immobilized instead of going forward in pursuit of our mission.

In the Breakthrough Experience, I have everybody scan their life and look at everything they believe was a mistake and then find out . how it served them and others, so they have something to be grateful for instead of something to be frustrated, burdened, or shamed by. That breakthrough dissolves their baggage and turns it into fuel. And then they break through their fears involving the future and instead allow their past experiences to catalyze them to do something amazing in their future. That is how you can overcome fear of rejection: by understanding that every perceived negative always holds great positive as well—so there is never really anything to be afraid of.

7. Fear of Somehow Not Having the Vitality, the Looks, or the Body Required to Fulfill Your Mission

This is a common fear, especially among people in middle age or older, but it is just as illusory as the other six fears we have examined. For example, I recently worked with a fifty-seven-year-old woman who was completely preoccupied with her looks and age. "I know there is no way that I can compete with thirty-five- or forty-year-olds," she said to me. "Those women are young and gorgeous, and I just know that I am going to lose my husband to one of them. And she'll be able to do a lot more with my kids, so I'll possibly even lose my family to her. And at my job, there are a whole crop of those beautiful young women coming along, and I'm sure that they are going to get the promotions I desire, or perhaps they'll even take my job. I just can't compete anymore."

I said, "If you truly value keeping your husband and your job, then upgrade what you are offering physically. Look in the mirror. You are not doing everything you could to compete. Today, for a moderate fee, you can upgrade your overall appearance, so that you could compete with any woman out there. If you are really worried about not having a thirty-five-year-old's looks, why don't you pay a body trainer, dermatologist, and plastic surgeon to upgrade your appearance and also advance your education or skills?"

She looked at me, appalled. "But I shouldn't have to do that!" she said.

"Listen," I said, "the reality of the world out there is that people are living according to their highest values, and youth, beauty, intelligence, and skills sell. If your husband and employer are not fulfilled by what they have, they are going to look for alternatives. It is wise to face a bit of reality. Even though you might be in a long-term relationship, if and when your highest values aren't being fulfilled, you sometimes start wondering whether your relationship is working for you. So you are not really in a relationship with another person. You are in a relationship with both of your highest values. If your loving, intimate partner is not even remotely fulfilling your highest values, you open the door for other people to potentially enter in. Relationships are often by default, enduring only until something perceived to be more fulfilling comes along. If nothing comes along that you perceive as more rewarding, you generally stay put.

"Now, how do you keep the relationship you are in, or the job, if you still want to do that? The best way to keep it is to empower your life. Shine, so that your loving partner and your employer are around somebody who appears beautiful, inspiring, and productive to them, and then master the art of communicating your talents in terms of their values [as we saw in Chapter 5]. When you do this—which might mean maintaining some of your competitive beauty and skills—they won't want to look at anyone else or go anywhere else because they won't be able to get a more fulfilling deal anyplace else. When you can stand up and look into the mirror and say, 'Hey, baby, I got something,' and mean it; when you can honor what you have; the world around you will treat you the way the world inside you is treating you.

"But if you keep minimizing yourself to somebody else, then they are going to minimize you to somebody else. You are fifty-seven years old. If you think a thirty-five- or forty-year-old woman has got something more than you, you are not honoring what you have—its equivalent. So you can either appreciate what you already have to offer, or you can upgrade your present package so you can compete with that younger woman on the grounds of appearance and skills. Or you can go and find out the benefits of your unique form of stability, intelligence, experience, and talent. You have a track record. An employer basically takes a gamble with that younger woman. Do you see what I mean?"

First I showed her what she *wasn't* missing. Then I helped her realize that if she wanted to compete on a physical level, she could do that with a little effort. But if we are frightened by what somebody else has physically that we imagine we don't, we minimize ourselves.

OVERCOMING THE SEVEN FEARS

So what happens when you begin to fear the rejection of loved ones, when you fear the loss of money, when you fear that you are going to "fail," fear that you are going to break the morals and ethics of the spiritual authority that you revere, and fear that you don't have the looks, vitality, or energy to become the leader that you might be or to fulfill the mission that you value above all else? Then your fears cause you to continue to further subordinate yourself to all the people that you believe have what you unwisely imagine that you don't: the people who might reject you, the people with money, the people whom you see as successful, the people whom you see as spiritual and righteous, the people whom you believe have the looks, vitality, and energy that you assume you don't.

And then, when you strive to achieve your goal, you find that very difficult to do, because the bottom line is, you are not likely to stay focused on your goals unless you live true to your highest values, and you are not going to live true to your highest values as long as you are minimizing yourself relative to any human being on earth. Respect them? Yes. Minimize yourself? No.

These fears cloud the clarity of what's inside your mind and heart, which is trying to express itself through your highest value: your mission.

Becoming a leader requires the kind of inner certainty that you can only get from living according to your own highest values. If you have to ask somebody else, "Where am I going?" you're not honoring your own inner leader. You are denying what you know inside. The person with the most certainty is the one who leads. Why? Because everybody is drawn to that person—to their certainty, to their clarity and poised equilibrium, to their ability to see the order and balance in the universe, and to their adaptability and ability to handle paradoxes involving complementary opposites. Everyone is drawn to the person who understands that every single one of us—every unique set of values—has an important role to play.

If you set goals that align with your highest values, you will awaken a feeling of certainty because you will "walk your walk": you will say what you intend to do, and then you will accomplish that very thing. By contrast, when you try to live according to someone else's highest values—when you live in any way that does not align with your own highest values—you will tend to doubt yourself. You'll become uncertain, preferring the security of remaining a follower rather than growing into your own authentic leadership.

If you'd like to awaken the latent leadership within you, your first step is to set goals that align with your highest values. Aligning your goals with your highest values helps you believe in yourself, take greater calculated risks, and act upon opportunities that no one else can even see. You claim your identity as a leader, and you identify yourself with your mission, which is another way of saying that you devote yourself fully to the fulfillment of your highest value.

In 1973, when I was still just a teenager, I became clear about what my mission was and I wrote out all my goals on some sheets of paper that I later stapled together. I set up a series of words of power about how I wanted my life to be so I could read them every day. Here are some of them:

I am clear on my inspiring mission.
I am a genius and I apply my wisdom.
I am a master of persistence, and I do what it takes.
I do what I love and I love what I do.
I am at the right place at the right time to meet the right people to make the right deal.
I am a master teacher, healer, and philosopher traveling the world.

I was very careful to write only what was inspiring and meaningful to me. I wanted to write down only those goals that I truly wanted to work toward. Every day, I would read these statements—sometimes many times a day. And I kept adding words of power along with goals and objectives as they arose.

Today those stapled typewritten pages have evolved into my more than fourteen-hundred-page *State of the Mission* book previously mentioned. In that book, I document whatever I set out to do. I document what I accomplish. I document what I am grateful for. I spend hours doing so, because I have learned that your innermost dominant thought becomes your outermost tangible reality. As we have seen, most people go through their lives setting goals that are not congruent with their highest values. As a result, they don't fully achieve their goals, and then they don't even want to set goals, because doing so is frustrating and unfulfilling when you doubt your ability to achieve them. Therefore most people basically live in other peoples' goals or vicariously through other people's lives instead of awakening their own inner leader.

But as we have seen in several chapters, Parkinson's Law states that if you don't fill your day with your own high-priority actions, your day will automatically be filled by other people's high-priority tasks. Likewise, if you don't plant flowers in the garden of your mind, showing how you want your life to be, somebody else plants those gardens, and you live other people's lives. You won't have fulfillment living somebody else's life, because you have your own unique set of values. You will really only feel fulfilled when you live by your own true highest values.

So to make sure that I was setting goals that were congruent with my highest values, I started writing down my goals and my accomplishments. At first the people I hung out with didn't see much difference. But within a decade they could see a great difference and now, more than four decades later, they can see a vast difference, and so can I.

The people who didn't list their congruent goals and didn't document their many accomplishments are still doing something that is less expansive and fulfilling. They have held themselves back. Deep inside, they certainly had big dreams, but they never gave themselves permission to let their dreams out and achieve them.

By contrast, as I started writing down my goals and accomplishments, as I documented what I had done and refined what I intended, I began to realize that although some of these actions took a bit of time, it was worth any amount of time it might take to become a true and more expansive leader. When you write down your goals and accomplishments, you are saying to yourself, "See, you are worth the time to structure the life that you dream about! You are worth Master-Planning[1] your life. You are worth breaking through the limitations.

---

[1] Master Planning for Life: This is the title of one of the seventy-two courses I present around the world designed to assist attendees in living more masterful and empowered lives. It consists of three intense days of answering two thousand questions about every area of their lives so as to help them create an inspired master plan to govern and live their more amazing and empowered lives by. Go to www.drdemartini.com and click "Programs" on the left-side menu.

You are worth defining how you would love your life to be. You are worth knowing what your highest values are and how to break through your fears and get on with you highest-priority actions, because *this is your life*. And at the end of your life, you are going to ask yourself a very simple question: did you do everything you could with everything you were given? You want to be able to say, "Yes. Absolutely."

MANIFESTING YOUR AUTHENTIC LEADER

If you avoid your own leadership potential:

- You will probably hold yourself back from your greatest service and accomplishments.
- You will probably perceive yourself to be a follower more than a leader.
- You will probably view yourself as worth less than others and thereby lessen your social influence.
- You will probably tend to subordinate yourself to others and live in their shadow.
- You will reduce the likelihood of leaving a legacy.
- You will probably give yourself less permission to make a big difference in the world.
- You will probably be less clear about your social cause or mission.
- You will probably be vulnerable to victim mentality rather than embracing victory mentality.
- You will probably stand down more than stand up and stand out.
- You will probably let others become the authors of your life.

If you align your intentions and goals with your highest values and link your actions to your mission for leadership, you will be more likely to:

continued...

> - Initiate social causes.
> - Communicate with and inspire people.
> - Lead and influence.
> - Transcend the distractions and influences of others.

DIFFERENT SCALES OF TIME AND SPACE

Now, as I've been saying, everybody has a vast potential. But that doesn't mean everybody recognizes that potential, acknowledges it, or wakes it all up. People wake up their potential for leadership to varying degrees, which is why our corporations and our governments are hierarchically tiered.

Which scale do you operate on? You might lead:

- a household.
- a home owners' association.
- a community or district.
- as city councilor.
- as mayor.
- as governor.
- as congressperson.
- as senator.
- as president, prime minister, or equivalent.

Each of these leaders has experienced different degrees of emergence and realization of their potential. It is the same thing in business. You might lead as a:

- factory worker.
- supervisor.
- lower-level manager.

- middle manager.
- upper manager.
- CEO.
- visionary.
- sage.

It simply depends on whether you allow yourself to honor your great inner potential.

The difference between becoming a sage and a factory worker has a lot to do with how well you know what your highest values are and how well you start organizing your life to live according to them. People in higher positions of leadership are masters of the art of delegating lower-priority tasks, and so, as they emerge into their potential, they move rapidly through the chain of authority and rise up in the game of leadership, shedding branches of their mighty tree along the way. They let go of lower priorities so that they can get on with their highest priorities—those most congruent with their highest values.

For some people, the potential for great leadership is there but because they are not honoring their own highest values, the probability of them realizing their leadership potential is low. After all, how can you be a great leader when you keep subordinating yourself to outside authorities and the social idealisms that surround you, rather than living by your own highest values? Once you give yourself permission to define your direction of leadership, you are then able to lead and to shine. The key, as always, is to begin living according to your highest values—to begin living consciously with congruency and integrity. That is how you increase the probability of bringing forth your great inborn leader.

At every level of leadership, you will experience a differently sized space and time horizon. In fact, your ability to see things in terms of larger horizons is one of the key factors enabling you to rise to higher levels of leadership.

Let's say that you are a factory worker on the shop floor. You will probably have a short time horizon and a small space horizon. You will likely think in term of hours and days, and you will bring order and organization to a small space. As a general rule, your sphere of influence will generally be smaller.

Now, if you're a supervisor, your time horizon is probably week to week. And you probably govern a little more space and bring order and organization to a somewhat wider area.

Lower management thinks in terms of month to month. Their space horizons are slightly wider.

Middle management thinks in terms of year to year. Their space horizons are wider still.

Upper management sees things in terms of decade to decade. They have greater space horizons than any of the levels below them.

A CEO might view life in terms of generations, and of course, their space horizon extends into every part of the globe where that company does business or might someday aspire to do business.

A visionary might run a giant corporation that owns several subsidiaries, each with its own CEO. The visionary's time horizon extends from a generation to a century. They can envision their company into the next century as they ensure that it will have some sort of longevity. They think in terms of the entire planet, usually in a very in-depth way.

The sage thinks in terms of centuries or even a millennium. They think outside the terrestrial sphere. I have met some people on that level. Sometimes they even think in terms of eternity. With regard to space horizons, they think in terms of the astronomical.

So the magnitude of space and time within your innermost dominant thought determines the level of conscious evolution you have mastered. How big a game are you playing? If you are a visionary and you try to talk to the factory worker to tell them about the vision that you are planning over the next century, all they are interested in is making sure that they have food for the day or possibly the week.

Their time horizons simply don't extend out to where the visionary's does. Not that they don't want to hear about the vision. But they won't relate to it. As you go down in the scale of time and space horizons, people want more immediate gratification; they live by more impulse, instinct, and passion rather than according to their inspired mission. As you go up, you'll find people who are willing to embrace ever greater pains and pleasures, eases and difficulties, challenges and supports, and ever-growing labels of villain and hero, sinner and saint, or vicious and virtuous to achieve their ever more effective, empowering, and inspiring causes.

Every time you set a clear intention or a goal that is congruent with your highest values, you will walk your talk, gain certainty, and grow. You will also tend to set the next goal even bigger. You tend to give yourself permission to expand, to see things in an even longer term, to create a longer, bigger vision.

This is a spontaneous evolution, because your innermost nature yearns to keep expanding. Nobody wants to shrink. Nobody gets up and says, "I want to be less spiritually aware, less mentally aware, less financially aware, less aware of family, less socially aware, less aware of my wellness, less aware of my career." Everybody wants to expand their horizons. They want to expand their sphere of awareness and influence. That is why I don't recommend going to a shrink. I recommend going to a stretcher!

One of the greatest ways I know of to expand your horizons is to begin to delegate to others whatever tasks that are not inspiring and that are not of highest priority to you, so that you can focus on only the most productive, profitable, meaningful, and inspiring activities. Use the following exercise to learn more about delegating.

Exercise 1: Assessing Productivity

Following Parkinson's Law (see Chapter 7), the way to optimize your productivity and potential is to identify the most productive and inspiring tasks and then focus only on those, delegating away everything else. Follow the instructions below to reorganize your day and your week according to what is most productive and inspiring.

Instructions:

STEP 1. List every activity you do in an average day within a typical week. Preferably, you would list your daily activities hour by hour.

STEP 2. In a column beside each activity, write down what income to the company or organization or household that activity produces per hour or even per minute, if that is more accurate.

STEP 3. In a column beside that, write how much money it would cost to delegate that business, organizational, or household activity to someone else. For example, if you dislike filing, how much would it cost to hire someone to come in and take care of your filing for you? If you don't feel inspired by driving your children to their lessons and activities, how much would it cost to hire someone else to do it?

STEP 4. In a column beside that, note how much of your time it takes *you* to do the task per day.

STEP 5. Finally, in the furthest column, rate how much meaning the task has for you a scale of one to seven, where one is "not meaningful at all" and seven is "the most meaningful task I can imagine performing." In some cases, the most fulfilling and important tasks are the ones that are exceptionally inspiring or meaningful, even though they may not be as financially productive. For example, you might have clients that would pay you $500 per hour to consult with them on business investments, whereas it would cost you only $20 per hour to hire someone to drive your kids to their after-school activities. Yet perhaps that time in the car with your kids is your chance to

connect with them and catch up on what they are doing, which might
be worth far more to you than $500 per hour.

STEP 6. Take action to delegate the least productive, least profitable, and/or least meaningful tasks to someone else who would love
to do them while focusing your own time on only the most inspiring,
productive, and most meaningful.

It was this exercise that helped set me free to live the inspiring life
I have today.

THE FIVE S'S OF LEADERSHIP

Now that we've seen what might *keep* you from being a leader, let's
look more closely at the Five S's that can *make* you a leader:

1. Service. True leaders know whom, what, and how to serve.
They know what they're here to contribute to the world. Whereas
most people shrink from tackling the world's challenges, the true
leader says, "No, my nature is to expand. The only way I can expand
is to seek and conquer new frontiers of the great unknown, to solve
significant problems, to answer great questions, to solve mysteries, to
fulfill some voids that are not being fulfilled, to take on challenges
that I see are really opportunities, or to transform some form of chaos
into order." They go after that which inspires them, which they recognize as their mission. They have their own particular issue in the
world—one particular problem or one collective group of problems
that they feel inspired to solve based on their highest values.

To serve, it helps to know what your service is. What void, what
problem, what mystery, what challenge, what question, what missing
item, what chaos in the world are you dedicated to solving or filling or bringing order to? A consultant answers questions that people

cannot answer for themselves. A specialist provides skills that people do not have for themselves. A parent provides nurturing, caring, affection, and guidance that children may feel they cannot provide for themselves. Those are all types of service.

My service is education. I help people learn about human behavior, human potential, and human achievement so people may have more inspiring, meaningful, and empowered lives. I have spent my life researching and studying these fields. My service is to learn what I can and then share what I know.

Another way to put it is that your service is your way of bringing your highest value to the greatest amount of people who value what you have to offer. Commitment to sharing your highest values in service is what makes you a leader.

2. Specialized knowledge. If you want to become a leader, identify your highest value and then follow your spontaneous desire to gain specialized knowledge in it. Whatever is highest on your values is where you love to seek growth and learning. One of the signs that you are living congruently with your highest values is that you don't have to be asked to go study and learn and read and take classes in educating yourself in your chosen field of service. You have tapped into your highest values so deeply that you spontaneously want to learn more to help you fulfill what is most important to you.

When you're deeply connected to your highest value, you automatically want to learn more about it. Nobody has to get you up in the morning to study the topic that matters most to you. You desire it so deeply that you pursue it naturally. And this specialized knowledge allows you to make a special contribution, because you naturally desire to become an expert in that particular field, whether that field is supplying the world with an adequate water supply or helping your children grow into responsible and loving adults. Whatever matters most to you, that is what you will run to learn about—and that is where you can become the authentic leader you were born to be.

Now, it may be that your present field of service requires mastery of specialized knowledge that currently does not inspire you. Perhaps the desire of the company you are working for, or leading, is to supply the world with adequate water by way of specialized engineering, but what inspires you is solving the political and economic problems of supplying that water—the engineering aspect does not inspire you at all. That's fine. Then as a leader, you may want to build a team of engineers that includes people who *are* inspired by the specialized engineering knowledge that leaves you feeling dry and cold. In this way, you can free yourself up to do what you are more perfectly designed and inspired to do—to solve the socioeconomic challenges. Either way—gaining the specialized knowledge yourself or building a team to provide it—is the sign of your leadership. You either want to know the most about a particular topic or to get the people who know the most about it onto your team.

By the way, if you study for thirty minutes a day in the field that you would love to master, at the end of seven years, you could be at the cutting edge of your chosen field. If you study an hour day in the field you want to master, in four years, you could be at the cutting edge. If you study for two hours a day, it will take you two and a half years, and three hours a day brings you to the cutting edge of a field in less than two years.

This type of study needs to be highly concentrated and focused to be effective. So I encourage you to take either my own or someone else's speed-reading and learning program to expedite that process. I personally have gained a great competitive advantage through learning how to speed-read, because this specialized knowledge has enabled me to read more than twenty-nine thousand books.

If you love serving, you will love learning about the service you are providing. And you will feel inspired and fulfilled because you are pursuing what is highest on your scale of values. So the different aspects of leadership all continue to reinforce each other and to increase your share of inspiration and fulfillment.

3. Speaking. Most people are terrified of public speaking, and many people are even nervous about speaking to strangers in a private setting, such as a party or office function. This is primarily due to your subordination or minimization to others. When you are too humble to admit that what you see in others is equally within you, you will feel too intimidated or insecure to confidently speak. But every time you set a goal that aligns with your highest values, and own the traits you see and look up to in others, you gain confidence and level the playing field. You say, "I know, I am, I can," and you come out of your shell. You want to express yourself because that is one of the greatest and most empowering ways of sharing your mission and inspiring others to help you fulfill both your highest values and their own.

I have a saying about speaking or teaching, which is that *your fluency is proportional to your congruency*. In other words, when you are speaking about a topic that is meaningful and inspiring and that is congruent with your highest values, your speaking confidence and fluency will come naturally. So challenging yourself to articulate your message and your vision through public or corporate speaking, or even through speaking in more intimate venues, such as to friends, spouse, or children, is extremely useful, because all of these types of speaking push you even closer to being congruent with your highest values. This is another power offered by the Values Factor.

Moreover, speaking well automatically gives you an advantage. By speaking well, you move into the top twenty percent of the world. This is a figure commonly used among those who teach or coach public speaking, and I have found it confirmed by my own experience. Those with a mission have a message, but if you can't share your message, fewer people are ever going to hear about it. The more people you meet and greet and speak to, the more people you get to work with. If you can get your message out on radio or television, you have that much more influence. Your voice is the instrument upon which you play the symphony of your life.

4. Selling. When I say "selling," I'm not necessarily limiting the concept to exchanging a product or service for money, though selling could also apply to that. But what I'm really talking about is how to sell what is important to you in terms of other people's highest values. How do you achieve what you value most by enrolling others on the basis of *their* highest values? That is what leaders learn to do because they realize that people ultimately act only in pursuit of what they value most. If you want people to participate in or become inspired by your mission, you have to help them see why it will fulfill *their* highest values. Then you influence and lead. Other people are only committed to the fulfillment of *their* highest values, not necessarily yours.

Selling is also a form of caring about people, because you take what inspires you—your product, service, or idea—and you communicate about it to others by showing them how it will serve their highest values. Obviously without sales, there is no growth, so sales is a key form of expanding your influence and becoming a leader.

This is true even in the intimate sphere of family and personal relations. For example, suppose you are concerned that your partner is not currently engaged in work that he or she finds inspiring. You might sell your partner on the idea of taking a course such as the Breakthrough Experience, reading a book such as *The Values Factor*, or simply completing one of the exercises in this book. Or you might sell your partner on taking a weekend retreat to think further about what he or she wants to do next, or perhaps sell them on pursuing a dream that they have often spoken about but never dared to try. All of these forms of selling reveal your deep caring, as well as your wish to share your own inspiration with others. Of course, as we have seen, any of these "sales jobs" will be most effective if you communicate your idea, suggestion, or sales pitch not just in terms of your own highest values also but in terms of your partner's, customer's, or client's. (For more on the notion of communicating in terms of another person's highest values, see Chapter 5.)

5. Saving. Leaders value themselves; therefore, they invest in themselves. If you want to initiate the emergence of your inner leader, save and invest your money and build financial wealth, or at least become credibly valuable enough to initiate a following from those who have. If you don't value yourself enough to pay yourself first, your money will end up going to other people and into depreciating consumables. Money goes where it's appreciated and managed wisely. Whoever has money attracts more money. So manifest your leadership by investing in yourself and the enterprises or projects you are inspired by. If you don't have money working for you, as its master, you will be working for it, as its slave. The greater your wealth, the greater will be your influence.

FOUNDING A COMPANY

One of the many forms of leadership that some people may identify with is leading a business or corporation. Founding a company generally begins with an inspiring vision—usually a right-brain holistic vision of the big idea followed by a left-brain detailed understanding to ground it. And then further specializations begin.

Now, the way a business evolves from this initial vision is very much the way life itself evolves. The greatest model of business growth is in fact life itself. The study of biology and ecology actually reveals how businesses grow because the growth of life is replicated in the growth of business.

We can see the process of economic exchange even on a cellular level. The cells within the human body exchange key biochemicals, such as neurotransmitters (the biochemical our brains use to create thought and emotion) or the chemical signals known as autocrine, paracrine, or endocrine secretions. This cellular exchange within each human mirrors the economic exchange that takes place between humans.

Thus, when human life begins—whether in many areas of the world or in one location, possibly Africa—humans begin to multiply and expand by having children, and at the same time, they begin to specialize. The men go out and hunt while the women remain in the village area and gather. This is the specialization of the sexes.

Then, as these early societies grow, new specializations begin to emerge. For example, one family lives close to another family for security. Then one is more efficient at cooking, and another is more efficient at gathering, and a third is good at weaving, and so they start specializing.

Little by little, as the population grows, everybody starts specializing and finding different niches to work in. Then they have to create an ecological system called "economics," which is a means of having some universal medium of exchange called money between many different specialties, so that they can express the different values of doing, say, an hour of weaving versus an hour of hunting. Thus, economics is the study of fair exchange between various specialties.

Then, once we started having vocational specialties, we developed social classes. Once we had social class systems, we started having differences of values, and so we started to develop the business world or market. Thus, when we found a business as an entrepreneur, the entire evolution of that business is actually duplicating what went on in human society. In all cases, we see a growing specialization.

In Chapter 7, I talked about the different specializations within a business, how you get the phototropic people reaching toward the light with their visions and their big ideas, and the gravitropic people hiding within the protection of the earth with their groundedness and their detail work. As a leader of any type—whether an entrepreneur or any other type of organizational leader—your job is to allow your company or organization to specialize, delegating the work you find least inspiring to those who find it more inspiring, and keeping for yourself the most inspiring and most productive work for you, the work that involves your highest values. Your job is also to manifest your highest values to guide the entire enterprise, extending throughout all its different specialties by communicating your own values in terms of the highest values and time horizons of the people to whom you delegate. Being in close touch with your own highest values allows you to guide the organization that you lead and to expand your influence in your organization, your community, your nation, and your planet. This ripple effect reflects the power of the Values Factor.

INSPIRING YOUR EMPLOYEES

If you take seriously the responsibility of guiding your organization through manifesting your own highest values, your next step is to consider how to inspire your employees to align their job duties with their own highest values as well as with your inspiring mission and vision. This is a service to them as well as to you or your investors. If you can inspire your employees to the degree that you have been inspired yourself, they will derive enormous fulfillment from working for your company, while you and your company will in turn receive the most productive expression of which those employees are capable.

The crucial importance of inspired employees was recognized by major investor Peter Lynch, who has said that if he is to invest in a company, he has four qualitative requirements:

1. People who work there are grateful for their jobs.

2. They love what they do.

3. They are inspired by the company's vision.

4. They are enthusiastically working.

Lynch has said that if he doesn't see those four qualities, he knows not to invest money into a company because it is not likely to grow or evolve.

So how do you achieve this level of inspiration and enthusiasm? One approach is to do a quarterly review of job duties and productivity. Every three months, have every employee working at your company prioritize their job descriptions according to what is most productive, profitable, and meaningful. Discover for each employee what their lowest priorities in their jobs are. Then either discard unproductive activities or combine those lowest priority duties into new jobs so that your current employees can get on with doing something that is more inspiring to them and for which their productivity and your company's profitability will consequently be higher, because inspired and congruent people are more productive. This extra productivity allows you to create new jobs, which helps to grow the economy.

At the same time, every three months, you refine, redefine, or update the purpose statement of your organization if it requires any form of evolutionary adaptation. In that way, you continually clarify what your company is striving for, which gives you the basis for developing your vision and your specialized teams. And now you can communicate the vision and the highest values of your company—which are congruent with your own highest values—to every single person who works for you.

As we have seen, you want to communicate your own highest values in terms of your employees' highest values. You want to go through with them the process you went through in Chapter 7, where you help them link their highest values to the highest values (purpose and vision) of your company, so that they see every three months exactly why their job is helping them achieve what is most important to them. That is the way to have productive employees who will take fewer sick days, who will work that extra amount when you need them to, who will mobilize their Attention Surplus Order, Retention Surplus Order, and Intention Surplus Order toward producing their greatest job performance for your company of which they are capable. That is the way to have grateful employees who literally cry tears of gratitude for the opportunity to fulfill their own highest values through working within your and their company.

Can you see how it all starts with you—with your highest values, with your communication, with your leadership? You are responsible for that clear and purposeful vision and direction. That is the primary purpose of the visionary, the inspired leader. The inspired leader is the one who has the vision. If you are an inspired leader, you are to translate your vision into objectives that are tangible for every single specialized employee in every department so together, you can all bring your inspiring mission of service to the world.

The key thing to remember is that nobody ever works for a company or is loyal to a company. *You* are not even loyal to your company. You are only ever committed to fulfilling your own highest values. Everyone who works for you is only ever committed to fulfilling their own highest values. That is really the only true commitment anyone ever truly has. Anyone's apparent loyalty to your company, including your own, is directly proportionate to how well they, or you, fulfill their, or your, highest values by working there. As soon as someone stops fulfilling his highest values, he will move on or at least let up in his productivity.

Now, whether you do this process or not, if someone feels that working for your company offers greater advantages than they might find working for any other company, they are going to give you the impression that they are loyal—to you, to your company, perhaps even to your mission. But don't ever live in the fantasy that somebody is loyal to your company. They are only loyal to the fulfillment of their own highest values. If you ever lose sight of what their highest values are, and misallocate their job duties, they might feel unfulfilled and end up moving on.

One of the greatest lessons an entrepreneur or organizational leader can learn is to only expect someone to live inside their own highest values. No one will attempt to subordinate their own highest values to yours over any extended period of time. Anytime you expect somebody to live outside their highest values, you automatically get resistance and resentment. Why? Because people just want to be loved and appreciated for who they are. They want to live according to their own true identity and genius. Anytime you project your highest values onto someone without regard for their own highest values, you are going to end up getting resistance. As management specialist Peter Drucker has said, anytime you get resistance from an employee, it is not because of them. It is because the management team during the hiring process did not match congruently the job description with the employee's highest values. Or, as author Jim Collins puts it, they didn't quite get the right person on the bus. The seemingly resistant employee was in an incongruent job for their highest values, or they did not link their job closely enough to their highest values. And so you have to motivate them to do what you want them to do, instead of counting on them to be inspired from within themselves.

If you have to motivate someone to do something, that means that the person's expected or delegated actions are not perceived as being congruent with their highest values—therefore, they require external motivation, because the internal inspiration is not present. Then, when they are resistant and uninspired and require constant motivation, you are going to be ungrateful for them and they are going to be ungrateful for your company. Do you think that if you have ingratitude between you and your employees you are growing your business as effectively as you would if you and they were grateful? I don't think so. Ingratitude is gravitational. It weighs your company down. But when you are grateful and inspired, you are phototropic, you are radiant, and you reach for the heavens. Then, as the saying goes, "The sky's the limit."

The key to inspired leadership is understanding that every single human is going to live according to his or her own highest values. Even if they work for you, they are not going to live according to your or your company's highest values—they are always going to make decisions according to their own highest values, just as you are. If you can get very clear on that and not expect anybody to live outside their own highest values, now you have realistic expectations of them and life. Now you are set free to get on with doing what you are inspired to do and in a way that will also inspire the people you lead. This is the importance of the Values Factor.

HIRING EMPLOYEES

When you are about to hire an employee, remember they are dedicated to neither you nor your company. They may have an expectation that by working for your company, they are going to fulfill their highest values. If so, they are going to energetically want to work for you. But it will be because they are dedicated to fulfilling *their* values, not *your* values. So, it is wise to start the hiring process from that reality: to the degree that a person's allocated job description fulfills their highest values, they are inspired to go and work for your company. It really is that simple.

So how would this affect your hiring process? How do you go on from this realistic perspective to choose the most value-aligned candidates for every specialization in your organization?

Let me tell you how I would do it. Suppose you narrowed it down to the top three candidates for a job by following the more classical hiring procedures so that now you are making your final decision. Here is a little exercise you can do to save yourself a lot of aggravation.

1. First, determine these three candidates' highest values, using the method I explained in Chapter 2.

2. Then use their answers to ask a simple question: "Ms. Jones, I see here that the five most important things in your life are [name her five highest values]. So I am going to ask you: how is the first job duty laid out in your overall job description going to help you fulfill your highest values?"

If Ms. Jones fluently rattles off an answer, what does this tell you? You can see clearly that she believes she will be able to fulfill her highest values by doing that particular duty. You can expect her to be self-reliant and inspired from within when it comes to that part of her job description. She won't need constant motivation and incentives, because she herself will be mobilizing her attention, retention, and intention to fulfill her highest values through that task. So you put a check mark beside that duty within the job description where she is highly congruent and fluent.

Then you go on to the next job duty within the proposed job description. You ask, "So how is doing this particular task going to help you fulfill your highest values?" Remember, your employee's highest values might have little to do with your or your company's, at least on the surface. They might involve raising a family, rising within the business world, buying a house, or planning a comfortable retirement. Whatever their highest values are, however, you want this prospective employee to see a deep connection between them, herself, and the specific duties you are hiring her to do. So if she hesitates for even a split second and if you see her eyes scanning the room or starting to look for an answer, you put an X by that duty within the job description, because that means she hasn't seen a connection between that duty of her job and her highest values. That means that you are going to probably have to help her to see a connection because, otherwise, she is not going to be inspired to go and do that work; in that area, she is going to need motivation and reminding from the outside.

If you do hire Ms. Jones, you will see a perfect correlation between her future productivity and the degree of her initial congruency and fluency between the various job duties and her highest values. She will keep hesitating and procrastinating and feeling frustrated about doing things that are disconnected or lower on her scale of values, whereas she will eagerly look forward to doing the things that are higher on her scale of values.

Ideally, you would be wise to have every person in your company doing what is most meaningful to them. So as you go down the list of duties in the job description, if you see eighty percent X's and twenty percent checks; what does that tell you? Is that someone you want to hire? No, because you are going to have to expend a tremendous amount of energy, time, and resources motivating her, putting in systems and bureaucracies to keep motivating her or other employees like her who are not inspired to do their jobs. Because, as we have repeatedly seen, nobody comes to work for a job. They come to fulfill their highest values.

Remember, if something is important to you, you love talking about it. If something is not important to you, you don't even know where to begin to speak about it. So if you are considering hiring someone and they eagerly talk about the duties in their job description, you can see that they already feel a strong connection between their job duties and their highest values. If they can't tell you how the work laid out in their job description will help them fulfill their highest values, then you can see right away that they are not inspired, because they have gone blank.

Can people fake these responses? Not really. Their body language will give away instantly whether or not they see a connection between this job and their highest values. Sometimes, when you are hiring potential employees, they will be eager to persuade you by telling you whatever they think you want to hear, usually because they may need a job. They want security, but that is not how you live an inspired life or create inspiring teams of employees as a leader. So it is wise to go through the questioning process I am describing for every duty within a prospective employee's job description to see how congruent each duty is with their highest values, as evidenced by how quickly and fluently they speak about it. (Although body language also reveals their true values, their ability to speak fluently about the links between your mission and their values is more important.)

3. Next, ask them about how the mission of your company will help them fulfill their highest values. You say, "Here is our company purpose and here are our primary objectives. How is fulfilling our mission and primary objectives going to help you fulfill *your* highest values or objectives?"

If they are stumped, then they are simply going to use you as a temporary job. They see no relationship between your company mission and vision and their highest values. It means little or nothing to them. They only want a nine-to-five job so that at the end of each day they can get out of there and go home.

That does not mean that they might not be somewhat productive. It just means that you are not going to get a person who is going to want to spontaneously grow in your company and constantly come up with creative and innovative ideas to tackle challenges. Instead, you will get a person who wants the easy path because they don't want to tackle challenges, because that is perceived to be painful.

This part of the questioning process can take anywhere from ten to thirty minutes or even longer, depending on how far you want to go with it. It can save you a lot of aggravation in your hiring, or ultimate firing, process if you choose to do it. It is a way of confirming congruency. Congruency is the key to leadership and productivity. And it is wise to recognize that leadership is not just at the top of the company. Leadership is in every department, every component of your company.

4. Finally, imagine that you are in the final stages of hiring someone. You really think that this is the candidate for the position. You have tested their skills, and you have made sure that their highest values will be met by doing the job you want to hire them for. Then you ask them this question: If I wrote you a check for $10 million and you never had to work another day in your life, what would you do?

That is a great question because if what they tell you doesn't even remotely match what is in their job description, you just say, "Thank you, that will be all." Why would you hire somebody who doesn't have a dream to do what you need to be done? This question is definitely worth taking a few extra moments on, because if you are hiring a manager, I assure you that they are going to manage your business according to their highest values. So if you and your company's highest values are primarily focused upon efficiently serving the world and maximizing brand awareness and profits, but their highest value is on social causes or on spending time with their family, they are going to tend to direct the people they manage in their own direction, without even being conscious of it. Even though they say that they are going to build the company and build a profit and everything else, they are still going to live and lead according to their own highest values. That is why it is worth knowing what their highest values are. This is another key dimension of the power of the Values Factor.

KNOWING YOUR MISSION

As the leader of your company, or of any organization or enterprise, you will find it very helpful to identify the highest values, primary mission, and central vision for both your company and yourself. Whether you are the company president, an aspiring entrepreneur, or a middle manager who seeks to grow within your company, I suggest writing a clear and concise company mission statement. What is your company really dedicated to? Write it down so clearly and honestly that everyone who reads it knows exactly what highest values and objectives your company is intending to fulfill.

Writing a mission statement that isn't really meaningful, valuable, and true is fruitless. Don't write social idealisms. Don't write something just for marketing. It is amazing how many people write down false ideals for their company, fantasies that nobody even pays attention to. Maybe they hired a consultant to write up a company mission statement that sounded savvy to the marketplace but had no heart and meaning to anyone within the company. How many of you have been to a company where nobody reads the mission statement, nobody pays attention to it, it has no meaning or inspiration whatsoever? It just sits there as a lifeless document.

That is not what a business mission statement is for. A business mission statement is meant to express what the core of your highest values and intended culture is about. It ideally reveals what you are dedicated to as a leader and what your life demonstrates—and, of course, what your company culture demonstrates as truly most important.

As mentioned previously, I once worked with a gentleman who had founded a paper company and who was, after many decades, still working as its CEO. I asked him what had inspired him to found and build his company. He told me that when he was a child his parents were poor. Due to changes in government and school policies, he was able to be sent to a religious school in the rich part of town, where he was one of the boys in his classes who didn't have paper. At the end of the day, he would go to the trash cans and take paper that wasn't written on and then he would make his own paper pads, so he wouldn't be humiliated going to school.

As an adult, this man went on to found a paper company that became one of the largest in Australia. His true inspiration was to make sure that no child would ever be without paper as he had been. The void of his childhood's relative poverty had inspired the value of his great service later on. But eventually his company became so big and time-consuming that after a while, he forgot his vision. He only remembered it when I asked him what had inspired him and given him his start.

When you lose conscious sight of the true highest values behind what your company is dedicated to, your company is likely to plateau. When you are clear about your highest values and acting congruently with them, your clarity of mission can inspire your entire company.

Once we recaptured this man's original vision, his company became more animated, productive, and profitable. In less than six months, he recaptured market share for his company. He had been blaming his company's difficulties on external factors, but company problems are seldom if ever truly due to anything from the outside. Most problems come from within.

So I suggest that you and every one of your employees ask for the sake of your organization, "How do my job responsibilities, and how do the mission and vision of this organization, help me fulfill my highest values?" Don't stop asking that question until you unveil a long and strong series of truthful and meaningful answers. Don't lie to yourself by saying you don't know or that you can't find them. Go and find them. Getting business leaders to link their own job responsibilities with their highest values is one of my most important jobs when I consult because the second they make this link, their work ethic, leadership capacities, and productivity escalates. That's because they are once again fulfilling their highest values.

It is wise to review your company mission statement every quarter and masterfully communicate it in a congruent way to all the employees in your company according to their job descriptions. That might take some strategic thought and a bit of time, but it is worth it. That little bit of time spent more than pays for itself in the productivity increases that result.

If you don't see how every single one of your job duties helps you to realize your vision and fulfill your highest values, the gaps in your vision will hold you back from your greatest possible vitality and productivity. On the other hand, once you recognize that your highest values and your work are fully congruent, your energy and your leadership influence soar.

I once presented before a real estate company that had dozens of separate offices throughout New Zealand. We spent almost three hours doing a vision- and values-linking exercise with the leaders and their employees. First we identified the company's mission, its overall hierarchy of values, and its primary objectives. Then we identified the highest values of each employee who worked within the company and his or her specific job duties. Finally, we linked each person's job duties and the company mission to each employee's highest values.

Throughout the company, gratitude, love, inspiration, and enthusiasm immediately rose for both the leaders and their employees. Once employees can see that they can fulfill what is most important to them, they take ownership of their position. That is worth a lot of money: it lowers overhead, solves a lot of management frustrations, gets more done in less time, and creates innovation and competitive edge and advantage. Creativity and innovation begin to soar, because when people throughout a company take on ownership, it means that their work at the company is higher on their list of values. Now they naturally want to solve problems for the company. Now they are willing to face equally both pain and pleasure in the pursuit of their inspiring goals. They start innovating, and everybody starts working toward getting more efficient instead of the person at the top always having to come up with the decisions of how to make everyone efficient.

Everybody has a unique set of values. No two people have the same. Money is an important medium because it allows us to exchange one person's value for any other person's value. But money may not be the most inspiring reward for everybody. So it is wise to find out each employee's highest values to be able to get the most out of them. The moment you communicate in a person's highest values, you get the greatest and most productive results.

YOUR VALUES DETERMINE YOUR
COMPANY'S FUTURE

If you are a CEO and your highest value is making the greatest profit, you will make absolutely certain that your company is efficient, productive, and profitable, with lots of revenue coming in. If your lowest value is family, you may run the risk of burning out people who have a high value on family because you will not be focusing on the family energy needs of the employees within the company.

Alternately, if you have a hierarchy of values in which family is at or near the top and financial profits comes third or lower, you probably will have a great family-friendly company but may not make as much profit.

Likewise, if you have social causes high on your values, you might concentrate on great social causes. But if you don't have a high value on productivity and profits, your profit margin could be fairly slim.

As we have seen throughout this book, the hierarchy of your values dictates your destiny as well as your company's destiny. So you don't want to live in a fantasy of how you are going to lead your company. Your highest values are going to guide your company's destiny, because you are going to make decisions according to your highest and most meaningful values.

Recently, I worked with a company based in Massachusetts. Its profit margins were extremely slim. So I wasn't really surprised to learn that nobody in upper management—neither the CEO nor the executives—were either financially driven or wealthy. They had a high value on social causes and a high value on "green" policies, but they didn't have a high value on actually increasing their profits. They expected that somehow they were going to make a profit someday. But the hierarchy of their values dictated their company's financial destiny—and the hierarchy of their values was keeping their company on the verge of unprofitability.

So if you are in a leadership position, knowing your hierarchy of values and where customer service and financial rewards fit in can result in a significant insight. Many people find out that customer service and financial rewards are not as high on the values list as they had previously believed. They have to think about readjusting and linking their highest values with their financial goals—or else they have to change their goals, as we saw in Chapter 2.

Remember, you can't just artificially make up your set of values. You just can't say, "These are going to be my values now." That is a delusion that some people have, and it is written about all over the marketplace. But it doesn't work. You have to face what is true or actively transform your values until they are congruent with your goals. You can use the process I've laid out earlier in this book to change your values—but first you have to know where you are. "Know thyself, be thyself, and love thyself" is an old adage.

I once worked with a guy who made $6.29 million in one year, but at the end of that year, he had to borrow $327,000 to pay off his taxes. You might think that a guy making that sort of income would not need to borrow money to pay off his taxes. It is hard to believe, isn't it? But remember, it is not about how much money you make, it is about how you manage what you make. This man had little value on paying his taxes. In fact, he resented them. He had a high value on a fancy lifestyle—fancy parties, fancy cars, fancy yachts, fancy houses, and fancy travels. He didn't have a value in saving any money. He didn't initially have a value on saving for or paying taxes, so at the end of the year, he had nothing in his savings to show for his labors, and he was behind on his taxes.

This man was disturbed by his situation and wanted to change his highest values to prevent being in a similar situation again. So I was able to have him realize that his current hierarchy of values was leading him to create his current reality and show him how to set more congruent and therefore reasonable goals for the future. By shifting a few of his highest values, he was finally able to place a higher value on paying taxes and saving for the future.

The irony is that his receptionist was making $2,000 every month, of which she saved twenty percent, or $400, a month. In other words, she was closer to reaching financial independence than he initially was! So it is not about how much you make, it is how you manage what you make—and the hierarchy of values determines how you manage it.

DISCOVERING YOUR CAPACITY FOR LEADERSHIP

Every single one of us has the potential to be an inspired leader. If you study very carefully, you will find that many of the leaders who did extraordinary things on this planet began their leadership activities in the face of amazing challenges that inspired some of their greatest accomplishments, whether founding a business, leading a cause, or establishing leadership on a smaller scale in their communities or families.

I once spoke at a South African prison where I asked the prisoners, "How many of you, no matter what you have done or have been through, still have deep inside you some meaningful and inspiring service that you would love to contribute to this planet?"

Almost every one of them raised their hands and said they had: They wanted to make a contribution. They may not have known how; they might have had all kinds of illusions in the way; they might have had all kinds of fears or excuses. They might have even become so accustomed to subordination that they believed they were oppressed victims of their history. But deep inside every human being is a yearning to contribute.

So it doesn't really matter where you come from or what you have gone through or what you are going through. What matters is your perception of these events. And what matters is that every one of us has within us the ability to be a leader if we live according to our own highest values. And when you are authentic, you are empowered—you are unique! Your greatest innovation, greatest genius, and greatest creativity are born when you are living according to your highest values and being your most authentic self. There is no competition with the true you. There is only a perception of competition when you are subordinating to other people and thinking that you are supposed to be somebody that you are not.

Anytime you minimize yourself to others, you become in turn ungrateful for yourself. Your heart shuts down to yourself and you think there is something wrong with you. Your confidence becomes eroded. You shroud your certainty. You cloud your vision.

Those without a vision perish, but those with a vision flourish. Because deep inside every human being there is a desire to live congruently, to live authentically, and to live by an inspired vision. So anybody who exemplifies that congruency automatically draws people to help them fulfill whatever it is that they are dedicated to.

Whenever you set a goal that is congruent with your highest values, you believe in that goal and you tend to walk your talk and add certainty to your life as you fulfill that goal. You become very affirmative. When I hire you for a job that is congruent with your highest values, you immediately say, "That is me! Let me have that job! I can do it, and I know what to do." You won't give up until you can find a way to achieve. But if I ask you to do some job that is not inspiring to you and that is not based on your highest values, you will say, "I don't know. That is not me. I can't do it."

As you can see, you become affirmative to the degree of your congruency. So again, if you are living congruently with your highest values, you become a master of your destiny. If not, you become a victim of your history.

So why not give yourself permission to set goals that are truly meaningful to you? Don't consume your time setting fantasies and delusions and end by beating yourself up! Instead, give yourself permission to do something extraordinary. Take advantage of the power of the Values Factor and awaken the inner leader that you are destined to be.

10

Unleashing
Your Vitality

We either make ourselves miserable, or we make
ourselves strong. The amount of work is the same.

—CARLOS CASTANEDA

first became interested in the healing arts and wellness as a teenager, when I discovered that I had a type of strychnine and cyanide
poisoning. As we saw in Chapter 1, this condition was the result of
insufficient nutrition in combination with my consumption of too
many toxic, psychedelic hallucinogens. Some of my symptoms lin-
gered for about twelve years, inspiring me to do everything I could
to dissolve them.

I did everything I could think of to restore my body to a state of
wellness. I changed my diet, I supplemented, I exercised, I fasted, I
did yoga, I meditated, and I studied many traditional and nontradi-
tional healing arts and related disciplines intensively and extensively.
As with many people who have experienced a health challenge, the
void I experienced concerning my illness inspired me to develop a
very a high value and strong drive to learn everything I could about
the field of wellness. Because I had also been diagnosed with dyslexia

as a child, I likewise developed a very strong value on learning, which led me to do advanced studies in the field of neurology.

Although I eventually won honors in premed as an undergraduate, I decided to go on to graduate school and become a doctor of chiropractic. I do believe that there's a place for every form of healing, including conventional, or allopathic, medicine as well as the various alternatives. But I was inspired by the principles of chiropractic, which are based upon the notion that wellness consists of a fully functioning nervous system and spine, and that we can create wellness by providing the body with the nutrients, the mental and physiological rest, and the balance that it needs. It seemed to me that too many conventional physicians believe that the solution to illness is to remove an organ, prescribe a medication, or kill a germ. But I did not believe that people's illnesses were due to an excess of organs, a deficiency of drugs, or an invasion of germs! Instead, I believed—and still believe—that the internal power that causes the body to evolve and develop has the power to return the body to wellness if the body's internal and external environments are brought back into balance and if the master governor—the nervous system—is allowed to fully orchestrate the show.

My belief in the innate wisdom of the body has been strengthened by the number of times I've seen how previously held medical wisdom and understanding has been humbled. So many concepts that we once believed were cutting-edge we now view as mere stages of incomplete awareness or even complete fallacies. For example, we used to think that our tonsils and our appendix were vestigial organs and unnecessary parts of the body; now we recognize that they are absolutely essential components of the lymphatic and immune systems and actually prevent many cancers and other disorders of the throat, tongue, mouth, and bowel. Such incorrect or incomplete hypotheses show us how much further and deeper our knowledge of the body must go. Yet the body itself has its own inner wisdom—it has always "known" that the tonsils and appendix were needed!

Of course, if I developed a serious disorder, I might well turn to specialists in various professions who would have much to contribute to my health. But my focus, when it comes to wellness, is not on just what specialists can do for me, but also on what I can do for myself. I believe that each of us has within us a vast power and potential to create our own illness or wellness. And this belief is confirmed the more I continue to explore the applied physiology and anatomy of the human body. The more I learn, the more deeply I believe in the power of the mind and the body to transform illness into wellness.

Here again, the Values Factor is crucial, for the key to harnessing the power of your healing mind and unleashing your vitality is to live in full congruence with your true highest values. Living by your highest values fills your life with wholeness and well-being.

HOW LIVING BY YOUR HIGHEST VALUES UNLEASHES YOUR VITALITY

If your intentions and actions are not aligned with your highest values and with true wellness, you are prey to certain ill effects:

- You may be vulnerable to experience more signs and symptoms of illness.
- You may experience less vitality.
- You may be less intuitive and responsive to your body's homeostatic feedback. You may be less balanced, centered, and clear-headed.
- You may become more vulnerable to the influence of drugs or addictive substances or behaviors.
- You may be more stressed.
- You may experience more anger, aggression, blame, feelings of betrayal, criticism, challenge, despair, and depression—the ABCD's of negativity.

continued...

- You may be more vulnerable to injuries.
- You may be less adaptable to stress.

By contrast, if your intentions and actions are aligned with your highest values and with true wellness and vitality you will lead a more energized life, manifesting all the physical states of wellness, stamina, and beauty of which you are capable.

ILLNESS AND IMBALANCE

In order to understand how the Values Factor can be a source of wellness, you will find it useful to understand the basic concept of universal balance. That is because wellness springs from balanced perspective and actions, whereas symptoms and illness frequently arise from imbalanced perspective and actions. So we begin this chapter with a discussion of the wisdom of balance.

Although many of us tend to judge events as "good" or "bad," these judgments actually represent an incomplete and biased awareness. In fact, all events are neutral. They are neither good nor bad. They simply are.

I realize this may be a new paradigm for many people, but there is enormous wisdom to be found in adopting this perspective. If you judge an event with an incomplete awareness, you are likely to say, "This is good, because it supports my highest values" or "This is bad because it challenges my highest values." This incomplete and biased perspective often leads you to create symptoms, which are nature's way of bringing you back to a more balanced and complete perspective. Anytime you perceive support without challenge or challenge without support, you are by definition missing something. Symptoms and illnesses are your intuition's way of revealing to your awareness the aspects of a situation that you are ignoring, so that you may return to a balanced orientation. But your biased evaluations often override your intuition, leading you to hold on to your one-sided views, and then, frequently, the symptoms persist.

Nature always provides you with both support and challenge, synchronously—at the exact same time. When your mother overprotects and supports you to make your life easier, your father or another member of your family or extended family will aggressively challenge you and make things difficult in order to break your addiction to her support. This is not necessarily conscious on the part of the challenger; it is just the way nature always maintains balance in every situation and gives you opportunities to grow. Likewise, when your classmates rally round you with support and encouragement for your freedom, your parents or perhaps your siblings will challenge or even constrain your actions at home. When you are being praised and honored at work by your colleagues and clients, your spouse will ridicule and humiliate you at home to level the game.

Again, none of these efforts is necessarily conscious on the part of either supporters or challengers. But just as the ecological world of nature maintains an inevitable balance of predator and prey, so does each moment of our daily lives provide that type of balance for us: if in one situation we are the predator, in another situation we will be the prey. Thus does nature help us to remain authentic. To paraphrase the insights of Ralph Waldo Emerson, as stated in his "Essay on Compensation," nature is continually seeking to level our playing field.

What this means is that anybody who seeks support without challenge is living an unrealistic expectation, a fantasy that is going to lead to the ABCD's of negativity: anger and aggression, betrayal and blame, criticism and challenge; despair and depression. These unrealistic expectations and their corresponding negative responses become correlated with symptoms of the body, producing illnesses as trivial as acne or as serious as cancer, along with everything in between.

These symptoms and illnesses may seem negative—a type of

challenge without support. In fact, they are an extraordinary opportunity intended to wake you up. As long as you view the world in an imbalanced way, you will create physiological symptoms in your body intended to awaken your conscious mind to that imbalance.

Without question, ingratitude is a great contributor to illness precisely because it results from an imbalanced state of mind. Ingratitude occurs when you assume that the balanced world around you is supposed to offer you more support than challenge, and more positive than negative. As a result, you are ungrateful because you want still more support and positives, but instead, you keep getting challenges and negatives that you don't want. You become ungrateful when you assume or perceive that you are about to lose or have just lost something that supports your highest values, or when you assume or perceive that you are about to gain or have just gained that which challenges your highest values.

To see how ingratitude results from an imbalanced perspective, let's consider the example of becoming infatuated with someone whom you perceive as offering you more support than challenge to your highest values. Because of your fantasy—because of your belief that it is possible to have support without challenge—you then assume that the object of your infatuation possesses attractive traits that you don't have to the same degree. If you are a man infatuated with a sexy, desirable woman, you might think, "She is so attractive! An ordinary guy like me is so lucky to have a beautiful woman like that!" If you are a woman infatuated with a powerful, high-achieving man, you might think, "He is so strong and capable. A man like that could take care of me better than I could take care of myself." In either case, your perception that the other person is somehow "better" than you produces the infatuation. Your focus is entirely on the traits you perceive as positive, with little or no awareness of the downside of those traits.

The biochemical expression of this one-sided infatuation is dopamine, a brain chemical related to thrills and excitement, and oxytocin, a brain chemical related to bonding and attachment. Both of these chemicals are very powerful. Dopamine is the chemical involved in addictive drugs and behaviors. Oxytocin is the chemical released at orgasm and when a mother nurses an infant, in both cases creating a powerful bond.

As a result of this chemically supported infatuation, you minimize yourself and become juvenilely dependent upon the object of your infatuation. You might think, "I'll never find another woman who is that wonderful—I don't know what I'd do if she left me" or "I can't imagine life without that man—I feel lost and helpless just thinking about trying to get along without him." Like a child who fears losing their parents, you enter into a state of juvenile dependence. And because you fear losing the object of your infatuation, you want to change yourself relative to them so as to preclude the possibility that they might reject you or leave you or in any way think less of you. In a sense, you are addicted to the dopamine and oxytocin that your brain generates in response to the relationship, and, like most addicts, you fear the pain of withdrawal and will do virtually anything to avoid it.

By contrast, when you are resentful of someone whom you perceive as offering you more challenge than support to your highest values, you consequently assume that they possess some repulsive traits that you don't have to the same degree. Now instead of dopamine and oxytocin, your brain produces cortisol and substance P. Cortisol is a brain chemical associated with stress and challenge, while substance P is a biochemical associated with pain.

So you decide that you dislike this person who challenges your highest values. Instead of minimizing yourself relative to them, as you did with the object of your infatuation, you exaggerate yourself relative to them. "Oh," you might think, "that person is so selfish! I'm not like that—and I can't stand that quality in others." Or, "Wow, that person is so boring and out of touch. I'm glad I'm a more interesting person who knows what the latest trends are." Instead of feeling juvenilely dependent upon that other person, you become precociously *in*dependent of them: you think, "I don't need that person in my life; in fact, I wish they were not even in my life at all." Instead of fearing the loss of the person with whom you are infatuated, you fear the "gain" of the person you don't like. Instead of changing yourself to protect yourself from a perceived rejection, you want to change the other person to protect yourself from having to endure their "unpleasant" traits. You wish they could be more like you, or at least you wish that they would support your highest values.

Most of us perceive the object of our infatuation as giving us pleasure, so we seek to obtain that person—to get them into our lives. We perceive the object of our dislike as causing us pain, so we seek to avoid that person—to get them out of our lives. We tend to view these two situations as very different from one another, but they are actually quite similar, *because they are both unbalanced.*

In one scenario, you minimize yourself relative to the object of your infatuation. You think, "I'm not sexy enough to deserve that woman" or "I'm not able to take care of myself without that man." As a result, you become ungrateful to yourself.

In the other scenario, you exaggerate yourself relative to the object of your dislike. You think, "I'm more generous or interesting or cool than that other person—and yet I have to deal with them anyway, even though I wish I didn't." As a result, you become ungrateful to them.

Either way, your one-sided perceptions cause you to feel ungrateful. Thus, *ingratitude is the result of an imbalanced, limited perspective.*

This is a key point to grasp when we are thinking about wellness and vitality, because ingratitude saps our vitality, ages us prematurely, and often leads our bodies to create symptoms or illnesses in an unconscious effort to restore balance and gratitude to our lives. To see how limited your perspective might be, think about an event that at the time you believed was terrible. Then, a day, a week, a month, or a year later, you found out that the event had a "hidden terrific" in it.

Likewise, think about an event that at the time you believed was terrific. Then, a day, a week, a month, or a year later, you found out that it had a "hidden terrible" in it. Terrific *and* terrible: *That* is the full equation.

Whenever you don't see the full equation, you unconsciously create symptoms to make sure that you *do* see it. So, by creating symptoms, you give yourself the opportunity to achieve wisdom, balance, and, ultimately, wellness. Seeing the whole equation can set you free from your imbalanced, unrealistic perspective—*and* from your physical symptoms. Instead of feeling ingratitude for the limited situation that you perceive, you are free to feel gratitude for the whole. That gratitude opens your heart so that you can again feel wholeness and love.

By contrast, when your mind is imbalanced, you cannot open your heart with gratitude. Nor can you be whole or well when you are judging anything in the universe either negatively or positively, either resisting "too many challenges" or welcoming "too many supports."

Instead, if you can look beyond your immediate challenges and supports, you can perceive the balance that is inherent in life: the full socio-ecosystem. Remember, maximum growth and development occur at the border of support and challenge. A full and balanced perspective allows you to live on that border, growing and developing to fulfill your utmost potential. Living according to your highest values and understanding the Values Factor will help you develop such a perspective and thereby achieve that potential.

Ingratitude is gravitational: you pull inward and contract yourself. Gratitude, however, is radiational: you grow outward and expand yourself, your horizons, and your awareness of space and time. The world opens up as your heart opens up, unleashing your inspiration, your fulfillment—and your vitality. It is your gratitude that also helps you fill your life with fulfillment and inspiration. It is your gratitude that brings about wellness.

THE NATURE OF EMOTIONS

As we just saw, wisdom and wellness flow from balance. Nature and our intuition are constantly showing us this balance. But our lopsided emotions reveal when we are out of balance.

In my signature seminar program, the Breakthrough Experience, I regularly demonstrate how to dissolve imbalanced emotions in order to awaken ourselves to wholeness, wellness, and balance. The basis of my method is to demonstrate clearly that nothing is ever lost—only transformed. And nothing is ever "good" or "bad"—there is always a balance of pleasure and pain, support and challenge, positive and negative. Understanding these universal truths opens the heart to create unconditional gratitude and love for everything that life brings us and everyone whom we encounter.

This new paradigm is often difficult for my students to grasp, so I offer a powerful demonstration of how it works during every Breakthrough Experience seminar. I invite students to raise their hands if they are in the process of experiencing the emotion that they identify as "grief." I have students vote on whose grief is the greatest, and then I work in front of the group with that student.

I have found that grief results from the imbalanced perception of a loss of some items, actions, traits, or behaviors without an equal gain; a loss of that which we previously assumed supported our highest values more than challenged them and "brought" us more pleasure than pain.

In a recent seminar, the student voted as displaying the most grief had undergone the death of his six-year-old daughter. I began by asking him what specifically he was missing or had lost since the moment his daughter had died.

Visibly overcome by sorrow, the man slowly began talking about his experience. "I miss spending time with my daughter," he said haltingly. "I miss tickling and playing and giggling with her."

"What else?" I asked.

"I miss watching her grow up."

"What else?"

"I miss coming home to see her every night and finding out about her day."

"What else?"

As I do each time, I continued to ask the man what things he missed until he had listed them all. Usually there are about ten items on the list—although sometimes more, sometimes less. The greatest number of items I have ever been given was twenty-eight.

Now, what my students do not yet realize is that all the things they miss represent infatuations fueled by dopamine and oxytocin. They miss the aspects of the person or relationship that induced pleasure, and so their grief results from their withdrawal from these two powerful brain chemicals. They never miss the dirty diapers, the screaming, the fighting back. They only miss the elements of the person or relationship that provoke pleasure.

So, once my grieving student has identified all the things that he or she is missing now, I ask a different kind of question, as I did with the man who had lost his daughter.

"The moment you perceived your daughter to be gone, what emerged in your life to bring the exact same traits and behaviors and make the exact same contribution to your life?" I asked.

As with most people, this man's initial response was to deny that possibility.

"No one emerged to take her place," he said angrily. "She was my daughter. She was unique. There is no one like her."

"Yes, but I didn't ask who emerged who was identical to your daughter," I pointed out. "I asked who or what is bringing into your life the same traits and behaviors that your daughter brought . . . the traits that you believe you have lost. So look again and see where those traits have emerged."

As with most people, the man was at first reluctant to consider this new perspective. But finally he said, "My sister has a daughter, and I've been spending more time with her."

"Exactly," I said. "Who else?"

"I have a client who has been bringing her daughter in to appointments with me," he said. "So I have had some time with her."

"All right," I said. "Who else?"

"I have been sort of spending time taking care of myself, babying myself," the man said. "In a way, I have been treating myself as a young child."

"All right," I said. "Who else?"

"Well, my mother and I have been talking about my childhood and what we used to do when I was my daughter's age," he said. "So in that way, too, those traits have been present."

By the time we had finished this portion of the grief-dissolving process, this man had seen that none of the specific traits or behaviors were actually lost; they were only transformed. And all of the traits and behaviors that he had been missing from the moment of his daughter's death had emerged since her death in other forms, whether in just one person or distributed over several people. He was able to acknowledge that while these traits were not *qualitatively* equal to his daughter—who was unique, as every human being is—they were *quantitatively* equal to the traits that she had brought into his life. This realization arises every time I go through this process, which as of this writing has been something like twelve hundred times.

The next step was to review the traits that this man had been infatuated with and was now missing and to help him look at the downsides of those traits. As we have seen, there are always two sides to every trait, even though our fantasies and imbalanced perspective might have us believe otherwise.

So I asked this man, "When you tickled and played with your daughter and she giggled and laughed with you, what were the downsides of those moments?"

The man at first said, "There are none." But then upon deeper reflection he finally said, "Well, spending time playing with my daughter was time-consuming. I would come home tired, and sometimes I just wanted to go and sit in front of the TV and relax, but as long as I was playing with my daughter, I couldn't. She would usually want to play as long as I was willing to, so by playing with her, I missed TV, my relaxation time, or getting other things done. I also missed spending time with my wife. Sometimes there were things that happened to me from the day that I didn't get a chance to process . . . And then sometimes when we played, she'd get hurt, and I had to deal with the injury . . ."

He went on and on, listing the downsides to all the positives he had just identified. In fact, he was demonstrating the universal truth of balance: there is no positive without a negative, no pleasure without pain, no support without challenge. Every trait has aspects that we label "positive" as well as traits that we label "negative," but we commonly blind ourselves to the "negative" aspects when we are grieving for someone whom we believe we have lost.

In fact, every trait is neutral until we create a fantasy around it. Then we hold on to our fantasy, negate the downsides of the trait, and remain mired in our grief.

So this step in my process asks the grieving person to find the downside of each trait that he or she is missing. Because all traits are neutral, we can always identify both benefits and drawbacks to each one. And because nothing is ever lost—because nature conserves everything and is continually transforming it into new forms—we can always find whatever we falsely believe we have lost, if we only know how to look for it.

The final step in my process is to ask the grieving person to identify the benefits of the new ways that the traits or behaviors of the lost person have emerged. So I asked this man to identify those benefits.

"Well," he said, "getting closer to my sister's daughter has also helped me to get closer to my sister. And playing with my client's daughter has given me new insights into my client . . ." He went on naming benefits. And so he proceeded through the stages of dissolving his grief: identifying the drawbacks of the old form and the benefits of the new. Finally we had leveled the playing field and the man could balance his perspective, let go of his fantasies, and release his grief. As he did, he momentarily paused, became silent, and sensed his daughter's virtual presence. He inwardly felt gratitude and love for the six years she was with him as well as for the new forms she had taken since her passing.

Now, what is the role of the Values Factor in this process? If you are living according to your highest values, you will find yourself acting and perceiving in a far more balanced way. Living according to your values makes it far easier for you to see a balance of support and challenge in every event, and to embrace everything that happens without judging it as good or bad—because you see ways in which any event can be made to pursue your inspired mission and further your highest values. Living according to your highest values makes you more resilient and more adaptable.

Lopsided emotions, by contrast, represent the misperceptions that keep you from being resilient. Illness is then the feedback that nature uses to try to get you to become aware of this balance, to adapt and evolve, and to live according to your highest values.

So the Values Factor is your path to wellness because it enables you to achieve a balanced perspective in which you welcome both pleasure and pain, both support and challenge, both positive and negative. Because you are willing to do anything in support of your highest values, you are able to welcome anything that comes your way.

WHERE DO EMOTIONS COME FROM?

As we have seen, your perceptions of the world are filtered through your hierarchy of values. A mother whose highest value is her children will walk through a mall and see a children's clothing store, a kiosk with children's books, and perhaps a children's play area. An entrepreneur whose highest value is business and profit sees occupancy rates, rental rates per square foot, foot traffic, and maintenance costs.

These value-based perceptions, in turn, generate your feelings. If the mother sees important items she can purchase for her children, she may feel fulfillment or satisfaction. If she sees food being sold that she believes won't be nutritious for her children, she may feel disappointed, frustrated, or even angry. If the entrepreneur believes the mall would be a good investment and he has no part in it, he may feel envy of the current investors or excitement about potentially becoming one of them. If the entrepreneur owns a part of the mall, his emotions may be positive or negative depending on his perception of how profitable his investment is.

These are examples of partial feelings—the types of imbalanced emotion that can often generate symptoms or illness. These imbalanced emotions result from an imbalanced perspective. If you feel happy when something seems good to you, then you are likely to feel sad when something seems bad to you. If you feel pleased when events appear to go your way, you are likely to feel angry when events appear to go against you. Instead of perceiving the positive in every apparent negative and the negative in every apparent positive—instead of perceiving every trait and event as neither good nor bad but simply "what it is"—an imbalanced perspective leads you to label and judge traits and events as "good" or "bad." Then you feel the emotions that fit those judgments, which will be, by definition, partial, imbalanced emotional feelings.

By contrast, whole and balanced feelings flow from a perspective that views the world as neutral, with every trait or event simultaneously including both so-called positives and so-called negatives. And what are these whole and balanced feelings? They are the four cardinal feelings of gratitude, love, inspiration, and enthusiasm. These whole, integrated feelings bring about wellness.

Thus, wellness results from the wholehearted embrace of every event that befalls you. Instead of getting caught up in feeling happy when something seems "good" to you or feeling sad when something seems "bad," you unconditionally embrace all that happens. Your heart is naturally filled with gratitude, love, inspiration, and enthusiasm, and your body becomes balanced and well.

In the Breakthrough Experience, I have helped tens of thousands of attendees realize the extraordinary effects of balance. They see that when they ask themselves specific questions that reveal both sides of an event simultaneously, and when they are able to recognize the ever-present complementary opposites—like the two poles of a magnet—they spontaneously experience a deep sense of gratitude and a feeling of love in their hearts for the inherent balance and order that underlies every event. Once we stop judging the world and simply embrace it as it is, love and gratitude flow into our hearts and we feel inspired and enthusiastic. This is the condition in which our body is most able to achieve wellness.

I have therefore redefined true gratitude and love as a synthesis of complementary opposites, experienced simultaneously. This is a very different paradigm for love than the one held by most people. What most people call love is merely the one-sided emotional feeling of passionate attraction, which I call infatuation. This response results whenever someone perceives more support than challenge to their highest values, which makes them vulnerable to the powerful effects of dopamine and oxytocin, to which they soon become addicted. By definition, infatuation sees only the good and ignores the bad. It results in a fantasy that gives rise to its corresponding nightmare.

True love, however, embraces both sides of the equation simultaneously. True love looks at a person and recognizes that every strength is also a weakness, every virtue is also a flaw, every positive is also a negative. The charming man who makes you laugh is a bit of a performer who is always seeking an audience. That outgoing woman who is so generous and kind is something of a martyr who sometimes seeks to control others through her "goodness." That self-confident entrepreneur is also arrogant; that humble worker is also passive. The child whom you adore also drains your energy; the friend you cherish asks you for help at inconvenient times.

If your vision of these people and their traits is whole and complete, your heart will well up in love and gratitude for the fullness of all that they are as you embrace them unconditionally. You will feel grateful to your child as you are changing her diapers; you will feel grateful to your friend as you are driving him to the airport on a cold, rainy night that you had planned to spend at home by the fire with your spouse. True gratitude and true love occur when you have a perfectly balanced state of mind, able to embrace pain and pleasure equally. This state of balance will open your heart.

If your vision is based on a one-sided fantasy, you will be happy when a person seems to support your highest values, and sad or angry when the person seems to challenge your highest values. Love and gratitude are feelings that bring wellness. One-sided feelings, by contrast, frequently cause your body to create symptoms and illnesses.

These partial emotions cover up the truth of the ever-present balanced state of love residing deep within. But, the moment you become aware of the balance of both sides and see the whole, you become grateful and spontaneously open your heart to feel this deep love.

These one-sided partial feelings occur because you put on the mask of happiness when you perceive more support than challenge, or because you put on the mask of sadness when you perceive more challenge than support. When you experience these polarized emotions, you tend to want to cover your face because you know unconsciously that they are distorting signs of incomplete awareness—only part of the whole truth. By contrast, you tend not to feel guilty or ashamed for experiencing gratitude, love, inspiration, or enthusiasm, because then you are authentic. You are seeing whole; and you know you are graced because you are honoring the balancing intelligence that governs all life in the world as it is, rather than imposing the evaluations made by your limited awareness.

Your intuition is always trying to take you from your polarized, incomplete emotions back to the feeling of wholeness, gratitude, and love. This process is accomplished as your intuition prompts questions in your mind to awaken your awareness of the other side of the equation. Your intuition pushes you to question the one-sided infatuation you have developed, and it also pushes you to reconsider your one-sided dislikes. Your intuition and your body understand that incomplete emotions are signs: they reveal that you are being blind to the whole picture, that you are inaccurately perceiving more support than challenge (and feeling happy as a result) or more challenge than support (and feeling angry or sad as a result).

Your intuition continually prompts you to return you to a balanced loving awareness of the whole. Your physiology, your symptoms, and your illness are also trying to bring you back from polarized emotions to the grace and wholeness of love. That is why polarized emotions frequently create symptoms and illness, while the balanced feelings of gratitude and love are the greatest healers, bringing us back to the state of wellness.

Positively polarized emotions are also a type of addiction. During certain types of experiences perceived as supportive, your brain releases dopamine, which as we have seen gives you the sensation of thrills and intense pleasure. For example, dopamine is released when you take cocaine, when you ride a roller-coaster, and when you first become infatuated with a person. And with anything you can become infatuated with, you can also fear the loss of. So when you feel an intense emotion of grief or sorrow over the loss of something you are attached to, it is because you are somewhat dopamine-addicted to that thing—and because you were infatuated with it, for you only feel the loss of that which you are infatuated with. You never fear the loss of that which you resent or things that you perceive to challenge your highest values. You celebrate *that* loss with relief, not grief! That is why you only experience remorse, bereavement, sorrow, or grief when you perceive that you have lost something with which you were infatuated or to which you were partly or wholly dopamine-addicted. Those partial emotions are actually dopamine withdrawal symptoms.

But as the man whose daughter died discovered, nothing in the world is ever truly lost. Just as energy and matter are continually changing their forms, so is every aspect of our lives continually changing: relationships, families, careers, enterprises, and even ourselves. The master is the one who embraces this world of transformation, knowing how to see the new form and honoring the laws of conservation and balance. The master embraces the laws that, on the one hand, caused my student's daughter to die, and, on the other hand, immediately brought into his life other aspects of children and childlikeness, to *balance* what he had apparently lost and to *conserve* the qualities that he valued.

As my student discovered, life holds no wholly positive experiences and no wholly negative ones: the laws of nature insist on an inseparable connection between the two. There were negative aspects to the time when his daughter was alive, and there were positive aspects to the time after her death. The laws of nature ensure that over time and through space, your pain and pleasure, your ease and difficulties, your overall amount of "positive" or "negative" will remain balanced. If you live in a fantasy that you will receive only support for your highest values, or that life will bring you only positivity, the complementary negativity will simultaneously emerge to help you crack that fantasy.

When you understand these universal laws, you can neutralize your fantasy. Instead of trying to obtain the unobtainable or avoid the unavoidable, you can set real goals in real time according to your highest values in a real world with a true balance. When you have set clear goals that you are certain are congruent with your highest values, your perception will become more balanced and less limited. No matter what happens, you will then demonstrate a higher probability of experiencing tears of inspiration and gratitude, because you will know that you are living with wholeness and with a balanced perspective. You will know that you are ultimately living your destiny.

This is why the Values Factor is so important, because the key to experiencing inspiration and gratitude is to know your highest values and then set goals in line with those values, while also knowing the laws of nature and setting realistic expectations. As Carl Sagan so beautifully emphasized, "The magnificence of the universe the way it is, is far greater than any fantasies we may keep imposing on it."

THE INTELLIGENCE OF THE BODY

Whole, integrated feelings have a tremendous impact on your physiology, and so do partial or imbalanced emotional feelings. Whole, integrated feelings—gratitude, love, inspiration, and enthusiasm—generate wellness. Partial, polarized emotions—joy *or* sorrow, happiness *or* sadness, attraction *or* repulsion—can create symptoms of illness.

Some people may have difficulty grasping the notion that joy, happiness, and attraction can create symptoms of illness. If this concept is challenging for you, recall the man we met in an earlier chapter who had met his "fantasy woman" at Club Med. For this man, those few days of amazing sex and passionate connection seemed like a completely positive experience. As a result, he created the fantasy that life could always be like that and that it was possible to have a relationship with a woman that would always be completely positive and never negative.

The ultimate result of this one-sided view was that the man was unable to appreciate his wife, who by definition would always fall short of a one-sided fantasy, as any real-life human being would. So those few days of one-sided emotion created mild lingering depression and misery—or, more accurately, the man's one-sided perception created a compensatory depression and misery. If you recall, the man's depression was dissolved when he recognized both the downside of his fantasy (his fantasy woman had an unpleasant voice, thin hair, unattractive buck teeth, etc., etc.) and the upside of his present life (his wife had many qualities that this man viewed as positive). Achieving a balanced perspective *both* about his so-called past joy *and* about his present unfulfillment enabled the man's heart to open, so that he felt real, balanced love for his wife and gratitude for his life.

Thus, symptoms of any kind—including depression and other mental illnesses—are a kind of call back to wellness, intended to alert you to the ill effects of one-sided, polarized emotions and bring you back to a deeper perception of reality in which you understand that the world is neither "positive" nor "negative"—it simply *is*. Then you have the opportunity to embrace the world wholeheartedly full of inspiration, enthusiasm, gratitude, and love.

Both whole and partial feelings work on your body through the autonomic nervous system. The autonomic nervous system controls the automatic aspects of your body—the actions your body performs without your conscious decision, such as breathing, heartbeat, digestion, and sexual arousal.

When your mind is fully balanced, seeing the universe whole and not limiting it through your polarized "value judgments," your autonomic nervous system maintains its equilibrium. When your mind is imbalanced, falsely perceiving more support than challenge or more challenge than support, your autonomic nervous system is imbalanced also.

This imbalance occurs between the two aspects of the autonomic nervous system: the *sympathetic* nervous system and the parasympathetic nervous system.

The Sympathetic Nervous System: This system rules the stress response, the so-called fight-or-flight reaction. It is therefore more active during the day, when you are more likely to perceive a challenging threat. This perceived threat might be a physical predator or an emotional demand, such as a work deadline, a fight with a loved one, or a difficult decision of some kind. What sets off the stress response is either a fear for your physical survival, a loss of what you depend upon, or a perceived challenge to your highest values.

When you perceive a physical or emotional threat, your sympathetic nervous system prepares your body for tremendous exertion. Your breathing becomes more rapid, your muscles tense, your heart beats faster, your pupils widen, and many other physiological changes also occur, all of which will make it easier to engage in the physical efforts required to fight or flee. However, you have the same stress response even if the challenge is not physical but rather challenges your highest values.

What many people do not realize is that the sympathetic nervous system also gears you up for *positive* experiences. Perhaps instead of referring to the fight-or-flight response, we ought to call it "the fight, flight, *or pursuit*" response. When you race to finish an important project, imagining the joy and satisfaction you will feel upon completion, your sympathetic nervous system is in high gear. When you are about to go out on a romantic date with a person to whom you are very much attracted, your sympathetic nervous system revs up for an exciting night. Think about the last time you had an exciting, pleasurable night—perhaps a birthday party given in your honor or a successful business meeting at which you achieved every one of your goals. Recall how hard it was to calm down and sleep after that night, and how revved up and alert you felt. Those are the physical signs that your sympathetic nervous system has kicked into high gear, producing the biochemical cortisol, adrenaline, and dopamine that in turn produce alertness, excitement, muscle tension, and wakefulness.

Whether your sympathetic nervous system is geared up to face pleasure or pain, the biochemical response is the same. This is a necessary aspect of life—but it is only one side of the equation.

The Parasympathetic Nervous System: The other aspect of your autonomic nervous system is called the parasympathetic nervous system. This system generally takes over at night, as it rules the rest-and-digest responses.

When you feel safe and protected—because you perceive physical safety or support for your highest values—your parasympathetic nervous system encourages your body to calm down. Your breathing slows, your muscles relax, your heartbeat slows, and your pupils contract. This is the optimal state in which to digest food, to relax, and, ultimately, to fall asleep, but it is not the optimal state in which to take on all the challenges of the day. Our bodies require a balance of both sympathetic and parasympathetic responses—enough challenge and excitement to wake us up, enough support and safety to allow us to sleep. Too much of a sympathetic response produces insomnia, anxiety, and a host of stress-related diseases. Too much of a parasympathetic response means that we never "get into gear," never rev up to create the life we want or pursue the goals that are important to us. In nature, the functions of the parasympathetic system put us at risk of becoming prey: we are never more vulnerable to a predator than when we are eating, sleeping, or having sex, or when we are simply relaxed and unmindful of potential danger. In life, an over-valuing of the parasympathetic would make us less likely to rise to the occasion, handle life's challenges, and pursue our highest goals.

Both the fight-or-flight and the rest-and-digest states are associated with polarized emotions. The sympathetic fight-or-flight response—aka the stress response—is associated with anger, fear, anxiety, frustration, resentment, and a host of other "negative" emotions, as well as such "positive" dopamine-fueled emotions as anticipation and excitement. The parasympathetic rest-and-digest state—aka the relaxation response—is associated with infatuation, happiness, sexual arousal, satisfaction, and a host of other "positive" emotions, as well such "negative" emotions as sorrow, boredom, lassitude, and depression.

These polarized emotions, in turn, affect your facial muscles, which tend to reveal your innermost thoughts and feelings. You tend to smile when you are happy, frown when you are angry or sad, wrinkle your brow when you are confused or thoughtful, and so forth.

Your body's muscles reveal your thoughts and feelings as well. When you experience yourself as being challenged, and feel awakened, you engage the sympathetic nervous system—and you tend to extend your muscles and *supinate*, or rotate your limbs, hands, and feet outward—like a cat stretching in the morning to face the day. When you experience yourself as being supported and feel relaxed, you engage the parasympathetic nervous system—and you tend to flex your muscles and *pronate*, or rotate your limbs, hands, and feet inward—like a cat curling up and positioning to sleep at night.

Your muscles and your posture reveal your psychology in other ways, too. When you have difficulty extending your wrist, your body may be saying, "I have difficulty saying *stop*." When you have difficulty flexing your wrist, your body may be saying, "I have difficulty saying *go forward*."

Likewise, if you have difficulty straightening your knee, you may be having difficulty standing up to authority. If you have difficulty bending your knee, you may be having difficulty giving in to authority.

If you are self-righteous and perceive that your highest values are being challenged, you might expect the world to match those values. As a result, you might engage your sympathetic nervous system in a fight-or-flight reaction that sends more oxygen and glucose (blood sugar) to your blood, fueling the body to fight or flee. When you feel challenged and become bitter, you tense up, engaging the sympathetic nervous system, which facilitates defense. Your circulatory system stores the glucose that has been sent into the bloodstream, and your blood sugar levels go up. As a result, if you express this personality type, you might be prone to high blood sugar and diabetes.

When you feel supported, you relax, engaging the parasympathetic nervous system, which facilitates digestion. Your body then absorbs the glucose that has been sent into the bloodstream, and your blood sugar levels go down.

Here you play out the personality type of someone who is more "self-wrongeous" and sweet, who minimizes themselves and likes to please other people. Whereas a self-righteous persona believes that he or she is usually right, a self-wrongeous persona believes that he or she is usually wrong and that *other* people are generally right. You generally act out the self-wrongeous persona when you perceive that your highest values are being supported, so you don't leap to a fight-or-flight reaction. Instead, you tend to minimize yourself and suppress your own reactions. This might suppress your blood sugar as well, and you may tend toward low blood sugar and hypoglycemia.

Interestingly, cats—who usually expect you to please them—have a higher incidence of diabetes. By contrast, dogs—who often try to please you—have a greater tendency to hypoglycemia.

Scientists have also discovered that if you have unrealistic expectations of yourself, particularly if you beat yourself up for attempting to live outside your highest values, the resultant stress will run down your immune system, and possibly alter your intestinal microbiome, or bacterial ecosystem, possibly resulting in an autoimmune disorder. Using the Demartini Method, you can discover the emotional charges that have created the imbalanced feedback system—the polarized emotions that are stressing your immune system. Then you can dissolve both the emotional charges and possibly the associated autoimmune disorder.

Ultimately, then, so-called illness and symptoms in your body can be traced to one-sided perceptions that result in an imbalance in the expression of either the parasympathetic or the sympathetic nervous system; and an excess or deficiency of some cell function governed by those systems. Your mind and body will store your imbalanced perceptions—"This is good, that is bad"—in the forms of memory or imagination, and in the subtle forms of cellular and subcellular compressions and tensions until you are ready for the truth of the balance.

However, when you adopt a balanced perspective, you can achieve *autonomic equilibrium*: the equilibrium of your autonomic nervous system in which your sympathetic and the parasympathetic nervous systems are perfectly balanced. This is the road to wellness.

DISEASE IS THE BODY GOING BACKWARD

Years ago, when I was in the midst of my illness and wellness studies, I made an amazing discovery: many of the body's illness states, including cancer, were initiated by cells that took a more "primitive" form—identical to an earlier stage of cell differentiation and development.

As a general principle, the more a cell has evolved, the less likely it is to multiply. By contrast, cancer cells and other cells involved in various disease processes have literally reverted to more primitive states.

That realization led me to another: I wondered whether illness is some sort of "devolution" back in time, transforming the body into an organism that functions with a less evolved perspective and a more primitive cellular tool kit. I began to believe that our bodies have the capacity to move backward or forward, heading toward either a primitive or a more evolved state, based on our more polarized or synthesized perceptions. Perhaps, by going backward in response to less evolved, more polarized, and one-sided perceptions, our cells and their symptoms are actually trying to give us feedback to try to wake us up and return us to a whole and balanced awareness.

Now, many people who have not yet fully embraced this paradigm might misunderstand this concept. They might inaccurately hear me saying, "If you're sick, it's your own fault" or "Anything bad that happens to you is because you attracted it into your life."

In fact, I am saying something quite different. I am saying that events are neither bad nor good—they simply *are*. I am also saying that when you view life from an imbalanced perspective—when you believe that an event *is* bad or good—you throw your sympathetic and parasympathetic nervous systems out of balance, which potentially creates symptoms or illnesses. These symptoms are your opportunity to create a more balanced perspective and could actually be perceived as just as much a blessing as they are assumed to be a curse.

Some people might say that this is a form of "blaming the victim." But that perspective—of "bad" events happening to an "innocent victim"—is childish, antiquated, and obsolete. From my perspective, there are no "bad" events and there are no "victims." There are only events and human beings within a perfectly balanced universe that contains equal amounts of positive and negative, support and challenge, pleasure and pain. Achieving a balanced perspective enables us to feel love and gratitude for everyone we meet, everything that happens to us, every experience we undergo. Achieving a balanced perspective enables us to embrace the reality that we are always both predator and prey, and so is every other creature on the planet. The rabbit preys upon the grass and is prey to the hawk; we go out to pursue our goals and then run up against obstacles that seem to challenge our highest values. If we resist this reality—as it is our animal nature to do—we will feel frustrated and unfulfilled, like a hamster running frantically inside its wheel. If we embrace this balanced reality—as is within our human potential to do—we will feel unconditional love, gratitude, inspiration, and enthusiasm, simply because we are alive and part of the universe.

From this perspective then, illness is not "bad." It's a wakeup call. Disease is not some terrible evil trying to destroy us—it's a valuable feedback mechanism to try to get us to balance our way of looking at life and also to balance our perceptions and actions.

Thus I have come to view illness and stress as offering valuable and meaningful insights into evolution (moving forward) and devolution (moving backward). I have learned that when we are under stress, we are more likely to activate the same immune pathways that are used by other mammals, reptiles, amphibians, and other less evolved or earlier forms of life. This is a survival mechanism, because when we are in fight-or-flight mode, alert to any danger, our bodies go back to primitive responses that are accustomed to handling the perceived danger, just as emotionally, when we are under stress, we will go back and repeat old patterns that we have otherwise left behind. In the same way, when society is stressed, it often goes back to old religious beliefs and other old patterns of behavior and even to older forms of architecture.

The more imbalanced your perceptions, the more primitively you respond. The more balanced your perceptions, the more you evolve and move forward. That's because, again, your optimal growth occurs at the border of support and challenge. When you perceive that your environment is perfectly balanced, you evolve and progress. When you perceive that your environment is out of balance, you regress.

When you are masterful, you understand that the world has a perfectly balanced dynamic of complementary opposites. When you see that perfect balance, you are graced and not stressed. But when you don't see that balance, you experience stress in the form of distress, boredom, or burnout.

Stress causes blood to flow to the most primitive part of your brain, which causes an imbalanced response—either an excess or a deficiency of some kind. So if you are in a state of infatuation or resentment, or if you perceive a high degree of support or challenge and your stress levels become elevated, you will actually revert to a more primitive physiology and brain function, with a more active amygdala, the part of the brain that controls our panic and fear responses. This physiological response often results in illness.

By contrast, when you are in a poised state of gratitude and love, blood goes to the most evolved part of your brain, known as the prefrontal cortex, the creative executive control center, or the telencephalon. Blood in that portion of your brain helps to generate a balanced or governed response.

This is yet another way in which the Values Factor contributes to wellness. If you are living according to your highest values, you have the highest probability of finding and embracing that optimal balance of support and challenge. If you are subordinating yourself to external influences and trying to live by somebody else's highest values, you will be more likely to impulsively seek immediate gratification and pleasure while instinctively trying to avoid pain. You are likely to end up in a state of juvenile dependency, behaving as a follower rather than a leader, perhaps even becoming an addict. Your imbalanced perceptions are also more likely to result in illness.

Wellness occurs when you are at one with the natural balance of life. But illness occurs when you perceive a false distinction between yourself and the world around you and then attempt to live in an imbalanced manner. Again, this illness has a purpose. Its symptoms are a kind of feedback to your conscious mind to make sure you live authentically according to your highest values and reawaken to a balanced awareness. The moment you do, your body dissolves the symptoms.

How do you know you are living authentically? You have tears of gratitude for your life and for what you love to do. That's why I have been saying for nearly four decades that gratitude and love are the two greatest promoters of wellness on this earth.

I have asked hundreds of thousands of people what they would do if they had only twenty-four hours to live, and they all said the same thing: They would use their final day on earth to say "Thank you" and "I love you" to everyone that has contributed to their life. Every human being on this planet wants to be appreciated and loved for who they are. This is why gratitude and love are the cardinal tools of wellness, along with certainty and presence. All four of these qualities spontaneously occur when you live congruently with your highest values.

THE JOY OF DEPRESSION

Some of the most popular medications dispensed in the world are for depression or bipolar disorder. What does that tell you? It tells me that many people on this planet are living with an imbalanced perspective and unrealistic expectations.

Every week, I work with people who believe they are depressed. But I have discovered that there is no such thing as a one-sided state of mind. What do I mean by that? Your depression is a comparison of your current reality—filtered by your senses and your value system—with a fantasy that you are partly addicted to about how your life is supposed to be. Your mind actually remains full and balanced, but you are not aware of that. So the degree of your depression is in direct proportion to the degree of your elating fantasies about happiness and support. A fantasy, as you may remember, is an assumption that you are "supposed" to experience more support than challenge to your highest values. If you didn't have such a manic fantasy, you would not be depressed. Instead, you would appreciate the balanced world as it is, and you would understand that maximal growth occurs not within your fantasy of total support, but on the balanced border of support and challenge.

This is why depressions and fantasies occur at the same time and to the same degree: the depression is a direct result of the manic fantasy, and an inevitable companion to it. However, you might be aware of only one side of the equation at a time and ignorantly diagnosed that way. The key to achieving wellness and wholeness is knowing how to ask the right questions to reveal the other side that simultaneously exists.

Infatuations, elation, and fantasies are all associated with dopamine, which, as we have seen, can be to some degree addictive. Depression, by contrast, is associated with completely different biochemicals. But it is closely related to your fantasies nonetheless.

Fantasies keep you addicted, dependent, and juvenile. In response, depression leads you to associate pain and challenge with your fantasies, helping you to break your addiction to them. In that sense, so-called depressive symptoms function as a kind of feedback mechanism to your conscious mind to help you break your dopamine-based addiction to your hidden fantasies.

That is why depression, in my opinion, is not so much an illness as it is a strategy. Yes, I have read the literature saying that depression is a biochemical imbalance in the brain with genetic roots. Certainly, the pharmacological industry likes to promote that viewpoint, as do many specialists. There may well be a biochemical imbalance in the brain of a depressed person, but that does not make biochemistry the sole or even the primary *cause* of depression. In fact, imbalanced biochemistry may well be an *effect*. I have assisted hundreds of people who have been considered or diagnosed "clinically depressed," and I have rarely found that label to contain the whole truth. The condition that some have called "depression" I would call instead a feedback mechanism to alert the conscious mind that it is addicted to an unrealistic expectation—a fantasy. As long as a mind holds on to that fantasy, it must create the symptoms of depression to break that addiction.

Your body is quite ingenious, and it does extraordinary things to try to wake you up to your authentic self so that you can fulfill your highest values. When you understand the Values Factor and live according to your highest values, you are willing to endure in equal measure pain and pleasure, support and challenge—you are willing to endure and even embrace virtually anything in the pursuit of your *telos*, purpose, or dream. But when you are attempting to live outside your highest values, you tend to feel unfulfilled. In that case, you want immediate gratification and so you awaken your addictive tendencies along with your masked personalities, which are one-sided personas or social roles and characters that you act or play out.

I am referring to what happens when you perceive only support and feel only infatuation, and so you put on a mask of comedy, as though you weren't capable of feeling anything else. Or when you perceive only challenge and feel only resentment, perhaps you put on a mask of tragedy. Both your one-sided perceptions and your one-sided emotions lead you to reveal the "mask" of one side of your personality and cover the other—an imbalanced perspective that tends to create illness rather than wellness. One result of this response is an addictive personality, which is the byproduct of a state in which your highest values are unfulfilled. You have the highest probability of awakening addiction—whether it be to food, alcohol, sex, drugs, stimulants, or to fantasies themselves—to the degree that you are unfulfilled in your highest values. In that case, you will be looking for immediate gratification because you don't feel fulfilled or inspired about your life.

The solution, as we have seen, is to adopt the balanced perspective about the world that will help free us from our addictions—and from the desire to experience support without challenge, pleasure without pain, happiness without sadness. That imbalanced perspective can never fulfill or inspire us. It can only drain us. Instead, we would be wise to set our goals not according to a fantasy but according to our highest values where we more fully embrace the balance of life.

That is why I say that I have given up the elusive search for a one-sided happiness. That imbalanced perspective turned out to be a fantasy that inevitably attracted its complementary sadness, pain, and challenges to help break me from my addiction. So I decided to give up happiness—because it made me too darn sad! Instead, I appreciate the fulfilling balance that life genuinely has to offer. The magnificence of the way life truly is, is far greater than any fantasy I could impose on to it.

THE HEALING POWER OF
THE VALUES FACTOR

A couple of years ago, I was involved in filming selected clients to develop a video for my Demartini Method–trained facilitators on the subtle details of my method. I worked with a wide variety of people: a former top movie executive who had been overcome by schizophrenia and became homeless; a man with a drug addiction; a woman who was working through her experience of a rape that she considered highly traumatic.

I also worked with a woman who struggled with compulsive eating whose story made a great impression on me. I thought she exemplified to me the prophetic words of William James, the father of modern psychology. James emphasized that the greatest discovery of his generation was that human beings can alter their lives by altering their perceptions and attitudes of mind. I have seen this happen with all sorts of issues, but his insight becomes particularly dramatic when it comes to the fields of wellness, well-being, and vitality. In fact, I actually saw his insight happening before my eyes, for this woman's life changed when her attitude changed.

So let me share with you how this story played out. This woman viewed herself as being addicted to food. I could see that she was grazing continuously, even while I was working with her. I believe she literally ate more during our session than I consumed in a week.

This woman said to me, "You have to help me. I can't stop eating. You have to help me!"

Well, that was her conscious mind saying, "I want to stop eating. This thing is killing me. Just look at me." But look a little deeper. Because what her conscious mind was *really* saying was, "I *should* stop. I *shouldn't* be eating this way. I *ought* to be eating differently." She was speaking out of "should" and "ought"—all this imperative language that came from those authorities whose values she had injected into herself and absorbed.

It doesn't matter whether she would have benefited from what she thought she "should" be doing. What matters is that her conscious mind was saying, "I *should* stop eating." But her unconscious mind was obviously saying, "I *want* to eat." And in any battle between the conscious and the unconscious mind, the unconscious mind generally wins. That was why she hadn't been able to stop.

So the first thing I said to her was, "I want us to identify the one hundred fifty benefits you are getting out of your eating."

She said, "There are no benefits."

I said, "I am certain that there are. No human being will ever move a muscle without a motive nor act in some way unless there are more advantages than disadvantages, more benefits than drawbacks. Deep inside you, there are benefits to your eating, and our first step is to uncover them. You are probably receiving benefits in all the different areas of your life: spiritually, mentally, professionally, financially, with your family, socially, and physically. So let's go through all those areas and look for the unconscious, hidden benefits of your continued overeating."

Well, first we found out that her mother was obese, her sister was obese, her brother was obese, and her father was obese. So if she wasn't obese, she didn't fit in with her family. When she realized that, tears came to her eyes.

Then we found out that her sister, who was two years older than she was, was bigger than she was and used to push her around and beat her up. So she grew up getting beaten up by her sister—until she decided that she was going to eat more than her sister so that *she* would be the bigger one and could push her sister back.

That was two benefits. I was shooting for one hundred fifty.

Then we found the third one. Every time she attempted to lose weight, she noticed that her skin sagged. She said, "I can't handle that," so she would eat to get her skin smooth again.

We uncovered something else. At one point, she had tried a radical diet and temporarily lost a lot of weight. At that point, a guy approached her and ended up having sex with her. She became pregnant—and then he dumped her. She had made herself very vulnerable to this guy, and when she became pregnant and he left, she was devastated and ended up choosing to have an abortion. So she unconsciously chose not to keep losing weight because that would make her vulnerable again and because she had associated losing weight with her ordeal.

We kept going like this, and by the end of our work that day, we had uncovered seventy-nine unconscious benefits accompanied by many tears of realization. That night, since she had gotten the hang of it, she went back for the rest of the one hundred fifty. She came in the next day and said to me, "I really have no intention of losing weight, do I?"

I didn't judge her. I didn't condemn her. I didn't say she was wrong. I simply said, "Now it's time to hug yourself."

She couldn't believe it. She asked why.

I said, "Because you are brilliant enough to create one hundred fifty benefits with one act—eating. That is ingenious. Give yourself a hug!"

She laughed, but she appreciated what I was saying. She said, "I am beginning to see how empowered I felt by that one act. I know it isn't healthy. But I did get a lot of benefits, didn't I?"

I said, "You surely did. And I am not ever going to tell you that you can't eat. But I am going to tell you that we will now pivot those one hundred fifty benefits into a variety of other actions, which I call viable alternatives. So you can take those actions, or you can eat without being right or wrong about it."

She said, "What do I do?"

For each one of the one hundred fifty benefits, I had her come up with four or five viable alternative ways of getting those same benefits, besides eating. For example, she could be part of her family by watching TV with them, going to church with them, or helping them with their garage sale. She could stand up to her sister by talking to her, learning martial arts, or asking a respected authority to mediate their conflict. She went through every single benefit and by the time we were done, she had more than five hundred viable alternatives to eating, although some of them were duplicates, so really it was more like a total of forty.

This discovery of viable alternatives is a crucial part of the process because contrary to much conventional wisdom, addiction is not a disease—it is a strategy. People become addicted to certain substances or behaviors because they believe that they will derive more benefit than disadvantage from those substances or behaviors. If they can see that they will derive more benefit from some other behaviors— the viable alternatives—they will drop the addiction and turn to those new behaviors.

After this woman had identified her key viable alternatives, I had her identify her own highest values—using the same procedure that I showed you in Chapter 2—so that she could relate these alternatives to the values that were most important to her.

Finally, I had her link her five most frequent and most viable alternatives with her highest values, creating hundreds of links between her top five viable alternatives and her top five highest values.

This creation of multiple links is not simply a psychological exercise. It is a way of literally reshaping the brain, creating hundreds of neural connections that did not exist before. Once the brain has been reshaped in this way, new actions and responses become possible.

This woman's top five viable alternatives to eating were:

- Go to church with my family.
- Watch television or go to movies with my family.
- Develop an attractive weight, fashion style, and overall look so that I feel less vulnerable to rejection from men because I

appreciate my looks and my desirability and will not rush into relationships blindly.

- Take a martial arts class so that I feel strong and powerful, and also so that my body will be toned and more attractive.
- Practice assertiveness so that I set strong boundaries with my sister, my family, the men I date, and others in my professional world, so that I no longer need layers of fat to protect myself.

This woman's five highest values were:

- Being close to my family
- Achieving recognition and acknowledgment
- Finding a loving partner and creating a family of my own
- Feeling sexual and desirable
- Feeling stylish and fashionable

So we began to create hundreds of links between each of her highest values and each of her new viable alternatives to eating. For example, here are some of the ways that we linked the value of "achieving recognition and acknowledgment" to "taking a martial arts class":

Taking a Martial Arts Class Will Help Me Achieve Recognition and Acknowledgment Because . . .

1. I will "fight fiercely" for the recognition I desire.

2. I will have a more toned body, which increases my chances of being hired for a job on television, which is my chosen path to recognition and acknowledgment.

3. I will receive recognition and acknowledgment from my martial arts teacher.

4. I will receive recognition and acknowledgment from my fellow students.

5. I will recognize and acknowledge *myself* for my achievements in this class.

6. Martial arts training includes developing a balanced mind, and this will be of great service in my efforts to pursue my goals of work in TV, because I will not feel disappointed or frustrated but will be a "warrior" for my goals.

7. I will be more likely to stand centered before my family, so I will not be affected by their various opinions of me.

We continued until we had from five to twenty links between each viable alternative and each highest value.

When this linking was complete, the woman was overcome with enthusiasm for the new actions she was inspired to take. Looking at her, I could see that she had already begun to restructure her brain.

Next we worked to detach her original behavior—overeating— from the five highest values she had just identified. I asked her, "How is overeating *interfering* with your top five values?" We began identifying the drawbacks to her overeating—no guilt, no shame, just the drawbacks. It is unwise to point out the assumed drawbacks to people's addictive behaviors until they have truly re-myelinated new viable alternatives into their brain. Otherwise, focusing on the drawbacks can create anxiety, guilt, and shame, which just add fuel to the addiction.

For example, if we had begun with this part of the process before identifying viable alternatives, all this woman would hear is, "Overeating is keeping you from achieving your highest values," making her feel ashamed, guilty, and self-deprecating. Without a viable alternative to overeating, she would feel unable to give up this strategy, and so proving to her that this strategy was not helpful to her would only make her feel worse.

By contrast, once you *have* a viable option to pursue, you become willing to understand how your previous strategy was once serving you but is no longer the most useful strategy, and so you become willing to give it up. But for the new strategy to become truly viable, you need to go through the linking process, creating hundreds of new neural connections in your brain. It is not enough simply to *understand* that you have new viable strategies open to you. That would be like saying that picking up a barbell *once* is enough to develop new muscle, because your body "understands" how to lift the weight. What changes your body is lifting the barbell many times, over and over, until the muscle has been developed. And what changes your brain is making hundreds of links between your new strategies and your highest values, until the new pathways within your brain have been developed.

The last step in the process was to help this woman identify the "subdictions" that were driving her addiction. A subdiction is something you want to avoid remembering—something that is extremely challenging to your highest values and that you perceive as painful in your life.

For example, this woman had a subdiction about her family's rejection of her. This was, in fact, a one-sided perception, because even if her family *did* reject her for losing weight, other people elsewhere in her life welcomed and embraced her. Yet the woman was so preoccupied with avoiding the pain of her family's rejection that she turned to the strategy of overeating in order to get her family to accept her and thereby avoid that pain. Helping her to develop a more balanced view—balancing her family's rejection of her with other people's openness—meant that she no longer had any need to avoid that pain and therefore no need to overeat.

Likewise, this woman had a subdiction about her loss of the man with whom she got pregnant and who then left. This was a very painful memory, and, as we have seen, part of the reason she overate was to avoid repeating such an occurrence in the future. But if she took a more balanced view—understanding that other men would stay with her if she communicated in terms of their highest values even though that man left—she would not need to overeat (or to do anything else) in order to prevent being abandoned, because she would understand that any loss is always balanced by a gain, and any man who left her would always be balanced by a potential mate who wanted to stay. A balanced perspective also helped her let go of the one-sided fantasy of an ideal man who would never think of abandoning her, and to embrace the realities of a universe that always contains equal measures of pain and pleasure, negative and positive, challenge and support.

So I went through and used the Demartini Method to dissolve each subdiction until there was nothing left to say except "Thank you." This woman was spontaneously filled with unconditional love and gratitude for her life just as it was—not as her fantasies would have it, but as it actually was: perfectly balanced, as all lives are, between pleasure and pain, support and challenge, positive and negative. In response, her eating disorder was dissolved, and she was able to go on to a new life.

Until those subdictions are dissolved to the point where you can say "Thank you" and where you can see that you are not a victim of your history, you won't master your destiny. Because whatever you try to run away from, you will keep running into. Whatever you condemn, you attract, breed, and become. Whatever you bury, buries you. Whatever you resist, persists. But once the subdictions are gone and there is appreciation, then wellness returns and your addiction subsides.

This entire process works in a remarkable fashion. I have completed it with heroin addicts who become completely inspired and can't wait to get up the next morning to fulfill their values on this new pathway. In fact, I worked with one man who had been addicted to heroin for six years but who came completely off the drug without side effects or withdrawal symptoms. That's because addictive behaviors and side effects are not so much caused by withdrawal from the drug as they are by withdrawal from the fantasies they have associated with the drug. If you dissolve the fantasies by means of the understanding the drawbacks, and clear the subdictions, those withdrawal symptoms subside. You are free to feel the wholeness of unconditional love and gratitude, and to let those feelings return you to the state and awareness of wellness.

RELEASING DIABETES: MY STUDENT ACHIEVES WELLNESS

Over the last several years I have had the opportunity to work alongside a noted psychologist, Ilze Alberts, who has been associated with the Demartini Institute in South Africa since 2005. Ilze has extensively used the Demartini Method in her work consulting patients, as well as in the seminars and workshops that she presented.

About two years ago, she attended my Prophecy II Experience seminar, a program that focused on the concept of "mind over body." As a result, Ilze realized that her insulin-dependent type 1 diabetes might well respond to the healing powers of her own mind. She agreed to share her story with me for this book: "I was so inspired to actually work with my mind and increase the value that I see on the ability of my mind to have power over my body. So I did a very intensive process using the Demartini Method."

Ilze's first step was realizing that her diabetes was not solely genetic but rather also resulted from her unconscious perception that the condition somehow gave her more benefits than drawbacks, more pleasure than pain, and more positives than negatives.

"So," Ilze told me, "I wanted to know, 'What is my hidden strategy? Why have I pulled this into my life?'"

Ilze completed a series of processes that she had learned in my seminar. First, she wrote down two hundred benefits that she derived from having have diabetes. For example, Ilze discovered that diabetes led her to eat in an extremely healthy fashion, to work out frequently, and to focus on maintaining a healthy weight. As Ilze told me:

People often comment how young I look, how well I look. So because I have diabetes, I became the master of the way my body looks. That was a very high value for me. After all, I have this chronic illness that goes completely out of control if I don't do those things. So for thirty years, diabetes gave me my very, very good reason to look great.

Ilze identified a second benefit: people admired her for being in such good control of her health. "The medical profession can't believe how healthy I am," she told me. "And I became quite a role model for lots of people. I see my life purpose and vision is to empower myself and others. I dedicate my life to that. So having diabetes is one form where I am truly an inspiration."

Ilze further discovered that she herself liked saying that she was managing a potentially life-threatening chronic illness "in this amazing way." So that was another value for her.

Altogether Ilze was eventually able to identify two hundred benefits from having diabetes. Then she went on to the next step of the process, asking herself what else she could do to experience the same benefits *without* having to use diabetes as a catalyst?

She realized that she didn't need to have diabetes to continue to exercise, because she loved exercise, which she used for stress release, as a time to think, to inspire herself, and to socialize. Ilze also realized that she could look for even more reasons to exercise so that her choice to exercise was higher on her values and not in any way dependent upon her illness. "Instead of having diabetes, I can look for other opportunities to achieve exactly the same benefits," Ilze said. "I can actually increase the value for me in having all those benefits, since then I wouldn't have to use a chronic illness."

For each of the two hundred benefits that Ilze had found for having diabetes, she then discovered five different viable alternatives or strategies for getting that same benefit.

"Instead of having to rely upon a chronic illness, I can use the power of my mind," she told me. "I can do those things out of choice, not because I have to."

So Ilze continued to identify the five most viable alternative ways of achieving each of the most important benefits she had discovered and listed for her having diabetes.

Then, she asked herself, "How can doing each of these five most viable alternatives help me fulfill my three present highest values?" She kept answering this question over and over again until she felt a shift in her perspective and then felt inspired to add these new viable alternatives in to her daily life.

Finally, Ilze wrote down two hundred drawbacks of continuing to have diabetes. "The more angles I could come at it from, the more my body would respond," she explained.

Upon completing this last step she began applying the Demartini Method on the traits or actions that she was feeling emotionally charged or bitter about within herself or others. As a result, Ilze decreased her insulin dependence up to eighty percent.

"It was quite amazing," she recounted. "I started to notice that I was in hypoglycemic states—my blood sugar level was dropping too low because the insulin dose I was used to taking was now too high for what I needed. My body was showing me that it didn't need that much insulin any more. I do test my blood sugar levels regularly throughout the day, and those tests bore out what I could feel for myself, which was that my blood sugar levels were very low—I felt very shaky, as though I wanted to pass out.

"I wasn't surprised by this—in fact, I expected it! I think I would have been surprised if it hadn't happened!"

Ilze stressed that her transformation was not an instant one, but occurred over time.

"My mind started to see more and more of the benefits of not having diabetes, and my body started to respond," she said. "It was a slow process—it didn't happen in a day. But over a month, my insulin dependence became less and less and less."

Ilze still needs some insulin to function optimally, but she is looking forward to needing less and less over time. She sees, however, that to achieve this goal—or even to maintain the transformation she has already accomplished—she still needs to repeatedly use the Demartini Method to release any emotional change that results from imbalanced emotions.

"I know that the emotional charges—the power of polarized emotions—affect my blood sugar," she told me. "So when I have those charges, which happens on a daily basis, I use the Demartini Method to release the imbalanced emotional charges. The more my mind is in a balanced state of calmness and not going into infatuations or resentments, the more my sugar levels are also balanced."

She continued, "The more I understand my behavior and my reactions to what life brings me, the more I have the tools and the skills and approaches to increasingly master my life. My body becomes more mastered as well. And my diabetes is more under control."

I asked Ilze what she wanted to share with others who might be interested in using the Demartini Method and the Values Factor to achieve wholeness and wellness. She responded, "The most important thing is to know that you will not achieve the results if you do not do the work. You cannot have fantasies around it. This all remains in the physical: putting pen to paper and doing the physical work. I am still continually doing the Demartini Method on my lopsided perceptions, because my mind can quickly go back into old patterns if I allow myself to go into those perceptions. And then I'm not being fair to my body. And of course, I still have to attend to my eating, exercise, and so on. If I ate a slice of chocolate cake, my blood sugar levels would be high! So I need to continue to take care of my body and feed it the right foods, in the right portions and in the right times. So this healing experience didn't give me license to go and become a glutton! I still require great self-governance on how I eat and what I eat, and I continue to exercise and train. Because if I don't do those things, my diabetes will probably re-emerge in an ungoverned form."

What was clear to me, hearing Ilze's story, was the centrality of the Values Factor. As long as her mind perceived more unconscious benefits than drawbacks to having her condition, she would likely continue to have diabetes in same form, where it was essentially controlling her body. But when she could see more benefits than drawbacks to *not* having diabetes, then she could change the way the illness affected her body. This in turn gave Ilze the power of her own mind to heal her body.

Ilze's story is very powerful, because it shows that ultimately, your body is doing everything it can to wake you up and teach you how to live a magnificent and inspired life, to be absolutely authentic. But when you live in ignorance, you tend to pay no attention. Instead, you have a doctor step in and prescribe an artificial drug to stimulate a part of the body that you believe is sedated . . . and then there are side effects from the drug.

Again, I am not saying that doctors and conventional medicine do not have their place. In acute situations, you may need them. But trying to transform bodily illness into wellness without treating the psychology is to disconnect two parts of who you are—your body and your mind—so that you don't get to the real source and psychology of what is underlying many of those conditions.

WELLNESS VALUES

When you live according to your highest values, you live your inspired destiny, deepen your relationships, activate your genius, fulfill your career, grow your financial freedom, expand your influence, and unleash your vitality. You bring Attention Surplus Order, Retention Surplus Order, and Intention Surplus Order to everything you attempt, and you create inspiration and fulfillment.

As I said on *The Secret*, when the voice and vision on the inside are more profound and louder than all the opinions on the outside, you have begun to master your life. You have also begun to unleash your vitality and discover the power of your mind to empower wellness. Once again, the Values Factor is the key.

11

Achieving Your Immortal Vision

The most powerful weapon on earth
is the human soul on fire.

—FERDINAND FOCH

Now you've explored the seven key areas of life: spiritual, love and family, mental, career, financial, social, and physical. Each of these seven areas of life forever calls you to expand, grow, and experience a different dimension of fulfillment. By creating a more inspiring life in each of these areas, you more effectively pave the way for others to climb their mountains and grow in *their* ability to fully express their highest nature. By giving yourself permission to live to the fullest and function at the highest, you exemplify what is possible and give permission for others to do the same.

The greater your life, the greater will be your contribution to the whole of humanity. And so at the end of your life, you will ask yourself at least one important question: did I do everything I could with everything I was given? You want to be able to say, "Absolutely, yes, I have." You are here to raise your standards for yourself and to stretch yourself beyond your previous limits. You are here to inspire others to do the same so that humanity can break through any stagnant ways previous generations followed and catapult forward to newer and ever more magnificent ways of being, doing, and having.

You identify yourself by your highest values. So when you live according to your highest values, your true essence or spirit is able to fully express itself through your actions. When you are inspired doing what you love, your leadership qualities emerge and you magnetize others into your sphere of influence. When you can see how all events ultimately help you fulfill your highest values, you feel grateful and your so-called greatest crises then become your greatest blessings.

Using the Values Factor to understand your highest values is the key to achieving your immortal vision. Earlier in this book, you learned how to identify your highest values by looking at the evidence demonstrated in your own life. You saw that you can recognize your highest values by the way you live: how you spend your time, money, and energy; where and how you feel inspired; where you show yourself to be organized, focused, and committed; which topics you choose to study and explore.

You have also seen the value of challenge and difficulty: how it calls you to enrich your life and expand your vision. You have learned how knowing your highest values can help you fulfill each key area of your life, bringing you an undreamed-of depth and richness.

Now I'd like to leave you with some final strategies for how the Values Factor can help you achieve your immortal vision.

Refine Your Goals

A key aspect of the Values Factor is to refine your goals, ensuring that they remain aligned with your ever-evolving values. Every day, I write down or edit the goals that are most important to me, and I keep reviewing them. I look to see how my highest values have evolved, and I refine my goals accordingly. Then I make sure that I am taking the wisest and most useful actions to reach my goals.

Surround Yourself with Inspiring People

At age twenty-three, I attended Texas Chiropractic College. About four or five months before I did, I decided to go and get the curriculum in advance and study the assigned textbooks. I wanted to make sure that I was one semester ahead of the school. As a result, I was one of the top students all the way through school, because I was always ahead. Then I really cemented my knowledge as a student teacher by teaching many of the classes I had just taken.

So the best thing to do as you are learning something is to share it with others and inspire them. The more people you have around you who are doing what you are, the higher the probability that you will stay with it and excel at it. Surround yourself with people who are committed to knowing their highest values, and who are aligning their goals with their values or their values with the goals, and living congruently with both. That helps you, too, to be mindful of the Values Factor and to live congruently with your highest values.

Every Day, Do Something That Inspires You

If you want to lead an inspired life, you want to take inspired actions. Choosing to do high-priority actions that inspire you every single day will keep reminding you of your highest values and mission and will inspire you further.

One way to inspire yourself is to compile and keep a "love list"—things you would love to do, be, have, explore, study, or create. As you keep adding new items to your list, you'll be continually reminded of what inspires you. The key is to add only what truly inspires you and what you are truly willing to work toward, not fantasies or injected values or objectives from others. As you keep doing things from your love list, you will remain inspired.

Cultivate Holy Curiosity

One of the most inspiring quotes I know comes from Albert Einstein: "The important thing is not to stop questioning. Curiosity has its own reason for existing. One cannot help but be in awe when he contemplates the mysteries of eternity, of life, of the marvelous structure of reality. It is enough if one tries merely to comprehend a little of this mystery every day. Never lose a holy curiosity."

This is something that highly effective and inspired people understand. For example, Donald Trump has stated that he spends four hours reading and engaging in personal development almost every day. He says he uses this "study time" to build momentum and mastery.

I have followed my holy curiosity as well. When I went to professional school, I read more books than anybody in my class, and possibly in the whole class combined. I listened to more audiobooks and attended more seminars than anybody there. I watched more educational videotapes than anybody there. I constantly listened, viewed, read, and learned as much as I possibly could, because I had a greater thirst for knowledge than anybody there.

As a result, today I am blessed with more financial wealth than probably my entire class combined. I reach and influence more people than probably the whole class combined. So, as you can see, I am highly dedicated to education. I read every single day of my life, and I work to learn something every day. I find that that is fulfilling. And my holy curiosity has helped me to create an inspiring life.

Keep Growing

If you aren't growing, you are probably decaying. So it is wise to learn and grow. There is no end to what you can learn, and you can never ever really be done. The sky is truly the limit.

We all have an inborn desire to go and do something extraordinary. Nobody gets up in the morning and says, "I want to shrink." We all want to stretch. We want to grow in all areas of life.

So you want to give yourself permission to do something extraordinary with your life. You don't want mediocrity. You don't want to lie to yourself and say you feel done or satisfied when in fact you are here to continue to grow. Every time I hear that someone is "completely enlightened," I ask, "How can that be when they have an infinite universe to explore?" We are wiser to be humble and keep growing and expanding and developing. As long as you're green, you're growing; as soon as you ripen, you rot.

Recognize Your Inner Leader

One of the most revelatory exercises in the Breakthrough Experience has you selecting some of the most powerful people on earth: the most powerful spiritual leaders, mental leaders, business leaders, financial leaders, and social leaders. Then you identify which traits they have individually or in common, and then you identify where you have those traits to the same degree, so you can overcome any subordination or self-minimization in that regard. Even though you are likely to swear that you *don't* have those traits to that degree, when you continue looking, you eventually discover to your astonishment that you do.

However, you will also likely discover that you have those traits in forms that are not always according to the highest values of these powerful people, but rather according to your *own* highest values. As long as you minimize your own highest values to those of other people, you will almost certainly have difficulty recognizing what you yourself have to offer to the world.

You have seven areas in your life: spiritual, mental, physical, family, vocational, financial, and social. In any area of your life that you don't empower, you will attract people who will overpower you. You are not a victim of their over-empowerment. You are just attracting over-empowerment by your very nature, to get you to raise the value of that area and empower it. The so-called victimization is actually giving you the opportunity to realize where you are not empowered, to frustrate you enough to *get* you empowered.

Understand That There Are No Mistakes

Once you understand the Values Factor, you see that every decision is based on your highest values. Therefore, you can't make a mistake: whatever decision you make is the most efficient with the data that you have.

However, you might *think* that you are making a mistake. Why? Because the moment you subordinate to somebody else and assume that you should be acting according to *their* highest values, the decisions you make based on your own highest values will look to you like a mistake.

There are no mistakes. There is only your injected superego judging your own highest values according to the highest values of another person.

Every week in the Breakthrough Experience, I do an exercise that blows people's minds. I make them identify every so-called mistake they believe they have made; everything in their life that makes them feel shame and guilt and self-minimization; everything that they believe is giving them difficulty in living congruently with their highest values. Then I help them see that according to *their* hierarchy of values, everything was in order. Only when they subordinate to somebody else's values do they think that they made a mistake. Mistakes are labels and projections of one person's values upon another.

Just as you can't live by someone else's highest values, other people cannot live by yours. So if you righteously project your highest values onto someone else and expect them to live by your values, you are going to feel angry and betrayed when they don't. Nobody ever betrays you; *you* betray you!

Communicate to Other People in Terms of Their Values, Not Yours

Every January, for the last twenty-nine years, I have presented a keynote speech to thousands of doctors and their staff gathered at a hotel convention center in Las Vegas. I generally have a few of my own staff members from my office in Houston accompany me so they can assist me in product sales during and after my speech. Recently, one single, female staff member who generally accompanies me was torn between coming to Las Vegas and staying in Houston with her daughter, who wanted her to stay home to watch a special equestrian event.

The event was important to her daughter, but this staff member's presence in Las Vegas was important to me. So I determined her highest values, her daughter's, and my own relative to the presentation. I then linked our values together as I showed you to do in Chapter 2. Having done that, I proceeded to effectively communicate my highest values and intentions in terms of her and her daughter's highest values.

First, I shared with her that this convention would be attended by many middle-age single male doctors, who would be gathering around our product table for about two hours, and I pointed out that she could certainly connect with and or go out with any of them that she fancied. I offered her the chance to stay on in Las Vegas for an additional two days and nights and go out to some shows for entertainment if she was interested. I also told her that she could bring her daughter to assist in sales, and that I would give them both a percentage of sales on top of her normal salary for an incentive bonus, which would help her to save some extra dollars for her daughter's college fund. I told her that she could also take her daughter to the nearby equestrian center if she wanted to.

In other words, I kept stacking up benefits in terms of her and her daughter's highest values. Accordingly, she went home to her daughter and shared the opportunity with her. As a result, they both decided to join me in Las Vegas, where they planned to visit the equestrian center so that the daughter could ride there, as well as take in a show. They both assisted me in sales and had a blast, and my staff member even went out one night with a doctor! She and her daughter were both jazzed by their trip, which became a memorable weekend together.

I could have just projected my values onto this woman and told her that she had to be in Las Vegas to cover my sales, but I would have received a lot of resistance, and I know that her sacrifice would eventually have had to have been compensated in some other way. Maybe she would have held this over me at her next salary negotiation, or perhaps the next time I needed her to go the extra mile, she would point to this experience as a reason why she didn't want to extend herself. Instead, by respecting her and her daughter's highest values and taking the time to communicate in terms of them, I was able to inspire both women to join me in Las Vegas, where all three of us got what we wanted: they had a memorable experience, and I had improved sales.

The message of this story is clear: When you help other people get what they would love in life, you increase the probability of *you* receiving what you would love.

In the case of the Las Vegas trip, all three of us were all able to fulfill our highest values. Accordingly, all three of us were fueled by the inspiration and were energized by doing what we love to do. Your vitality and creativity rise whenever you do the same. And your energy can soar when you master the art of communicating your highest values in terms of other people's highest values. This is one of the key powers of the Values Factor.

After all, you always have energy for the things that are high on your hierarchy of values. As the saying goes, "When the *why* is big enough, the *hows* take care of themselves." When something is high enough on your hierarchy of values, you don't let yourself down. You will endure whatever it takes to get the outcome.

And so, if you use the Values Factor to communicate to other people in terms of *their* values, you will get far greater results. Projecting expectations onto others in terms of *your* values leads to feelings of betrayal and to the ABCD's of negativity: anger and aggression, blame and feelings of betrayal, criticism and challenge, and depression and despair. Communicating in terms of *other people's* values leads to understanding and deeper connections.

Fill Your Life with High-Priority Activities

As we have seen in earlier chapters, anytime you don't fill your day with high-priority activities, lower-priority activities will flood in to take up your time, energy, and focus. So to remain inspired, it is wise to fill up your day with high-priority activities that inspire you.

High-priority activities raise your self-worth and empower you as well as inspire you. Meanwhile, any area of your life that you *don't* empower by filling it with high-priority activities will automatically fill with low-priority activities that will disempower you. If you don't get up in the morning and organize your day according to your own highest values what is most important and inspiring to do and then fill your day with those activities, you will automatically attract into your day low-priority activities based on other people's highest values. And these disempowering, uninspiring activities will simply consume your day in order to frustrate you enough to finally get you to be authentic with yourself and reprioritize your day.

Donald Trump used to have a golden glass timer. He found out that if he gave people an hour, they would waste the first forty-five minutes and not get to business until the last fifteen minutes. So then he just gave everybody fifteen minutes. He would turn the glass timer over and say, "You have fifteen minutes. If you haven't sold me by then—time is up!" The other person would get more efficient, and Trump would get more done with his day. He insisted on filling every minute of his day with high-priority activities, and so he remained inspired and empowered.

This principle is not just true for space and time; it is also true for energy and matter. Any energy or resource that you don't target for high-priority purposes will automatically be consumed by low-priority purposes.

For example, if you don't take the money that you earn and put it toward your highest-priority actions and your personal wealth, you will automatically attract unexpected bills. These bills will erode your wealth as they lead you to put money into less important priorities. They are a reminder from the world around you to live more in line with your true highest values, because any area of your life that you don't empower, somebody else will overpower you. So your physiology, psychology, sociology, and even the universe around you is doing whatever it can to assist you in maximizing your most authentic being.

It is wise, therefore, to prioritize your expenditures. The wealthy have learned to pay themselves first, so it is wise for you to do so, too. Then figure out which bill will cause you the most penalty if you don't pay it, the second-most penalty, the third-most penalty, and so on, all the way to least penalty of paying. Pay your bills in order of priority, because when you start to manage your money wisely, you get more to manage. On the other hand, if you *don't* spend your money in order of priority, you will automatically attract low-priority items and unexpected bills that will eat up your resources.

Likewise, any area of your space that you don't fill with high-priority items will attract low-priority items. When your space is full of highest-priority items, everything has a place. Things that are high on your values, you organize.

So if you want to empower and inspire every area of your life, allocate your time, space, energy, and resources for things that are of highest priority to you. Be aware that whenever you don't do this, you'll attract low-priority things that frustrate you, because your innermost being and the world around you are working together to help you wake up and create a life congruent with your highest values.

Find the Contribution That Is Unique to You

What are you the greatest at? What is your unique contribution? What you are on the cutting edge with? What is it that you can't wait to solve? What do you have that is valuable that nobody else expresses in quite your way?

If you can identify your unique contribution, you can choose to focus your life around making and expanding that contribution. That becomes your highest priority. That becomes your way of filling your day, your space, your life with inspiring activities and people and things. And that is the secret to a fulfilling life.

Once again, the Values Factor is the key to your fulfillment because your unique contribution and your highest priorities and your sources of inspiration all flow from your highest values. Understanding your highest values and then living congruently with them is the key to knowing yourself, being yourself, loving yourself, and creating an inspiring life.

If You Can't Do What You Love, Love What You Do

Very often, people come to me and say, "I would love to do what I love, but right now, I have this job that has some duties that I don't like, and it is holding me back."

I tell them, "If you don't see how every single aspect of your job is helping you to realize your highest values, then you are holding back your own vitality. Your energy is infinite once you recognize its source—and the source of your energy is living congruently with your highest values."

In the Breakthrough Experience, I ask people to identify any obligation, task, person, or activity in their lives that they think is
weighing them down. Then I ask, "How is that very thing helping
you to fulfill your vision? How is it helping you to fulfill your highest
values?" And the instant they see that every single aspect of their lives
is helping them to fulfill their highest values, their energy lightens
up. They are freed.

So you don't want to sit there and say, "This particular activity
doesn't help me." You want to ask, "How does it help me; how can it
help me?" Because once you answer that, instead of going to work
every day and doing something that is not inspiring to you, you become liberated and inspired. You can masterfully learn to love what
you do by linking it to your highest values. That is the power of the
Values Factor. And that is what you are here to master.

Permission to Be *You*

For more than forty years, since I was eighteen, I have had this affirmation: *I will do whatever it takes, travel whatever distance, pay
whatever price, to give my service of love.* For the things or actions that
are highest among your values, you will not let yourself down. Nothing mortal that you can experience has to interfere with your immortal vision, something that is truly inspiring to you. Because when
you continually set and state goals that are in alignment with your
highest values, and when you congruently walk your talk and go on
to achieve those goals, you give yourself permission to continually
expand your space and time horizons with any succeeding goals . . .
and to *keep* expanding them until they in turn extend in space and
time even beyond your mortal life. It is then that you awaken your
most immortal goals, which give rise to your greatest legacy. That is
why your hierarchy of values is so important: because it dictates your
destiny.

It doesn't matter where you come from, it doesn't matter what you have gone through, it doesn't matter what you are going through. What matters is how you choose to apply the Values Factor. If you apply it now, your past could become your fuel, and your future can be unbelievable. I am a firm believer that you are a result of the decisions that you make today and the actions that you take tomorrow. If you start making decisions that are wise and meaningful and take actions that are inspired and powerful, you will end up with an inspired and meaningful life.

I consistently say that we have an amazing capacity within us, so here's permission to discover yours. Because after all, the most authentic you can be is *you*. No fantasy will compare with you. Just imagine what might happen if you gave yourself permission to be the authentic *you*. That is where you are creative. That is where your genius is born. That is where you are inspired. That is where your vitality comes out and where you have the most life.

You want to live your life to the fullest. And, as Aristotle implied, fulfillment means filling the greatest number of voids in your life. I would add, fulfillment means understanding the Values Factor and then choosing to live congruently with your highest values.

We have such an extraordinary opportunity being and living on this planet to do the most amazing things. Fill every one of your days with your highest priorities—live congruently with your highest values—and watch what happens in your life. That is the ultimate power of the Values Factor.